Contents

iv

Chapter 9   **Discipline or Solidarity:
A Tale of Two Housing Estates** **153**

Acknowledgements

This book draws upon the findings of two research programmes. The first, was a comparative study of child-protection social work in England and France, funded in the UK by the ESRC. In this study I worked with Karen Baistow, Andrew Cooper, Veronique Freund, Alain Grevôt, Rachael Hetherington, Brynna Kroll, Philip Smith and Angela Spriggs, as well as social workers from Paris, Oise and Greater London. It was within this talented group that I learnt most of what I know about transnational comparative research. Thanks are also due to Alex Gazzard who laboured long, hard and fast to enable me to bluff my way through in French. It was largely as a result of this research that Andrew Cooper, Alan Dearling, Rachael Hetherington, Geoffrey Mann, Philip Smith and I launched the journal *Social Work in Europe* and, because of their unstinting efforts and, in particular, the efforts of Philip Smith, who unstints like no other, the journal continues to this day.

The second research programme involved action research, conducted in London, Merseyside and eventually Paris, which aimed to devise ways of reducing the violent victimisation of school students. The initial victimisation study was commissioned by the Home Office Repeat Victimisation Initiative and the subsequent Anglo-French comparison was funded by the ESRC Crime and Social Order Research Programme. Here, once again, I worked with Philip Smith whose ability to devise original and witty methods for eliciting information from young people is unsurpassed. Latterly we were joined by Jenny Pearce who worked with the young people we found hardest to reach. She showed a rare capacity to empathise with these youngsters and to work with them to conceptualise their predicament. We were more than ably assisted by Kemi Onibuje and Karl Phillips, two remarkably mature Probation students, who moved the project along with energy, insight, good humour and a genuine concern for the children and young people with whom we were working.

None of this would have been possible without the 'Charles Dickens School' (not its real name) Staff-Student Anti-Violence Working Party; and so especial thanks to Carol, Danielle, Farid, Graham, Irene, Kerry, Louie, Mike and Peter who put the ideas into action and really made a difference. More recently we have worked in another school 'Sidney Burnell' (not its real name) in another London borough, and our work here, supported by the ESRC Violence Research Programme, has involved a protracted ethnographic study of young people involved in inter-racial violence in neighbourhoods adjacent to the school. Alan Marlow and David Porteous developed the work in the school and helped to co-ordinate the efforts of a range of agencies with those of students, teachers and parents, while Ian Toon undertook the ethnography – a dream team indeed. Special thanks go to Phil, Charley, the staff-student working party, and all the young people who allowed us to spend time finding out about them and their lives. The Anglo-French element of the project would not have been possible without the help and support of Jean-Marie Pujol, the Director, and Alain Grevôt, the Research Director, of Association Jeunesse, Culture, Loisirs, Technique (JCLT) (Paris) and their teams in Beauvais and Mantes la Jolie, and Nicole Brenôt of the Centre Nationale Formation et d'Etudes de la Protection Judiciaire de la Jeunesse.

The ESRC Crime and Social Order Programme brought me into contact for the first time with its director, Tim Hope. Tim is, at once, scholarly, practical, committed, far too modest and great fun. This book has been enriched by our subsequent work together and the many things I have learnt from him. I am also indebted to Barry Goldson, whose knowledge of youth justice is second to none. This is a better book because of the time and attention Barry has given to reading the proofs but, of course, I remain responsible for the mistakes.

Alarmingly, I have been talking about youth crime, youth justice and related matters with Cathy Aymer, John Dennington, Charley Burr, Dave Crimmens, John Lea, Roger Matthews, Toyin Opitikpi, Geoff Pearson, Phil Smith and Jock Young for the best part of a quarter of a century and I remain indebted to them. I have been having a fascinating conversation with Andrew Cooper about the fit, or otherwise, between psychoanalytical and sociological understandings of social class, gender, race culture and crime for almost as long. He complicates things enormously and I am very grateful to him for it. More recently this doughty crew of crucial referents has been joined by Patricia Gray at the University of Plymouth and John Hagedorn of the University of Illinois in Chicago. At the University of Luton I have had the good fortune to find David Barrett, Alyson Brown, Isabelle Brodie, Fiona Factor, Alan Marlow, Margaret Melrose, Suzella Palmer, David Porteous, Mike Thomas, Ian Toon and Marilyn Wolfson, who have all helped me think about old intellectual problems in new, and often more practical, ways. Working with Geoffrey Mann at Russell House Publishing is a delight. He is utterly, yet somehow surreptitiously, efficient, so that he doesn't scare the authors. But he is also interested in the issues and deeply committed to disadvantaged children and young people, as his involvement in youth work testifies, and this makes publishing with him a very good experience. The fruits of my discussions with Geoffrey and all the other friends and colleagues mentioned here permeate this book.

And as for Deborah, and all that she has done, I would not know where to begin.

About the Author

John Pitts is Vauxhall Professor of Socio-legal Studies at the University of Luton. He has worked as a 'special needs' teacher, a street and club-based youth worker, a youth justice development officer, a residential social worker in a remand and assessment centre, a group worker in a Young Offender Institution and a consultant to youth justice, legal professionals and the police in the UK, mainland Europe, the Caribbean, the Russian Federation and the People's Republic of China. His publications include *The Politics of Juvenile Crime* (1998), *Developing Services for Young People in Crisis* (1991), *Preventing School Bullying* (1995), *Working with Young Offenders* (1990 and 1999), *Planning Safer Communities* (1998), *Positive Residential Practice: Learning the Lessons of the 1990s* (2000), *Crime Disorder and Community Safety* (2001) and *The Russell House Companion to Working with Young People* (2001). He is a member of the editorial and advisory board of *Youth Justice, The Community Safety Journal, Social Work in Europe* and the UNESCO journal *Juvenile Justice Worldwide*.

x

For Deborah

Always to be right, always to trample forward, and never to doubt, are these not the great qualities with which dullness takes the lead in the world?

(William Makepiece Thackery, *Vanity Fair*, 1848)

Tears of rage, tears of grief
Why must I always be the thief
Come to me now, you know
We're so alone
And life is brief

(Bob Dylan, *Tears of Rage*, 1968)

Chapter 1

The Disciplinary Tradition

Our party alone challenges the indiscipline in our schools which has led to disorder in our streets. We alone robustly proclaim the overriding need to defend life and property. Whatever the threat and whatever the consequences, our mission is to defend the rule of law and the values of freedom wherever they are in peril.

(Speech to the Conservative Party Conference, Leon Brittan, Home Secretary, 1983)

You say there's a race of men in the trees, you're for tough legislation. Thanks for calling; we wait all night for calls like these. (Donald Fagan, *Nightfly*, 1982)

The Political Utility of 'Youth Crime'

In Britain, the relationship between criminal justice policy and youth crime is, at best, oblique. Policy is seldom informed by a dispassionate assessment of the nature, dimensions and effects of youth crime. Moreover, the new laws and administrative measures set in train by policy rarely, if ever, have the impact the political rhetoric suggests they should. This is because, since the 1960s, governments, originally of the 'right' but latterly of the 'left', have usually been more interested in 'youth crime' as a *political issue* than youth crime *per se*.

'Youth crime', the political issue, is characteristically mobilised by opposition parties during elections to highlight the social disintegration and moral decay fostered by the government's complacency and inaction, or its muddle-headed policies which reward moral turpitude and discourage moral continence among the young. Incumbent governments usually turn to 'youth crime' when the economy is faltering and they need to deflect attention to an alternative arena in which they can mount dramatic, but inexpensive, demonstrations of their political grit. Governments rarely dwell upon the fact that rising crime, because it represents a rejection or abandonment of the values, norms and laws which are the prerequisite of social cohesion and social solidarity, calls into question their own political legitimacy. More recently, 'youth crime', and the fear of it, has emerged in Anglo-American politics as a kind of electoral glue. On the one hand, fear of 'youth crime' can bind together an otherwise disparate band of electors into a new 'post-industrial' political constituency which transcends traditional class affiliations. On the other, it may be used to repair rifts within political parties, generating an impression of unity and common purpose.

The erratic twists and turns in the politics, policy and practice of youth justice in the UK in the post-war period are best understood as a product of governmental attempts to manage the tensions between political ideology, economic reality and electoral viability. This has meant that the issue of youth crime has sometimes occupied the centre of the political stage, most notably in 1970, 1979–83 and 1992–98, while at others it has been pushed out of the political limelight and placed in the hands of administrators and justice system professionals (Goldson, 1999).

The Spectre of Indiscipline

The meaning of 'youth crime' is not simply imposed by politicians however. Political meaning emerges from a complex interaction between government, the media, the police, quasi-governmental organisations, 'think-tanks', the church, the entertainment industry, selected academics, and political and occupational pressure groups which, together, elaborate the discourses which shape political action (Hall et al., 1978). This network constitutes a kind of semiotic 'power elite' whose definition of the situation has all too real consequences for the children and young people who break, or are suspected of breaking, the law.

Although the meaning of 'youth crime' is a complex, contemporary, political fabrication, the semiotic traces employed in its construction come from a bygone age. With relentless banality, the monologue which passes for the 'law and order' debate recycles the same time-honoured anxieties, expressed in the rhetoric of indiscipline and social deterioration. Accordingly, familiar, because interchangeable, 'experts' offer accounts of the latest disciplinary technology, only to be upstaged by politicians on the make, demanding that we 'condemn' more and 'understand' less. Together, they promise to return us to a golden age of civility and moral continence, when people were bound together by ties of mutual respect, an acceptance of tried and tested social conventions, and a subtle code of sociability.

One of the paradoxes of contemporary British politics, it appears, is that to win power, 'progressive' politicians must capture 'law and order'. But to capture it requires them to cast themselves as the natural inheritors and defenders of a tradition rooted in the celebration of a society simultaneously held together and held apart by fine gradations of deference and patronage, and kept in place by the 'the rule of law'. The discourse of law and order is therefore essentially backward looking because law and order is almost always depicted as something which must be 'restored'. As such, 'law and order' finds itself congenitally opposed to ideas of social 'progress' and, by implication, the possibility of a 'progressive' political intervention to reduce crime, finding the solution to the contemporary malaise in the restoration of the values and disciplines of a former era. It is for this reason that conservatives across the political spectrum tend to welcome most warmly those penal reforms which reintroduce measures whose origins lie in the eighteenth and early nineteenth centuries, and why they pay homage to 'the family'. But this is no simple celebration of a still popular social institution, with a mum, a dad, 2.4 children, a red setter and a vasectomy. It is a coded invocation of a complex nexus of cultural symbols which celebrate the capacity of powerful adults to instil, by violent means if necessary, the deferential conformity which, in this world-view, was the highest achievement of the Victorian age.

In the modern age, we learn, this world is in jeopardy, and responsibility falls to politicians, in partnership with an honest yeomanry, to fight a lonely rearguard action. Thus a Gloucestershire 'mum' having listened to Tony Blair's widely reported Wellingborough speech in 1996, where he spoke of teaching 'the value of what is right and what is wrong', warning of impending 'moral chaos' if we failed in this task, writes:

> *I'm just a member of the usually silent majority and a mum and like millions of others am sickened by our society today. Having heard you talking about the subject of young offenders, although I'm a lifelong Tory I feel you have the right ideas. We have to get the youngsters long before they are teenagers to instil in them discipline, respect and the knowledge of telling right from wrong.*

Here, a loyal, and clearly furious, yeo-person, betrayed by a corrupt political elite she was once proud to serve, pledges her allegiance to a new elite which has promised to 'turn back the clock', in order to retrieve that lost past of civility and moral continence which these honest folk hold to be their birthright. The actors come and go, the script remains the same.

The key to our recurrent, *and extraordinary*, preoccupation with young offenders and the motor of the contemporary British debate about law and order is not, ultimately, to be found in the crime committed by young people out there in the world, but in the terror in the face of indiscipline from below which lies at the heart of our culture. This discourse has its origins in Tudor times, when the enclosure of feudal lands created an impoverished, itinerant, 'mob', driven to begging, petty crime and periodic bouts of public disorder. Needless to say, this engendered profound anxieties in the aristocracy. As Thomas Moore (1516) observed:

> *And when they have wandered abroad till that be spent, what can they do then else but steal, and then justly pardy be hanged, or else go about a begging and yet then also they be cast in prison as vagabonds, because they go about and work not: whom no man will set to work, though they never so willing proffer themselves thereto.*

(In Cloward and Fox-Piven, 1972)

Our subsequent history is punctuated with such anxieties, as the ruling class recurrently armed itself against indiscipline bubbling up from below. And it was around the endeavour to suppress this indiscipline that our youth justice system and the arcane rhetoric of 'youth crime' and 'law and order' coalesced.

And this is why it is still possible for a government minister to observe, without tongue in cheek, that young offenders represent 'a rising tide of anarchy and violence threatening to engulf our shores', and be taken seriously by the media and the public. This rousing phrase, which could have been uttered at any time in the preceding 300 years, was actually borrowed from the Duke of Edinburgh by Sir Patrick Mayhew in September 1979, two years after the death of Elvis Presley.

From 'Dark Hearts' to the 'Heart of Darkness': The Politicisation of Youth Crime

A 'rising tide of anarchy and violence' was just what Margaret Thatcher needed to get her 1979 election campaign off to a good start. But her depiction of 'youth crime' subsumed this older rhetoric of class insubordination within a more toxic discourse of 'race' and 'nation'. Thus, in a clear reference to the threat posed by young Black men to White families, she claimed that 'our culture' was being 'swamped', and pledged to 'turn the clock back' in order 'to make the streets of Britain safe, once more, for law-abiding citizens' (Hall et al., 1978; Lea and Young, 1984; Pitts, 1996). The addition of 'race' to the, by now, somewhat anachronistic rhetoric of class, rendered her appeal more topical and more urgent and, thus emboldened, she waxed ever more visceral, invoking the spectre of the 'stranger on the stair', the 'knife at our throats' and 'blood on the streets' – fears which she claimed to divine within the electorate:

> People have asked me whether I am going to make the fight against crime an issue at the next General Election. No, I am not going to make it an issue. It is the people of Britain who are going to make it an issue.
>
> (Margaret Thatcher, speech to the Conservative Party Conference, 1977)

However, despite the obvious electoral appeal of her rhetoric, Margaret Thatcher's first term in office looked, for a time, as if it might also be her last. The economic recession deepened, unemployment soared, and the prospect of electoral defeat loomed, prompting vigorous ideological activity at Conservative Central Office, culminating in the renaissance of the deteriorationist rhetoric of traditional conservativism in an attempt to transform an impending economic calamity into a moral crisis at the epicentre of which were those contemporary descendants of the Elizabethan 'mob', 'the enemy within', Black delinquents and White trade unionists.

In their muddled but different ways, the vandals on the picket line and the muggers on our streets have got the same confused message: 'We want our demands met or else...' and 'Get out of the way and give us your handbag'.

(Margaret Thatcher, 1987)

However, in the event, it was not the 'enemy within' who saved Margaret Thatcher's political bacon, but an 'enemy without', in the shape of General Galtieri and the young men of the Argentinian armed forces who, by invading the Falkland Islands, provided the arena, *par excellence*, where she could demonstrate her political 'grit'. And she did.

Balancing the Books

The Criminal Justice Act 1982 (CJA) marked the first important bridgehead of the first Thatcher administration's 'fight against crime'. The Act was heralded as the law which, by restoring the powers of the police and the bench, would make good Mrs Thatcher's 'law and order' pledges. Yet, behind the scenes, it was clear that the youth justice system inherited by the Thatcher government was a mess; an incoherent mixture of welfare-oriented measures introduced by the Children and Young Persons Act 1969 and the attendance centres, detention centres and borstals of a previous era. It was a system, moreover, which was locking up more and more less-problematic children and young people. This was forcing older juveniles up into adult jails where their presence was placing enormous strains on a prison system which was itself at bursting point (Pitts, 1988). Moreover, youth justice was one of the many areas of government spending perceived to be spiralling out of control, and this was acutely embarrassing for an administration committed to 'small government' and 'good housekeeping' (Scull, 1977). Having been saved from electoral defeat by the Falklands War, the second Thatcher administration, now in the thrall of monetarism, confronted the reality of Britain's fiscal crisis (Scull, 1977). The crisis centred upon the inability of the state to maintain existing welfare and crime control services in the face of rising costs, competing demands on state expenditure (largely from unemployment benefit), mounting political pressure to reduce taxation and a significant reduction in the taxpaying population. As a result, the period between 1982 and 1992 witnessed a sustained attempt to contain and reduce the burgeoning costs of the criminal justice apparatus.

The De-politicisation of Youth Crime

This political *volte-face* led the Home Office to reconsider the costs and benefits of existing penal measures, and the political and fiscal viability of 'alternatives' to custody. Not surprisingly, in this new, hard-headed, political and fiscal environment, prison was revealed

[handwritten note: NOTE THE CHANGE IN LANG — LAW + ORDER TO DELINQ. MANAG.]

as expensive, inefficient and counter-productive. In consequence, between 1983 and 1992, a series of reforming Conservative Home Secretaries, Brittan, Hurd, Waddington and Baker, supported a, more or less, 'depoliticised' strategy of 'delinquency management' which aimed to handle offenders more efficiently and so more cheaply. As a result, they were also handled more humanely. *[handwritten note: → CONSEQUENCE, NOT THE MAIN AIM.]*

> *If we are to keep in prison for a proper time those who must go to prison, then we must keep out of prison those minor offenders for whom alternative punishments will suffice. For those convicted of the common, less serious and non-violent offences, which comprise the majority of all recorded offences, the argument that custody should be used sparingly...seems to me entirely persuasive.*
>
> (Douglas Hurd, Home Secretary 1985–89, lecture to New Bridge, Sept. 1985)

The Criminal Justice Act 1982, its blood-curdling rhetoric notwithstanding, was the law which initiated the rationalisation of the youth justice system in England and Wales.

Community Corrections

In 1983 the DHSS launched the Intermediate Treatment (IT) Initiative in which £15m was granted to non-governmental agencies to develop 4,500 alternatives to custody, over three years, in collaboration with the police and juvenile court magistrates. Between 1981 and 1990 the numbers of juveniles sentenced to custody fell from 7,700 to 1,900 per annum. Apparently the juvenile magistrates had been persuaded by the Lord Chancellor's Department which appointed them, the Home Office which regulated them, and the youth justice professionals who served them, to give 'alternatives' a chance (Bottoms et al., 1990).

However, on closer scrutiny, it is difficult to attribute the radical reduction in custodial sentencing during this period simply to changes in 'sentencing culture', although this may have played a minor role. If these reductions in custodial sentencing were a product of changed sentencing patterns, we might reasonably expect the proportion of custodial sentences imposed by juvenile courts to have dropped markedly vis-a-vis non-custodial sentences. In fact, as Anthony Bottoms and his colleagues (1990) discovered in their evaluation of the IT Initiative, sentencing patterns within the juvenile courts remained remarkably constant during the Initiative period. If the reductions in custodial sentences were not produced by diverting young offenders away from custody and into alternatives to custody, the argument that custody was reduced simply by the provision of plausible alternatives to custody cannot be sustained. The level of custodial sentencing in areas where Initiative projects were established tended to be two or three per cent below the national average (9 per cent versus 11.4 per cent of all sentences) (NACRO, 1988).

While supporters of the Initiative maintain that this lower rate testifies to its effectiveness, it could also be the case that Initiatives were established in areas which already had low custody rates, since a precondition for funding was that the police and the juvenile bench should be in favour of, and willing to use, alternatives to custody. Moreover there were, at the same time, reductions in custodial sentencing in many non-Initiative areas where no additional 'alternatives to custody' were established, or popularised by project workers. Arguably, the major contributory factor to the reduction in custodial sentencing during this period was the marked reduction in the numbers of children and young people entering juvenile courts. Whereas in 1980 71,000 boys and girls aged 14–16 were sentenced by the juvenile courts in England and Wales, by 1987 this figure had dropped to 37,300, a reduction of over 52 per cent. Police cautioning and other, less formal, modes of pre-court diversion were 'starving' the courts of juvenile offenders, causing some youth justice workers to proclaim, prematurely in the event, the advent of 'custody-free zones'. Between 1980 and 1987 the cautioning rate for girls aged 14–16 rose from 58 to 82 per cent. For boys the figures were 34 and 58 per cent respectively.

Nonetheless, so enthused were Home Office ministers by the results of the 'alternatives to custody' pioneered in the 'Initiative' that they decided to launch a similar strategy for young adult offenders, whose custody rate was climbing, and to enshrine in law many of the practices developed in the 1983 IT Initiative, in the Criminal Justice Act 1991. As the junior Home Office minister John Patten (1991), rather quaintly put it: 'I want to promote a cultural change not just in the probation service but among the sentencing classes... The punishing classes and the helping classes are now talking to each other in a way they never did before' (*The Guardian*, 12 April 1991).

A Marriage of Convenience

These remarkable reforms, coming as they did from an administration elected a few years before on a draconian law and order ticket, required an unusual, and on the face of it unlikely, political alliance, between the government and a youth justice lobby composed of youth justice professionals, penal reform groups, progressive Home Office civil servants and academic criminologists.

The IT Initiative succeeded because the Thatcher administration's cost-cutting imperatives and its commitment to 'small government', articulated with the desire of the youth justice lobby to limit the state's intervention in the lives of children and young people in trouble. This 'non-interventionism' had its roots in the disillusionment of Anglo-American political activists, scholars and welfare professionals, with the welfare state (Gouldner, 1971; Pearson, 1975). Persuaded that public and professional intervention in private lives must, of necessity, boomerang, yielding outcomes at stark variance with professional intentions, they strove to do 'less harm' rather than 'more good'. Their critique pointed to the ways in which behaviour, perfectly acceptable in its own social milieu, was transformed into pathology by the heavy-handed interventions of agents of the state (Becker, 1963; Matza, 1969). Thus, progressive policy makers and radical practitioners with young people in trouble insisted that whenever and wherever possible, we should 'leave the kids alone', maintaining that the most effective intervention was 'radical non-intervention' (Schur, 1973). This political stance was rooted in four related assertions:

- That the crime perpetrated by working-class children and young people was more or less innocuous and that intervention in their lives was motivated by elitist, middle-class, concerns about the morality of the poor rather than the crime perpetrated by their children.
- That victimisation was not therefore a serious problem, and was best dealt with by indigenous mechanisms of social control rather than state intervention.
- That rehabilitation, treatment, or social and economic intervention, to prevent or eradicate crime was demonstrably ineffective and that young people in trouble should be granted their right to due process of law.
- That, left to their own devices, children and young people would simply 'grow out of crime'.

For 'progressive' Tories, like Kenneth Baker, Home Secretary from 1990 to 1992, youth imprisonment was, to all intents and purposes, an expensive irrelevance in a modern penal system:

> *Prison breaks up families. It is hard for prisoners to retain or subsequently secure law-abiding jobs. Imprisonment can lessen people's sense of responsibility for their actions. Some, often the young and less experienced, acquire in prison a wider knowledge of criminal activity. Imprisonment is costly for the individual, for the prisoner's family and for the community.*

(Response to the Woolf Inquiry recommendations of imprisonment, Sept. 1991)

For the neo-liberals who were gaining increasing influence within government, the state had no mandate and no competence to intervene in the 'social causes of crime' (Wilson, 1975). If the problem was to be solved at all, it would be solved by punishing serious criminals harshly and, in so doing, sending those on the threshold of crime an unequivocal message about the likely consequences of their actions. Thus, in Britain, until 1992, ministers chose to deal with less serious young offenders via police warnings and cautions, and the bulk of the more serious ones in 'community-based', 'offending' programmes. Many politicians were aware that the social changes wrought by neo-conservative economic policy probably fostered youth crime but, such was the power of neo-conservative ideology, and so intoxicated were they by the economic boom of the mid-1980s, that there appeared to be a tacit acceptance that increased youth crime was probably a price worth paying.

A Culture of Cynicism

It is at least doubtful whether many members of the youth justice lobby or, indeed, Home Office ministers, actually believed that Intermediate Treatment 'worked', in the sense that it prevented future offending in any significant ways. Indeed, it is doubtful whether, by the late 1980s, they believed that it *mattered* whether they believed that it worked or not. By then, politics, policy and practice in youth justice, like most other areas of public administration, was concerned first and foremost with the manipulation of images and the re-presentation of reality in administratively convenient and media-friendly forms. Thus, both halves of this unlikely coalition chose to live in this state of 'bad faith' because the alliance they had entered was working so well that to 'rock the boat' by revealing the fiction which underlay it was unthinkable (Zizeck, 1989).

The Crime Rate Steepens

But the bubble was about to burst. In the late 1980s the British economy went into a deep and protracted recession and, suddenly, the fact that between 1981 and the early 1990s, recorded crime in the UK increased by 111 per cent, mattered. Crime in general and youth crime in particular were rapidly re-politicised and placed at the top of the agenda of the 'natural party of law and order', the Conservatives. The government went on to the offensive, placing the blame for the failure to achieve its 'law and order' objectives on the probation service, social workers and the police. Pointing to a real increase of 87 per cent in expenditure on policing during the Conservatives' time in office, a splenetic Kenneth Baker demanded: 'Where is the value for money?' Worse; on the basis of some patently mischievous advice from 'situational' crime prevention buffs in the Home Office, at the 1991 Conservative Party Conference, Baker attempted to explain away the 17 per cent hike in the crime rate in 1990 by suggesting that its victims should take better care of their property. But the booing and stamping from the auditorium indicated that this would not wash, that the government needed to 'get a grip' and that Kenneth Baker should start looking for a new job.

Re-politicisation

The non-interventionist project, as we have noted, was predicated on four assumptions: that youth crime was largely innocuous, that victimisation was relatively unproblematic, that rehabilitation or social intervention was fruitless and that young people simply grew out of crime. Yet, by the early 1990s, it was evident to most observers that:

- Some of the crime perpetrated by working-class children and young people could be serious, damaging, dangerous and, in certain cases, lethal.

- Victimisation was a serious problem, which had been redistributed towards high-crime, low-income 'ghettos' where socially disadvantaged residents bemoaned the lack of official intervention.

- Where other nations had responded to the social consequences of economic globalisation by robust social intervention, crime rates had not risen.

- Many young people in high-crime neighbourhoods were not growing out of crime.

In March 1992, the Home Office revealed another huge, 16 per cent, rise in recorded crime. There was rioting on out-of-town housing estates in Bristol, Salford, Burnley and Carlisle in which young people used petrol bombs and in one case firearms against the police. These disturbances were all the more worrying for the government because they appeared to continue a trend established in the 1991 riots in Oxford, Cardiff and Tyneside. 'Ram-raiding' and 'twocking' (taking a car without the owner's consent) were in the news. The press carried reports of 'rat boys', 'under-age criminals the law can't touch' with 'countless' offences to their names 'making their neighbours' lives a misery'. In Moss Side, a 14-year-old boy was shot dead, an apparently innocent victim of the 'crack wars'. Also in Manchester, a 15-year-old girl was abducted, imprisoned and eventually tortured to death by her 'friends'. In south London a 12-year-old was savagely stabbed in his school playground by a 'class-mate'. And then, in February 1993, two-year-old James Bulger was brutally murdered by two truanting ten-year-olds. The political storm which accompanied this murder, and the ensuing trial, focused national attention on the government's capacity to fulfil the primary rationale for its very existence, the maintenance of the 'rule of law' (for an account of the enduring impact of the Bulger case on child care and youth justice, see Goldson, 1998).

Chapter 2

New Labour and the Criminology of the Third Way

Contemporary politics is similarly constrained by an unacknowledged impossibility. Tony Blair and Bill Clinton make minor changes to the style and presentation of public life but leave unanswered broader questions of how society should be governed…genuine political action is virtually impossible now because capitalism has won the ideological war and nobody is seriously questioning its values or rules. But just like post-modern culture persuades itself that it lives in an age of freedom so politicians mask their limitations with a façade of energetic political activity.

(Zizeck, 1998)

We will deliver on our pledge on court delays, just as we are cutting class sizes, reducing waiting lists, helping young people off benefit and into work, and building a platform for long term growth and prosperity. We will work tirelessly to build the modern and fairer society that Express readers want.

('How we're fighting teenage tearaways', Tony Blair, *Sunday Express*, 7 March 1999)

A Major Crisis

By early 1993, John Major's government was on the ropes. Weakened by the narrowest of electoral victories in 1992, the Conservatives knew that they had to do something radical to assuage the public concern generated by the Bulger case. On 21 February 1993, Kenneth Clarke, who was now Home Secretary, told the *Sunday Times* that in future, persistent and serious offenders under 15 would be 'locked up'. He urged fellow MPs to 'catch up with the mood of the people' and attacked 'laggard police authorities'. On the inside pages, John Major, in one of the rhetorical flourishes for which he was renowned, laid the blame at the door of 'parents, the church and opinion generally, for failing to disapprove of criminal behaviour'. He called for a 'crusade against crime', declaiming that 'society needs to condemn a little more and understand a little less'. The following day, Education Secretary, John Patten, announced a £10m clampdown on truancy. 'Show me a persistent young truant' he roared, 'and I will show you a young criminal'.

As David Downes (1995) has astutely observed, the Major government appeared to be trying to peddle an account of youth crime which bore many resemblances to the explanations concocted by the Kremlin during the Soviet era. Thus, economic causes were deemed irrelevant because, in the new, classless 'Opportunity Britain', brought into being by the 'free-market revolution', citizens were 'at ease with themselves'. It followed that youth crime must be attributable to either biological, psychological or intellectual deficiencies or indiscipline. This indiscipline was fostered, it seemed, by counter-revolutionary elements within the professions of teaching, social work and the probation service, deviationists (Tory wets), lone mothers and reactionary parents, born in the 1960s, who were the bearers of a false and subversive pre-revolutionary consciousness. Their depredations were worsened, of course, by the Labour Party and the trades unions, who were struggling to forestall the realisation of the universal reign of the free market, and the final withering away of the state. The convergence between the world according to Conservative Central Office (circa 1992), and New Labour's evolving stance on crime, the family, the economy, 'Old Labour' and the trades unions was, as we shall observe, remarkable.

Labour Joins the Fray

Labour struck. They mounted a full-scale attack on the Tory 'law and order' record, orchestrated and led by their new shadow Home Secretary, Tony Blair. Under the Tories, Blair claimed, crime in general and youth crime in particular was running out of control. Not only had they created a moral vacuum in which crime flourished, the Tories had shown themselves to be incapable of forging the radical measures needed to contain it. Labour, Blair maintained, would be 'tough on crime and tough on the causes of crime' and, in the ensuing debate, the Labour Party deployed the entire lexicon of 'get tough' sound-bites in an attempt to wrest the political initiative on 'law and order' from the Conservatives' grasp (Chapman and Savage, 1999).

If Labour's message was unfamiliar, its delivery held even more surprises. Ken Livingstone, who as leader of the GLC, had entertained Sinn Fein's Gerry Adams and Martin McGuinness at County Hall, called for longer prison sentences. David Blunkett, shadow Health Secretary and erstwhile leader of Sheffield City Council, once known as the 'Socialist Republic of South Yorkshire', demanded the reintroduction of national service. And, with that touch of ambiguity which was to become his political hallmark, Tony Blair called for a regime of 'tough love', a phrase he had borrowed from US President, Bill Clinton, in which secure confinement would be tempered with a responsiveness to the offender's needs.

> *There is a school in my constituency, which is for kids who have committed serious criminal offences, and a very large proportion of those have been sexually abused in childhood. And that's terrible. But if you don't secure them, some poor person who*

has done no harm to anyone is going to find their life ruined. Although I passionately believe in trying to rehabilitate young offenders, to divert them from the path of crime, these people who come into my surgery have got to be helped. And my generation sees no inconsistency in dealing with both kinds of problems.

The Pre-Pubescent Super-Predators from Purgatory

In response to the murder of James Bulger, in 1993 the Conservative government had asked the House of Commons Home Affairs Committee to inquire into 'issues affecting juvenile offenders and the particular problems of persistent offenders'. The Committee commissioned research (Graham and Bowling, 1995) and took evidence from relevant organisations and individuals. In their evidence to the Committee, the Association of Chief Police Officers (ACPO) argued that despite Home Office data which showed a significant decline in the numbers of young offenders apprehended by the police in the 1980s, recorded offences committed by 10 to 17-year-olds had risen by 54 per cent between 1981 and 1991. This suggested to ACPO that we were witnessing the emergence of a small band of younger offenders who were committing a larger number of offences, the so-called 'one-boy crime waves'. This led the Committee to observe that (para. 15):

> *…one possible explanation for the apparent discrepancy between ACPO's picture of greater juvenile offending and the decline in the number of juvenile offenders is a growth in the numbers of persistent offenders… If there is a small but growing number of juvenile offenders responsible for many offences (some of which they may be convicted or cautioned for, and some of which may go undetected) it is possible to reconcile the indisputable fact that the number (and rate to a lesser extent) of known juvenile offenders has fallen over time with the more speculative assertion that the number of offences committed by juveniles has risen.*

However, Home Secretary Kenneth Clarke was not a man to let such nit-picking stand between him and a good sound-bite. In a late-night TV interview he declared that 200 10 to 15-year-olds were responsible for 60 per cent of all juvenile crime in the UK. Those with a pocket calculator and a copy of the criminal statistics handy could have worked out that this gave an annual total of 15,900 offences per head, or one every 22 minutes.

For the media, the idea of a pre-pubescent 'super-predator', which was holding the nation to ransom, was a hard one to resist. And they did not:

> *Yesterday police in Newcastle upon Tyne were questioning a youth after a hunt for a 13-year-old burglar nicknamed the 'Rat Boy' who scurried through the ventilation shafts of the Byker Wall housing complex to rob his elderly victims, a monster figure straight out of the steamy New York tenement blocks. Indeed it is now the turn of*

the people of the Bronx to sympathise with Britain. From being an issue only mentioned by 9% of the public in October, law and order has leapt above the economy and the health service and ranked second only to unemployment in the list of most crucial matters facing the country.

(*The Sunday Times*, 28 February 1993)

The Bulger case and the furore surrounding 'Rat Boy' facilitated the emergence of a new-style, 'realistic', 'compassionate' yet 'hard headed', Labour Party, unconstrained by the old party political divisions which had cast the Conservatives as 'the natural party of law and order' and Labour as the party of penal reform. This new Labour Party was in touch with the fears and anxieties of 'ordinary people' and pre-eminent among these anxieties, they maintained, was a 'new breed of under-age criminals', the most notorious of whom were, of course, John Venables and Robert Thompson, the killers of James Bulger. Thus, New Labour placed criminality among the under 10s, the capacity of the youth justice system to deal with it, and the role of government in supporting the family to nip it in the bud, at the heart of its 'law and order' strategy. As Jack Straw was to later observe:

> …*all the serious research shows that one of the biggest causes of serious juvenile delinquency is inconsistent parenting. We need to bring parenting out as a public issue so people feel able to talk about it. It is not easy, but one of my tenets in politics is that we should try the difficult issues.*

(*The Observer*, 1 February 1998)

Tony Blair put it more succinctly when he said: 'A young country that wants to be a strong country cannot be morally neutral about the family'.

The Gates Slam Shut

In March 1993, under sustained pressure from the Labour front bench, the Conservative government abandoned the key reforms of the 1991 Criminal Justice Act. Thus, only five months after the newly implemented Act had ended the imprisonment of children under 15, Kenneth Clarke promised to create 200 places in new secure training centres for the hard core of persistent and serious 12 to 15-year-old young offenders identified by the House of Commons Committee. Tony Blair opposed this measure arguing, unsuccessfully, that the government should carry out its promise to expand local authority secure accommodation in order that young offenders could be contained closer to their homes and families. This *volte-face* on child imprisonment signalled a new era in which crime in general, and youth crime in particular, was to be moved back to the centre of the political stage. These changes dealt a deathblow to the non-interventionist delinquency management strategies of the 1980s.

'Prison Works' – But Not for the Tories

Within weeks of his appointment as Home Secretary in July 1993, Michael Howard began putting his personal stamp upon youth justice policy. In October of that year, at the Conservative Party Conference he propounded his belief that:

> *Prison works; it ensures that we are protected from murderers, muggers and rapists – and it makes many who are tempted to commit crime think twice. This may mean that many more people will go to prison. I do not flinch from that. We shall no longer judge the success of our system of justice by a fall in our prison population.*

Whereas his predecessor Kenneth Clarke had been a pragmatic hatchet man, robustly cutting government expenditure as he was promoted from department to department, Howard was an ambitious, neo-liberal ideologue who took it upon himself to wage a populist war against the criminal justice and penal establishments. Howard's strategy involved placing himself consistently in breach of the law in order to precipitate high-profile, vote-winning, confrontations with the courts and criminal justice agencies. In 1994, he set about toughening the Probation Service by allowing direct recruitment of ex-NCOs and police officers and severing probation's traditional links with social work education. Taking inspiration from some of the more punitive practices within the US correctional system, in February 1995 he announced plans for 'tougher and more demanding' 'house of pain' regimes, 'aimed at knocking criminal tendencies out of young offenders' (*The Times*, 5 February 1995). With this *mélange* of toughened teenage prison regimes and new rehabilitations enshrined in the new, more restrictive, more punitive Criminal Justice and Public Order Act 1994, Howard set out to restore the government's political legitimacy and the Conservative Party's electoral fortunes.

While not subscribing directly to Howard's proposition that 'prison works', Straw emphasised his commitment to:

> *… consistent and progressive sentencing so that criminals know far more readily what they can expect. At present so many of them think they are living a charmed life and are too often surprised when they end up in jail. It is one of the reasons there are so many prison suicides.*   (*The Observer*, 1 February 1998)

The Youth Court bench, realising which way the wind was blowing, began to impose custodial sentences in earnest. The numbers of young offenders under sentence in penal establishments, a population which had fallen steadily between 1980 and 1993, rose by nearly 60 per cent in the four years to 1997.

Jack Straw's Stratagem

In July 1994 Tony Blair became leader of the Labour Party, and Jack Straw became shadow Home Secretary. Straw's job was at once simple and daunting. He had to retain the political initiative which Tony Blair had seized in the furore surrounding the Bulger case. This task was central to the New Labour project, not least because Blair's claim to the leadership of the Labour Party was predicated, in large part, upon his virtuoso parliamentary performances, which simultaneously enabled the party to speak with one, albeit meticulously rehearsed, voice, and give expression to 'the mood of the country' on an issue previously viewed as the sole preserve of the Tories. Straw's task was to plant firmly in popular consciousness the idea that New Labour was now the 'natural party of law and order', and yet to stress that Labour offered not a radical departure from, or a reversal of, the Conservatives' stated objectives on youth crime, but rather a policy which integrated popular Conservative 'law and order' themes with vastly improved economy, efficiency and effectiveness.

Jack Straw's strategy was to force the pace on policy, anticipating and pre-empting Howard in order to claim any new policy initiative for Labour. Meanwhile, he endeavoured to discredit Howard's political credibility by attacking his personal integrity. This latter objective, discrediting Howard, should have been relatively easy for a seasoned political 'hit man' like Straw, since Howard was disliked and mistrusted by MPs of all political hues. However, Howard regularly beat Straw in debate, most notably over the sacking of Derek Lewis, head of the prison service, in 1995. On the other tack, the attempt to force the pace on policy in order to outflank the Tories on the right, Straw was somewhat more successful, earning himself the dubious epithet from the Liberal Democrats of 'Howard lite'.

As the 1997 general election approached, Jack Straw had to contend with the fallout from Michael Howard's decision to become the 'hard right candidate' in the impending, post-defeat, Conservative Party leadership contest. Knowing that he would probably never have to 'deliver', Howard's 'law and order' promises became ever more extravagant. But now Jack Straw was committed, and his only option was to match Howard's increasingly eccentric bids. Howard had toughened the Probation Service; Straw said it should be tougher still. Secure training centres; New Labour now liked them, but wanted 10- and 11-year-olds sent there too. Youth on the streets; Howard told the police to act decisively, Straw promised to pass a law against it (Chapman and Savage, 1999).

The Final Straw

But this game of 'madman's poker' into which he had been lured by Howard rendered Jack Straw particularly vulnerable to media provocation:

> *In June last year the Observer was compiling a feature on the zero tolerance in the United States of anyone deemed anti-social. I phoned Jack Straw, then the Opposition's home affairs spokesman, and asked if he would be following the Americans' hard*

line. *'Now Jack,' I said, with that slightly hysterical laugh it is always wise to use when addressing the New Labour leadership. 'You won't be introducing Yankee curfews on kiddies out after bedtime will you?'*

My certainty was misplaced. Straw, thinking off the top of his head, decided child curfews were a splendid idea. Once he began considering their charms there was no stopping him. 'There are a lot of complaints about youngsters out on the streets until late at night,' he said. 'I see them when I'm driving back from the Commons and wonder where their parents are.'

I put the phone down and went to tell the editor we had a story. An hour later, Straw called back. He didn't mean what he had said, he implied, and had not been authorised to make an announcement. Would I pull the article? Journalism's machismo culture demands that you always reject politicians' attempts to tell you what to write. And I did, reasonably and politely.

But machismo can often lead to ruin and the curfews case was no exception. Because we printed the story, New Labour decided they would look weak if they did not clamp down on tots. The party's intellectuals considered curfews with a solemn respect for the integrity of public policy and cobbled together a curfew package on the back of a fag packet. If I had not run the article, it would not have happened. I'm very sorry.

(Nick Cohen, *The Observer*, 28 September 1997)

By 1997, many of the key elements of New Labour's youth justice strategy were already established. The fact that, in many cases, they were cribbed directly from Michael Howard's Crime, Sentencing Bill (1997), was not viewed by New Labour strategists as a particularly bad thing since, they believed, such political kleptomania would deliver an important message about strength of purpose and continuity, thereby assuaging voters' anxieties that the Blair administration would be soft on crime.

This message was reinforced with a steady stream of 'on-message' anecdotes from Jack Straw, his assistants and advisers about conversations, which had helped to ground policy in the lived experience of ordinary people; conversations with parents who wanted help in controlling their adolescent children, with young people who did not understand the consequences of their actions, and with young offenders who had been let down by a system which was nowhere near tough enough. Happily, one such encounter, between Jack Straw and David Farley, described as 'a member of the loaded generation' (sic), was recorded by a *Guardian* journalist:

JS   *One of the criticisms that are raised at some social workers is that they indulge the people that they are working with…*

DF   *Yeah, They're like 'poor you' and this and that and the other but at the end of the*

day that's not what I needed. I needed someone to give me a kick up the arse.
JS   *In a metaphorical sense.*

(The Guardian, 31 May 1998)

This strategy, which all too often teetered on the brink of pantomime, aimed to simultaneously outflank the Tories and disarm the Labour Party's left wing, by presenting New Labour as a party which listened to the people who were 'going through it', rather than those whom Alistair Campbell, New Labour's media supremo, referred to as 'Guardian-reading Trots and wankers'. As Jack Straw was to tell the self-same organ:

> *...empowering the community is very important. We have proposals for child curfew orders and it won't be the government saying kids have to be in at a certain time. It will be the mothers saying 'What are we going to do about this?' And putting a demand on the local council or police to have this order. I have seen plenty of examples ... where it's the women, the mums, who have had enough and are setting up homework classes and so on.*

But New Labour was not wholly reliant upon the Tories for its policies on youth crime; it was also influenced by focus groups, 'think-tanks' and the 'American experience'.

God Bless America

The American influence upon New Labour has taken four main forms. Firstly, many of the ideas and assumptions, about the changing nature of economic life and the role of government in a globalised economy, which have gained currency in the USA in recent years, have played a key role in the reshaping of the 'agenda' for the reform of the welfare state and the criminal justice system in the UK. Secondly, New Labour has imported a range of laws, policies and administrative strategies with which to flesh out its social and criminal justice policies. Thirdly, technologies of behavioural change and professional practices developed in the welfare and criminal justice systems of the USA have been introduced into relevant public services in the UK. Fourthly, New Labour is deeply indebted to Bill Clinton's campaign team for an electoral strategy which rescued the Labour Party from perpetual opposition.

Following its defeat in the 1992 general election, Labour's leading 'modernisers', policy 'wonks' from Demos and the Fabian Society, wannabe MPs and an assortment of Millbank 'spinners' shuttled between London, Washington and Massachusetts Institute of Technology (MIT), in an attempt to discover Clinton's recipe for re-inventing an apparently moribund political party and building, and then holding together, a political constituency which could elect it. As Jack Straw was later to confirm, on questions of crime and justice '...the two governments are learning more from one another all the time. There is now a deep ideological relationship but it is not all one-way traffic' (*The Observer*, 1 February 1998). Indeed, it was three days after his return from the USA in January 1993, that Tony Blair, by now shadow Home Secretary, voiced the famous Clintonism: 'tough on crime and tough on the causes of crime' for the first time, on BBC Radio 4's Today programme (King and Wickham Jones, 1999). That much has been learnt is evident; whether what was learnt was either relevant to or desirable for, the UK situation is another question.

The modern era in American politics began with the election of Jimmy Carter (1977–81) whose presidency paralleled the emergence of the religious right as a significant political force. It is, in large part, a result of their influence that youth justice systems in the USA today have such a strongly retributive character. By the mid-1980s most US states had passed laws restricting the jurisdiction of the juvenile courts and reallocating specified groups of offences and offenders to adult criminal jurisdictions (Feld, 1987; Szymanski, 1987; Wilson, 1994). These changes were justified on the basis that juvenile courts offered inadequate retribution for serious crimes committed by juveniles, no effective deterrence and little community protection, via incarceration in secure facilities (Feld, 1988; Wilson, 1983; Wolfgang, 1982).

In this vein, Attorney-General Edwin Meese, a personal friend of Ronald Reagan, had argued against the wisdom of diverting 'status' offenders, juveniles apprehended for under-age drinking, curfew busting, etc., from secure institutions since these were, he believed, the same young people who either 'went missing' only to become involved in prostitution, 'hustling' and drug dealing, or were drawn into the pornography industry. These preoccupations were expressed via substantial federal grants for 'juvenile intelligence' and 'enhanced prosecution programmes' for the juvenile bureaux of state police forces. The most obvious outcome of these developments was a growth in juvenile incarceration in the USA between 1979 and 1989 of 103.5 per cent. 'Minority youth' constituted 93 per cent of this increase. By 1985 two-thirds of the nation's training schools were officially deemed 'chronically overcrowded' (Krisberg and Austin, 1993). In the same year Attorney-General Meese called for the execution of teenage murderers (Lilley et al., 1995).

Don't Stop Thinking About Tomorrow

To the consternation of many traditional 'liberals' and 'progressives' in the Democratic ranks, far from rejecting the Reagan/Bush strategy on youth crime, Bill Clinton proved to be just as 'tough on crime' as his Republican predecessors.

> *Clinton has learned to play the dull reactive media like the virtuoso he is, and Dole, if not God, can't think what to do about him. No matter what new bêtise the Right comes up with, Clinton has got there at least a day early and has made their issue his. Currently, everyone hates (when not raping or corrupting on the Internet) teenagers. What is to be done with these layabouts? This is a crucial Republican-family-values*

issue, the result of all that money (practically none in fact) thrown at the poor, who, by nature, are lawless, drugged, sexy, violent. But before the Doleful could get around to the death penalty for pubescent vagrants, Clinton struck. Curfews for teenagers, he proclaimed. Whoever said freedom to assemble applied to anyone with acne? All Dole could gasp was, 'Character, Integrity. Or whatever. That's what it's about, America.' Clinton struck again. No more violence on television (the freedom to censor is the hallmark of a democracy). No teenage sex, much less smoking.

(Gore Vidal, 1998)

It is important to remind ourselves that 'getting tough' in the USA is a significantly different activity from 'getting tough' in the UK. The 1980s in America saw the reintroduction of the death penalty in all but 17 states. As governor of Arkansas, in 1992, in the midst of the crucial New Hampshire presidential primary election campaign, Clinton returned home to personally supervise the execution of Rickey Ray Rector, a brain-damaged, Black, double murderer and long-term resident of death row.

As a presidential candidate, Clinton reworked the traditional 'get tough' formula (as Tony Blair was to do in the run-up to the 1997 election), representing the vulnerability of citizens to drug-related violence and disorder spilling out from the ghetto, as a violation of their civil rights and liberties. In the USA, 1992 saw riots in south-central Los Angeles triggered by the acquittal of the police officers who had brutally assaulted Rodney King. This was the worst incident of civil disorder in the USA this century, and many residents, Black, White and Asian, believing, correctly, that the police were powerless to protect them, armed themselves in anticipation of imminent anarchy.

Unsurprisingly, Clinton's commitment to stem the rising tide of violence in and from the ghetto, proved to be a popular electoral pitch. But Clinton was not only politically astute, he was also lucky, and in the mid-1990s the US murder rate levelled off. So, in 1995, beset by burgeoning political and personal problems, but presiding over an apparently buoyant economy, Clinton called upon the American people to give him a second term in which to 'finish the job' on the law and order front. And in 1996 he entered the White House once again, promising to secure the death penalty for a broader range of offenders and a larger number of offences, and pledging continuing support for the draconian 'three strikes and out' sentencing strategy which was clogging up the country's jails with Black and Hispanic petty offenders.

These tough policies were accompanied by a presidential proposal for extensive crime prevention programmes which targeted vulnerable children in their early years. Thus, in 1996, Clinton called for an extra $21.7bn (£13.5bn) spending over five years to improve child-care facilities which were, he said, 'the single largest commitment to child care in the history of the United States'. This included a $3bn increase for Headstart and other

US pre-school programmes, and $12bn to cut class sizes for the first three grades from 22 to 18, and to take on an additional 100,000 teachers. But, as Norman Mailer (1998) observed:

> *It was, when all was said, a cosmetician's catalogue, but it had been developed by a consummate pitchman who could project a sweetness of mien, a steadfastness of purpose, and the healthy earnest suggestion that no citizen of America who was in want could possibly be alien to him. Like all the other major speeches Clinton had given, very few of the proposed programmes would be obtainable once they entered the jaws of the Republican Congress. And whatever did get done would not change much.*

On Not Tolerating Broken Windows

While in America, New Labour's scouts also learnt that broken windows could be fixed by zero tolerance. The 'broken windows' thesis was first aired by James Q. Wilson, Ronald Reagan's adviser on crime and justice, and George Kelling, a senior New York police officer turned criminologist, in 1982. They write:

> *A piece of property is abandoned, weeds grow up, a window is smashed. Adults stop scolding rowdy children; the children emboldened, become more rowdy. Families move out, unmarried adults move in. Teenagers gather in front of the corner store. The merchant asks them to move, they refuse. Fights occur. Litter accumulates. People start drinking in front of the grocery, in time an inebriate slumps to the sidewalk and is allowed to sleep it off. Pedestrians are approached by panhandlers.*

(Wilson and Kelling, 1982)

What Wilson and Kelling describe so graphically is the onset of the process of social deterioration which has transformed many North American city centres into urban wastelands (Moore, 1997; Hagedorn, 1998). What is remarkable about this thesis, however, is its implicit assertion that robust policing of these low-level 'incivilities' which, the authors maintain, presage such social deterioration, can arrest, and indeed reverse, this process. The form of policing the authors commend, known variously as targeted or zero-tolerance policing was practised most notably by William Bratton, the erstwhile New York police chief. He writes:

> *...every day over 200,000 fare evaders jumped turnstiles as shakedown artists vandalised turnstiles and demanded paying passengers handed over their fare tokens. Beggars were on every train. Every platform had a cardboard city where the homeless had taken up residence. This city had stopped caring about itself. There was a sense of a society that allowed things that would not have been permitted before. The city had lost control*

and was the epitome of what Senator Daniel P. Moynihan had described as 'defining social deviancy down' – explaining away bad behaviour instead of correcting it.

(W. Bratton, The Guardian, 14 April 1997)

To the criticism, that by prioritising the policing of incivilities, the police neglect more serious crime, Kelling and Bratton (1998) have argued that 'experiences on the subway taught us that chronic, serious offenders also behave in a disorderly fashion and commit minor offences like fare beating.' While acknowledging that 'social change' might affect the volume and nature of crime, Kelling and Bratton's work stresses that the 'urban crisis' is, first and foremost, a product of the weakening of informal social control and the erosion of a shared moral base. In vindication of their position they cite a staggering 37 per cent reduction in crime in general in New York City between 1994 and 1997, and a 50 per cent drop in the murder rate as a result of their policing strategy (Bratton, 1997).

However, as Jock Young (1998) and Charles Pollard (1997) have observed, similar reductions in crime were achieved in San Diego and many other major US cities during the same period, using very different policing methods, more akin to what, in the UK, would be described as 'community' or 'problem-solving' policing, based upon partnerships with local agencies, businesses and citizen groups.

Naming and Shaming

The philosophical corollary of the 'broken windows' thesis is the highly influential version of 'communitarianism' offered by Amitiri Etzioni (1995), a social philosophy cited approvingly by both Tony Blair and Jack Straw. Etzioni (1995, p.ix) writes: 'Communitarians call to restore civic virtues, for people to live up to their responsibilities and not merely focus on their entitlements, and to shore up the moral foundations of society.' He speaks of a pressing need to address the collapse of a common moral base and to inject a moral dimension into the task of social reconstruction. For Etzioni, the public humiliation of wrongdoers, 'naming and shaming', serves 'to underscore society's disapproval of crime', 'temporarily marking out those convicted in open court, after due process, seems a legitimate community-building device' (1995). He indicates that the 'community' must act as 'a reinforcer of pro-social mores' and, with Wilson and Kelling (1982) and Bratton (1997), argues that in this endeavour there is little room for tolerance of minor infringements of rules, laws or norms, or minor acts of public disorder.

Over There

America's crime problem is peculiarly and emphatically American. History, culture, social structure and the widespread availability of firearms have determined that the scale, severity and impact of crime in America set it apart from other advanced industrial societies (Messner and Rosenfeld, 1994). The common-sense observation that what happens in the USA today happens here in the UK tomorrow may hold true for hula hoops and Big Macs, but crime is another matter.

By 1997, the USA was spending $100bn per year on law enforcement, completing three new prisons each week. California was the biggest spender, devoting 18 per cent of the state's budget to law enforcement. At this time, 40 per cent of California's African-American males were in jail. Black Americans make up 12 per cent of the population of the USA, 13 per cent of estimated drug abusers, 35 per cent of narcotic arrests, 55 per cent of criminal convictions and 74 per cent of those receiving prison sentences. The criminologist Jerome Miller has predicted that, on current trends, by the year 2010, 50 per cent of adult Black men under the age of 30 in the USA will be in jail.

By 1999, US jails held 2 million prisoners. This represented an imprisonment rate of over 600 per 100,000 of the population, compared with a UK rate of 120 per 100,000. Thus the USA had a higher pro rata prison population than the former USSR at the height of Stalin's purges. Meanwhile, a further 3.75 million Americans were on probation or parole. Contemplating these figures, the American criminologist Elliott Currie has observed that, 'If this is what winning the "war against crime" looks like, I'd sure hate to lose.'

A major problem with the uncritical absorption of US-style social philosophies, and electoral strategies rooted in the fear of crime, is that UK politicians have sometimes come to act as if we really were facing American-style crime problems. Yet as Gavin Essler (1998) has observed:

> *Taking care of business in Little Rock in 1993, a small town of 180,000 people, meant 76 murders. For comparison, in Northern Ireland in the early 1990s with a population of 1,700,000 and in the middle of a terrorist emergency, there were about 100 murders a year. Translate a Little Rock level of violence to Belfast and you would expect roughly 800 murders a year. Every day in the United States approximately 60 Americans will die of gunshot wounds. In almost any American city in the early 1990s you were between five and ten times more likely to be murdered than in Northern Ireland.*

Yet, as the 1997 election approached, Jack Straw fulminated against 'aggressive beggars', human windscreen wipers, and unaccompanied ten-year-olds who hung around the fish and chip shops of the Old Kent Road after dark, as if he were talking about Chicago's South Side ghetto where firearms-related homicides, rather than mumbled requests for 'spare change', are an everyday reality.

Left Realism

At the core of the debate about 'law and order' in the USA in the 1980s and 1990s was the question of the heavy involvement of Black and Latino people in crime. New Labour has steered clear of the highly contentious issue of ethnic minorities as perpetrators, turning its attention instead to the question of Black people as victims of crime, most notably in the public inquiry into the killing of the Black teenager Stephen Lawrence. However, its criminal justice thinking has been profoundly influenced by the heated debate about race, crime and justice between left-wing criminologists in the 1980s and 1990s.

This debate was triggered by the publication, in 1984, of *What is to be Done about Law and Order?* (Lea and Young, 1984). The central strands of Lea and Young's argument asserted that:

- In certain neighbourhoods impoverished Black young people committed a disproportionate amount of crime.
- Its victims tended to be other poor Black people.
- As such, rather than an expression of resistance to oppression, such crime simply compounded their victim's oppression.

In such a situation, they said, socialists and radical criminologists could not, in any straightforward way, be 'on the side' of the socially deprived perpetrators since to indulge in such unreflective partisanship was to ignore the plight of the Black community as a whole. They commended a position of 'left realism' in contrast with the 'left idealism' of which they accused their critics.

The ensuing debate did not concern the 'evidence', of which there was very little. Rather, it focused upon praxis; upon the way Lea and Young, as radical criminologists, had conducted themselves. Their adversaries (Gilroy and Sim, 1985) replied that by their acceptance of the category of 'Black youth crime' as the 'problem', a category generated by the control culture, they had broken with a central tenet of the radical criminological project and given comfort to the MAN. By assisting in the transformation of Black young people into 'folk devils', it was argued, they were contributing to the mystificatory process of political displacement in which the crisis in the social relations of production is transformed into a crisis of race relations. Put simply, they had changed sides.

Lea and Young replied that for too long radical criminology had denied politically inconvenient aspects of social reality. It had, they claimed, espoused a romantic and idealistic view of the world, which while 'politically correct' was factually and epistemologically flawed. They called for the abandonment of illusions and a return to realism. *What is to be Done about Law and Order?* attempted to delineate the territory which a radical criminology could inhabit in the neo-liberal era of the 1980s. In espousing left realism Lea and Young tried to seize the political initiative by articulating the concerns of the working-class victims of crime and mounting an assault upon police inefficiency and governmental indifference. This was a struggle between a Marxism which 'read' street crime as a fabrication of the 'ideological state apparatus' (Althusser, 1965) and one which viewed it as apolitical, egotistical behaviour generated by poverty. What they shared was a belief in social structure as the primary determinant of human behaviour and class struggle as the motor of social processes.

That left realism became a major influence in academic criminology was not surprising. That it also gained currency on the Conservative front bench and among New Labour modernisers was remarkable, in view of the resistance of both groups to both Marxism and the kind of 'joined-up thinking' in which left-wing academics engage. For good or ill, left realism was an idea whose time had come. For Conservative politicians left realism turned the spotlight on the victims of crime; a surprise endorsement of the party line from an unexpected quarter. Left realism also strengthened the arm of the, university-educated, progressives in the upper echelons of the police force who, by the mid-1980s, were railing against Thatcher's 'criminogenic social and economic policies'. Labour modernisers found in left realism's insistence on the Tory failure to protect underprivileged victims, a route into the 'law and order' debate and out of the ghetto of 'penal reform', previously regarded as Labour's 'natural' terrain on these matters. Indeed many people within New Labour and beyond now regard left realism as a crucial vertebra in the intellectual backbone of New Labour's third way on crime, disorder and community safety (Giddens, 1998).

Welfare Mothers, Barbaric Sons

Meanwhile, other kinds of intellectuals were going to work on 'the family'. In the USA in the 1970s, and the UK in the 1980s, the question of the 'family', or more specifically, the 'lower class', 'welfare-dependent' family and the crimes perpetrated by its children, taxed the imagination and the rhetoric of politicians and social commentators across the political spectrum. As Monica Barry (1998) suggests:

> *Variations on the theme of an underclass have long been in common parlance to illustrate the presence of a residual, scapegoat 'class' within society: the (non-deserving) poor and criminal, dangerous, disturbed, work-shy and idle people. However, as a concept to denote the troubles of the late twentieth century, the term was popularised by Auletta (1982) in the USA. His definition included cultural as well as economic differences, but nevertheless emphasised that such people were unable or unwilling to be assimilated into the American way of life rather than being denied the opportunity. Auletta's diagnosis has been broadly accepted as the epitome of an underclass – economically marginal, culturally opposed and personally culpable.*

The Rise of the Neo-Suburban Intelligentsia

In Britain the 'underclass' debate has offered a raison d'être for what had previously been regarded as something of an oxymoron – a right-wing intelligentsia. This original group of dyspeptic pundits was augmented through the 1980s by disenchanted Fabians, disoriented 'post-Marxists', and any number of discarded 'policy wonks' scratching a living penning tracts for obscure 'think-tanks', under aliases culled from 1960s TV shows. Their lament, in essence, was that the rules of civilised social life were no longer observed, that absolute moral values and their associated norms and practices had been trashed and abandoned by irresponsible 'intellectuals' on the one hand, and lower-class malcontents on the other. Moreover, a culture which had once placed a premium on duty and responsibility had now been supplanted by a culture of complaint, dependency and entitlement.

Once in the vanguard of modernism, these erstwhile progressives confronted the moral and cultural cacophony of a post-traditional world. Just as, in the 1950s and 1960s, they dismantled and cannibalised the cultural practices, values and social mores of an earlier generation, now they confronted a similar fate. No longer able to support the libertarian ideas which first brought them to public notice, unable to bear the thought of their own passing, and unwilling to step aside, this generation of fading luminaries strove to reclaim the once reviled, albeit largely imaginary, world of suburban respectability into which most of them had been born. This would all be just another tragic tale of vanity, self-delusion and the eventual collapse into an undistinguished and unloved old age, however, were it not for their influence upon New Labour's front bench.

These neo-suburban intellectuals were united in their rejection of traditional approaches to the welfare state, which emphasised the rights of the poor, focusing instead upon the economic burden placed by welfare claimants upon those who subsidised them. In its dealings with families, they maintained, the welfare state had been counterproductive because it:

> … failed to reinforce the work ethic; the goal of self-sufficiency, self-support and self-initiative; the importance of intact families; the fiscal responsibility of the parents to the child; and the notion of reciprocity, the idea that recipients have a social obligation to perform in return for receiving assistance.

(Karger and Stoesz, 1990)

Thus Charles Murray (1994) imported for the purpose by Andrew Neil and the *Sunday Times*, argued that the US government should scrap its Aid to Families with Dependent Children (AFDC) programme, Medicaid, food stamps and unemployment insurance, in order to 'drive young women back into marriage'. For Murray (1994) the link between lone parenthood and youth crime is clear:

> I am arguing that the civilising process cannot occur in communities where the two parent family is not the norm, and this will turn out to be as true in England as America. The real problem with the 'alternative' of unmarried parenthood is that it offers no ethical alternative for socialising little boys. For males, the ethical code of the two-parent family is the only game in town.

Norman Dennis (1997) developed an analogous argument on the basis of, similarly anecdotal, investigations of the lives of council tenants on housing estates in the north-east of England. Unencumbered by complex or ambiguous data, Dennis was able to trace a clear line from welfare-dependent mothers, via unregulated sexual intercourse among their early adolescent offspring, to youth crime and public disorder.

The journalist Melanie Phillips was one of the first public figures on the British left to embrace this critique, and in her writings she has gleefully monitored its colonisation of metropolitan opinion (1994):

> *Peter Lilley and Sue Slipman, doughty defenders of single parents, are suddenly singing in close harmony. In a speech last week, the Social Security Secretary blamed low pay and unemployment for turning young men into unmarriageable prospects. Miss Slipman talks about how the collapse of the male role through lack of work is manufacturing the kind of yob no self-respecting woman would choose as a spouse. Suddenly a government widely assumed to be hostile to single mothers seems to agree that the real problem is men... The question being asked is how can we civilise young men when family structures, employment and moral authority are so weakened?*

For Phillips, the rot set during the 1960s with the advent of 'moral relativism'. Thus she urges parents to specify clear moral values which accord with those of the right-thinking majority.

In a somewhat similar vein, out on the 'post-Marxist left', Beatrix Campbell (1993) argues that unemployment and the 'collapse of the male role' force men back into spaces which, by day, have traditionally belonged to women. However, far from:

> *...co-operating in the creation of a democratic domesticity...what they admired and serviced was the criminalised brotherhood; what they harassed and hurt was community politics. It was an entirely and explicitly gendered formation.*

Thus, for Campbell, there is 'an underclass' but it is a gendered underclass made up exclusively of men. What unites these critiques is their conflation of ethical and fiscal concerns, a somewhat paradoxical desire for the state to control the bad behaviour of young men and their feckless fathers and, with the exception of Slipman and Campbell, a demand for the state to withdraw support from their welfare-dependent mothers. Yet, as Michael Moore (1997) observes, the assault upon 'welfare mothers', whose claims upon the state are actually fairly modest, may be serving to distract attention from a far more serious manifestation of welfare dependency:

> *I hate welfare mothers. Lazy, shiftless, always trying to get something for nothing. They expect the rest of us to take care of them instead of getting up off their collective ass and taking care of themselves. Always looking for a handout, they simply expect*

us average, hardworking, decent, taxpayers to underwrite their illicit behaviour as they churn 'em out, one after another. How long are we going to tolerate big business acting in this way? Each year freeloading corporations grab nearly $170 billion in tax-funded federal handouts to help them do the things they should be paying for themselves. That's $1,388 from each of us going to provide welfare to the rich! By contrast, all of our social programmes combined, from AFDC to school lunches to housing assistance, amount to just $50 billion a year. That breaks down to only $1.14 a day for each of us.

Misspent Energies

The contemporary assault upon welfare mothers finds its corollary in the assault upon public professionals. And it too has its origins in the neo-conservative critique of the welfare state which gained currency in the 1980s and maintains that:

> *...the true purpose of the state is to further the interests of its constituent groups. A cadre of human service professionals such as health and care personnel, social workers, psychologists, counsellors and administrators would be out of work if the welfare state was abolished.*

(Stoesz and Midgley, 1991)

The strategy, initially commended by the radical right but subsequently embraced by the emergent neo-suburban intelligentsia, was to replace government intervention with alternative, informal, social institutions. In this vision of the world, the non-governmental and private sectors would provide radically 'slimmed-down', 'bottom line', services for those in abject need. Meanwhile, 'empowered' by the removal of the dead hand of the state, new 'mediating structures' – the family, the neighbourhood, the church, the PTA – would arise spontaneously to revitalise informal systems of social support and social control, thus obviating the need for professional intervention.

In Britain, anti-professional ire is characteristically directed against teachers and social workers, although the police are not always exempt, as Campbell's account of their collusive involvement in the 1991 youth riots in England testifies. Teachers are castigated as defenders of entrenched, outmoded and almost invariably 'permissive', professional doctrines to which they cling, even in the face of 'widely accepted contrary scientific evidence', and 'informed opinion'. Melanie Phillips, for example, traces contemporary problems in education, and in 'society generally', to the introduction of 'progressive' educational methods in the 1960s and urges teachers to return to traditional classroom techniques. In this she echoes earlier utterances of Margaret Thatcher (1987) who observed that: 'These teachers are so indoctrinated with their alien political creed that they convince kids that it's all the fault of the system…and social workers, who turn a blind eye, sometimes connive at offences by children in their care'.

Social workers, as this snippet indicates, are also viewed as part of the problem, not part of the solution. Thus, the problem of youth crime is reduced, ideologically, not simply to a by-product of the moral failure of families, but also to the stupidity, incompetence or bloody-mindedness of the professionals who are supposed to contain and educate the offspring of these morally flawed and incomplete households. These themes are articulated succinctly in *The Blair Revolution* by Peter Mandelson and Roger Liddle (1996), who subsequently achieved greater media exposure by dint of their alleged involvement in the 'cash for access' debacle in the spring of 1998 and, in the case of Peter Mandelson, an alleged misunderstanding about a mortgage in the December of that year, and latterly a further alleged misunderstanding about a passport application. They write:

> *Schools require a new, much tougher, set of disciplinary sanctions to deal with unruly and uncooperative pupils, such as compulsory homework on school premises, weekend and Saturday night detention, and the banning of favourite leisure pursuits such as football matches. This greater emphasis on discipline should be matched in the local community. The police, schools and local authority services must work together closely to crack down on vandalism and other anti-social behaviour. Excessive tolerance of low-level sub-criminal behaviour by unruly young people undermines general respect for the rule of law, ruins the environment and makes a misery of the lives of many innocent people – and provides a breeding ground for more serious crime.*

A Third Way

New Labour placed youth crime at the core of its social and criminal justice policies, alongside, and inextricably linked with, the assault upon 'welfare mothers', 'failing families', laggard education authorities, self-serving public professionals and 'neighbours from hell'. Together with the adoption of Tory public spending limits, this was a strategy which aimed to annex the defining concerns of traditional Conservatism, 'law and order', 'the family', 'fiscal prudence' and 'freedom' – from fear and from threat. For this was the essence of the discussions with Bill Clinton, the burden of the message from the 'think-tanks' and the focus groups, the *raison d'être* of the third way, that, with the decline in the size of the industrial working class, the diminishing power of the trades unions, and the widespread rejection of the electoral process by the urban poor, modern 'centre-left' parties must build a new political constituency. It follows that, because it is the more prosperous sections of the 'working' and 'middle' classes who remain politically engaged, it is in the suburbs, the small towns and the gentrified urban enclaves that elections will be won and lost. This new constituency of the centre is, the argument runs, 'post-political', in that it has rejected both right and left wing dogmatism, preferring governments which administer the state in accordance with the dictates of common sense, administrative and technical competence and value for money. This is, however, a constituency which, next to job security, is most concerned about the threat of criminal victimisation posed by an expanding 'underclass', with a distinctive anti-social culture, dwelling in the 'unemployed ghettos' of the inner city.

However, the fiscal constraints placed upon national governments in a global economy, by the financial markets (Hutton, 1995), the IMF and the European Central Bank (Bourdieu, 1998), mean that national governments lack both the means and the political mandate to effect radical social and economic change; change which is necessary to protect society from the social dislocation generated by globalisation, of which rising lower-class crime is the most obvious manifestation. In these circumstances, in order to maintain political legitimacy, modern, centre-left governments must be seen to be intervening robustly, efficiently, and effectively, to control the lifestyles, low-level crime and the 'incivilities' which the new centre-left constituencies find most offensive, and most threatening to their quality of life and freedom of action.

This is, as Peter Mair (2000) has argued, a politics which aims to remove the politics of party from the governing process by appealing directly to 'the people' who count electorally, via focus groups, opinion polls and informal contact between senior government ministers and 'ordinary people'. This 'politics of good governance' is therefore a politics driven by the anxieties of both potential electors and those who may be elected by them. In a socially and culturally heterogeneous, economically polarised, society in which those who can make a difference electorally are disproportionately older, more prosperous and white, it is hardly surprising that the beliefs, behaviour and attitudes of those who are young, relatively poor and non-white become a major focus of social and criminal justice policy.

But this was social and criminal justice policy millennium-style, not an over-ambitious, Twentieth Century social policy which strove to engineer social justice and extend the bounds of 'citizenship'. This social policy aimed only to iron out those anomalies which hampered economic efficiency and inhibited individual freedom. As New Labour's policy emerged, the modesty of its ambitions became apparent. Whereas Thatcherism had offered us a 'grand narrative' of the free market triumphant and socialism vanquished, Blair proffered a 'post-modern' politics, of appearance rather than substance, which offered only modest disruption on the margins, not a transformation of the centre. And at the core of this politics without a core, was youth crime, in your neighbourhood, making your life a misery.

Kicking 'Ass' in Worcester

The issue of youth crime offers the example par excellence of the lessons Labour election strategists learnt from Bill Clinton. For Clinton, 'youth crime' in general, and the implicit promise to contain the threat posed by socially and economically marginal African-American and Latino ghetto youth, towards those in the social and economic mainstream, was an electoral hermetic which served to solidify an otherwise socially disparate political constituency. John F. Kennedy knew that he could only win the presidency if, like his Republican predecessor, Dwight D. Eisenhower, he could win the cities; and this meant carrying the 'Black' and the 'blue collar' votes. Thirty years on, Bill Clinton's appeal was to the suburbs, not the cities, because the demographic changes which had occurred in the USA through the 1970s and 1980s meant that those who could leave the 'hollowed-out' inner cities of the USA had done so, leaving behind a residual population of, overwhelmingly poor, Black and Latino Americans most of whom had given up on politics and simply did not vote any more (Wacquant, 1986; Wilson, 1987).

Although such spatial polarisation had not occurred in the UK on anything like the same scale, like Clinton, Blair opted for an electoral strategy of 'suburbanisation'. New Labour calculated that to gain and hold political power they had to get to 'Worcester woman' rather than 'Clapham claimant' or 'Jarrow job seeker'. And if 'Worcester woman' was to change her voting habits, New Labour strategists reasoned, she must be made to feel that the government would contain the threat posed to her property, person and peace of mind, not to mention the educational opportunities of her children, by the roughly spoken, badly behaved, young people who haunted the streets of the inner city and the estates on its periphery. This strategy was designed to have a double pay-off for the Blair campaign, pulling in the traditional Tory vote while bridging political divisions in his own party by promising to be both 'tough' enough 'on crime' for the 'modernisers' and 'tough' enough on the 'causes of crime' for old Labour's remaining 'social engineers'. And it worked.

Chapter 3

Hard Labour

In difficult times it is tempting to avert the gaze from problems whose remedy will require a profound reorganisation of social and economic life and to fasten one's eyes, instead, on the promise that the continuity of things as they are can be somehow enforced by the imposition of social order and discipline from above.

(Hall, 1980)

I fail to comprehend how the discourse of criminology has been able to go on at this level. One has the impression that it is of such utility, is needed so urgently and rendered so vital to the working of the system, that it does not even need to seek a theoretical justification for itself, or even simply a coherent framework. It is entirely utilitarian. (Foucault, 1980)

No More Excuses

New Labour's youth justice legislation hit the statute books in record time. Following a brief consultation period in 1997, which changed very little, the *No More Excuses* White Paper became the Crime and Disorder Act on 31 July 1998. It took Harold Wilson's government five years to get the Children and Young Persons Act (1969), on to the statute books. Mrs Thatcher, her 'law and order' bluster notwithstanding, took three years to enshrine her ideas in the Criminal Justice Act (1982). New Labour did it in 14 months.

However, even the most ardent supporters of New Labour's youth justice policy would have to agree that the Crime and Disorder Act (1998) was 'cobbled together' in a bit of a hurry. In a speech in London in October 1997, Alun Michael, one of the chief architects of the 1998 Act observed that:

In the years leading up to the 1997 general election, there has been an enormous amount of detailed thinking on the actions needed to target specific problems. A few examples are, Jack Straw's proposed Community Safety Order which will deal with violent and abusive neighbours; plans to encourage and support good parenting; ways in which the needs of victims can be made more central to the criminal justice system; positive proposals to improve consistency and progression in sentencing:

plans to make the Crown Prosecution Service much more effective and plans for a fast track system to deal with persistent young offenders.

The measures to which Alun Michael alluded were indeed new, and it was true that, 'in the years leading up to the 1997 general election there had been an enormous amount of detailed thinking…' However, as we have seen, not too much of this thinking had been undertaken by New Labour. Their youth justice strategy was derived, largely, from Michael Howard's 1994 Criminal Justice and Public Order Act, and the Crime (Sentences) Act (1997), key sections of which were simply pasted into the 1998 Act. The community safety provisions of the Act were lifted from the Morgan Report, commissioned by the Tories in 1991. The problem of youth crime was conceptualised, and targets for intervention specified, by the Home Office Study, *Young People and Crime* (Graham and Bowling, 1995), commissioned by the Conservative-dominated Parliamentary Home Affairs Select Committee in 1992. And *Misspent Youth* (1996), the report of the Audit Commission, the quango founded by Lady Thatcher, subsumed all of the foregoing and placed them in a new administrative framework which New Labour adopted as its own.

Misspent Youth

Misspent Youth was primarily concerned with whether, or not, the youth justice system of England and Wales offered 'value for money'. Its authors brought extensive experience and considerable expertise in economics and social policy to their task but, in consultation with criminologists, they also deliberated upon the origins of youth crime and the likely impact of a range of interventions upon young offenders. The central message of *Misspent Youth* was that, of the £1bn spent annually on youth justice services in England and Wales, 70 per cent was spent on administration while the remaining 30 per cent was spent on, largely ineffective, interventions with young offenders when they eventually completed their journey to the serious end of the system. Nothing, they noted, was spent on preventing young people getting into trouble in the first place:

> The current system for dealing with youth crime is inefficient and expensive, while little is being done to deal effectively with juvenile nuisance. The present arrangements are failing the young people – who are not being guided away from offending towards constructive activities. They are also failing victims; those who suffer from young people's inconsiderate behaviour and from vandalism and loss of property from thefts and burglaries. And they lead to waste in a variety of forms; including lost time, as public servants process the same young offenders through the courts time and again; lost rents, as people refuse to live in high crime areas; lost business, as people steer clear of troubled areas; and waste of young people's potential.

More alarmingly, the authors suggested that if nothing was done, young offenders would continue to perpetrate an estimated 7 million offences per year. But was the youth justice system really as abysmal as *Misspent Youth* had suggested, and was youth crime really running out of control?

The Administration of Discipline

The Crime and Disorder Act 1998 epitomised the New Labour project. That the ideas it embodied came from across the political spectrum, though mainly from the political right, attested to New Labour's newfound 'toughness'. The criminal justice provisions of the Act promised the victims of crime a voice in the outcome of criminal cases, while the new civil measures offered to 'empower' 'middle England' by handing it the legal and administrative means to re-establish order and civility in its 'communities'. The entire system was to be robustly managed at a local level, to ensure that it all 'joined up' and offered 'best value' to the public.

Home Secretary Jack Straw described the Crime and Disorder Act 1998 as 'the most radical shake-up of youth justice in 30 years'. Yet, while it is true that it represented the most radical administrative 'shake-up' of the youth justice system for 30 years, the measures the Act introduced were another matter altogether.

The Act brought into being the Youth Justice Board of England and Wales, chaired by Norman Warner, Jack Straw's adviser on youth justice. The chief executive of the Board was Mark Perfect, the co-author of *Misspent Youth* (Audit Commision, 1996). The Act required chief executives of local authorities to bring into being youth offending teams (YOTs), staffed by personnel from the police, the probation service, education, social and health services. YOTs were required to produce a youth offending plan specifying how the team would be organised, how it would discharge its functions and how it would liaise with other statutory and voluntary bodies. The Youth Justice Board of England and Wales was to audit, and in some cases formally inspect, YOTs. If, following this, the Board remained unsatisfied, it could send in its own officers to bring the YOT up to scratch. Under the Act, the Youth Justice Board also assumed responsibility for the rationalisation and modernisation of the 'secure estate', the multiplicity of penal and child-care institutions to which young offenders could be remanded or in which they could be imprisoned. Meanwhile local authorities and police services were identified as 'joint stakeholders' with a new statutory responsibility to develop community safety partnerships with the voluntary sector. They were required to form a 'leadership group'; this group was subject to a legal requirement to undertake a local crime audit, involving extensive public consultation; to devise and publish a local community safety strategy, which specified targets and timescales for intervention, and the roles and responsibilities of the agencies and groups involved in these interventions. For its part, the Home Office was granted reserve powers to call for reports from 'leadership groups' on the discharge of their duties and to specify the agencies which were to be involved in the 'delivery' process.

Inasmuch as these changes represented the devolution of power and responsibility to the local level, they also represented a significant move towards a national system of youth justice and community safety in England and Wales. The new, centralised, managerial structure established a 'steering and rowing' relationship between central and local government with direction coming from above, and the effort, evoked if necessary by sanctions, coming from below (Crawford, 1998). In this way, the government hoped to establish local accountability and national standards to which, over the period, local areas would rise. As such, the Act promised to inject a greater degree of equity between areas into a system which, as *Misspent Youth* had observed, was characterised by significant variations in provision, quality of service and sentencing outcomes.

The political message of the Criminal Justice Act 1998 was clear. And it was, pre-eminently, a message to the Conservative voters who had defected to Labour in 1997. It said, 'We will keep our promises, we will fulfil your expectations, we will assuage your fears and confound your enemies, and because of this, you may safely re-elect us.' The Act symbolised all that was new about New Labour and so it was imperative that if New Labour was to consolidate and strengthen its political legitimacy in this major policy area, it should start 'delivering' quickly.

Alacrity

Both government ministers, and the new cadre of politically canny professionals swept into the new administration in the wake of New Labour's 1997 victory, shared the belief that eradication of delay was crucial to both governmental legitimacy and the cost-effective operation of the justice system. Beyond this, there was also a belief that these delays were sending a message to young offenders that nobody really cared about what they were doing. As Mark Perfect, later to become Chief Executive of the Youth Justice Board of England and Wales, observed (1998):

> The present system replicates the inconsistent parenting which most young offenders have received, making it necessary to replace it with a fast, efficient system with a progressive, comprehensible sentencing tariff, which offers the consistency and predictability which replicate 'good parenting'.

Such delays, ministers indicated, were to be dealt with by sanctions upon the relevant agencies for failure to meet the new statutory time limits. Moreover, the 1998 Act had made provision for 'serious and persistent' offenders, the 'pre-pubescent super-predators' mentioned above, to be 'fast-tracked', in order to get them into court quickly and ensure that their past and prospective victims would get some respite from their depredations.

The idea of speed was attractive to New Labour because it suggested a new dynamism in public affairs. Moreover, it accorded with the dictates of popular psychology which hold that the sooner the proscribed act is punished, the more effective that punishment is likely to be and, conversely, that the longer the interval between the act and the punishment, the more likely it is that other acts would be committed, because the link between the original act and its consequences would be weakened. Hoghughi (1983) notes that, in order to work, punishment must induce 'an unpleasant state of emotional arousal in the form of fear and anxiety in relation to the proscribed act' while the work of Church (1963) and Bandura (1969) indicates that in the case of children, the punishment must follow the act more or less immediately.

However, in reality, even if the time between apprehension and sentence were reduced significantly, the routine functioning of the youth justice system is likely, of itself, to undermine the process, purpose and impact of punishment:

> The time interval between apprehension and the Court's sentence is taken up with interviews (by police, solicitors, social workers et al.), court appearances, bail, remand in custody as well as the humdrum daily life of the young offender which has nothing to do with the legal processing. Unless we are to regard these processes as the punishment and the Court's sentence as simply another element in the total package, then clearly many other events intervene between the offence and the punishment. When the punishment is imposed, from the court's point of view, it is for the offence. At a verbal, intellectual level even the young offender may agree. But from the viewpoint of strict conditioning, the behaviour being punished is standing in the dock and possibly other proximal events of the day, and not the original offence. Punishment, however harsh, could not hope to be effective after such a long interval, unless it were to be mediated by explicit anticipatory rehearsals of the punishment to come.
>
> (Hoghughi, 1983: p.275)

The Systemic Parent

Beyond these technical issues however, is the question of whether the youth justice system is actually experienced as a kind of quasi-parent by the children and young people who pass through it. Although the representation of administrative and judicial systems as a symbolic parent, more usually a father, has a long pedigree, it is extremely problematic. In the 1950s and 1960s, for example, some psychoanalysts came to regard the encounter between, usually fatherless, boys and young men and the youth justice system, as an oedipal struggle in which the imposition of legal penalties represented the constraining hand of the symbolic parent, and a prerequisite for the healthy development of the troubled adolescent's ego. Today, the crude reductionism represented by this simplistic interpretation of Freud's theories is rightly rejected, and few scientists now believe that young offenders project parental attributes or attitudes onto administrative systems with which they neither identify, nor wish to have a relationship. Of course, the suggestion that state institutions, in their dealings with children and young people, should replicate the tenets of good parenting holds out some intriguing possibilities. What would happen, one wonders, if the Department of Employment, the Board of Trade and the Inland Revenue took to heart the oft repeated parental injunction that children should share their toys and sweets, and that mums and dads should not have favourites. Would this mean that New Labour should place the means of production, distribution and exchange in the hands of the poor?

Alacrity and the Italians

The only research we have on the impact of delays in youth justice systems was done by Edwin Lemert (1986) who, in the mid-1980s, undertook a comparative study of youth justice systems in Italy and California. Lemert notes that by the early 1980s, the Italian youth justice system was underfunded, understaffed, inefficient and phenomenally slow, generating backlogs of two to three years. Indeed, so intractable were the administrative problems of the Italian youth justice system that, every year or so, amnesties were declared, and the vast majority of the young people in the system were simply pardoned. Why did the Italians not improve their youth justice system?

The juvenile court was introduced into Italy in 1934 by Benito Mussolini, following a visit to London, during which he sat in an English juvenile court. Clearly Mussolini thought that such a juvenile court would be 'just the ticket' for an up-and-coming fascist state but most Italians were far happier with the existing system in which problems of youthful misbehaviour were dealt with either by the family, or the family supported by the church or church-based charitable organisations. Because it was such a cultural anomaly, the juvenile court was never popular in Italy and this was reflected in the paucity of political, administrative and financial support it attracted.

What was the effect of the system's failure to forge a link between proscribed behaviour and the official response to it on recorded youth crime? Lemert found no discernible impact upon rates of youth offending whatsoever. They remained very low. Meanwhile in California which, in the 1970s and 1980s probably had the most extensively researched, efficient and generously funded juvenile justice system the world has ever seen, youth crime rates were over ten times higher, resulting in 28 times as many juvenile arrests than in Italy. Not only does this finding cast doubt upon the deterrent or rehabilitative effects of speedy systems, it raises important questions about what relationship, if any, exists between youth crime rates and the operation of youth justice systems.

Alacrity and Electoral Anxiety

Nonetheless, a central plank of the Crime and Disorder Act (1998) was the pledge to end delays in the youth justice system by attacking what Jack Straw (1997) had described as the 'adjournment culture' of the youth courts. The Audit Commission Report, *Misspent Youth*, had suggested that delays were occurring at all points in the system and that magistrates, lawyers, the police, youth justice workers and probation officers were all implicated. As Tony Blair observed 'these same hardened young offenders could wait months between arrest and sentence' and he therefore pledged that:

> We will deliver on…court delays… Before, hardened young offenders could wait months between arrest and sentence with an average delay of 142 days… Our aim, as a first step this year is to hit our target of 72 days for persistent offenders in 50 per cent of cases.
> (*The Sunday Express*, 7 March 1999)

Somewhat rashly, the Prime Minister invited the electorate to sanction the government if it failed to 'deliver' on this pledge. Thus when, at the end of 2000, it emerged that the time between arrest and sentence had been reduced to around 96, rather than the promised 72 days, an obviously delighted shadow Home Secretary, Anne Widdecombe, came out fighting. On the BBC's *Today* Programme Lord Warner of Brockley, now a Labour peer and chair of the Youth Justice Board (YJB), blustered that the time-scale for the promised reduction had been five calendar years rather than one parliamentary term but Ms. Widdecombe was not to be fobbed off, administering a monumental verbal drubbing to the hapless peer. Meanwhile, behind the scenes, the YJB was frantically dispatching 'gagging orders' to YOT managers, forbidding them to speak to the press about the unmet time targets.

This profoundly uninteresting fracas was, however, the logical outcome of New Labour's commitment to a strategy of 'good governance' (Mair, 2000) in which, on the one hand the government makes promises to the electorate and asks to be judged on 'hard outcomes' while on the other it attempted to establish a 'direct' relationship with the electorate through 'meet the people' sessions, opinion polls and endless focus groups, to see how these promises are 'playing' on the ground. But as John Humphreys has observed:

> The political technicians and strategists are now adept at identifying the relatively small number of people who can swing an election and put their clients in power, and they are the people they will listen to most carefully. All of Gould's focus groups consisted only of people who had voted Tory in 1992 and had become 'floaters'. So no one else gets a look in.
> (Humphreys, 2000)

If this is so, we would expect New Labour's policies on youth crime to resonate with the central tenets of traditional Conservatism. Thus, politics as a struggle between opposing

interests or a public competition of ideas collapses. In consequence, we wit~~~~
Slavoj Zizeck (2000) has called 'the zombification of social democracy'.

Populist Criminal Justice Policy

The implications of 'good governance' for youth justice policy are all too clear. New Labour's criminal justice policy-making perpetuates the movement away from 'elitism' towards 'populism' set in train by their Tory predecessors:

> The Home Secretary, Jack Straw (the minister responsible for penal policy), has suggested that the elites, who from their comfortable social position pushed penal policy in a liberal and humane direction, were oblivious to the concerns of those less well positioned who suffer most from shocking rises in crime rates... Accordingly, Straw declared that, in devising its plans to tackle crime, the government would listen not just to 'interest groups' but also and primarily to 'ordinary people' living in areas undermined by crime and disorder.
>
> (Johnstone, 2000)

A strategy of 'penal populism' requires that, both policy ends and policy means must accord with the dictates of an invariably retributive 'common sense'. The senior civil servants, criminal justice and penal professionals, pressure groups, judges and magistrates, who once determined the shape of criminal justice policy, are now moved to the margins of the policy-making process. New policy initiatives are no longer justified by reference to the criteria of these 'experts'. Now the experts are called upon to advise on the means whereby populist policy goals may be realised, rather than the ends to which policy should strive. Whereas, in an earlier period, growing penal populations were represented as a shameful error on the part of the authorities because they were both wasteful and inhumane, now a steadily rising penal population is celebrated as a political success.

In this new era of populist 'good governance', policies must go all the way down. David Marquand (2000) has written of a 'Prussian discipline' within the Labour government, enforced, as often as not, by a new political cadre, part political *apparatchik*, part public servant, brought into being to keep public services, and their privatised surrogates, firmly 'on-message'. It is their job to establish 'robust' and 'rigorous' mechanisms for ensuring that neither policy ends nor policy means are subverted by managerial drift or professional self-interest. There is to be no slippage between intention and implementation; no space for discretion, innovation, cupidity, stupidity or idleness. Everybody at all levels – the policy makers, administrators, managers, professionals, private and voluntary sector agencies, and even volunteers if they are needed – must be heard to be singing 'from the same hymn-sheet'. Moreover, this hymn must be sung with optimum efficiency, economy and effectiveness because, like 'law and order' and sexual continence, fiscal prudence is dear to the hearts of the Tory defectors whose ephemeral loyalties these policies aim to secure.

ix main strategies; centralisation, monitoring and evaluation, -professionalisation, the narrowing of the aetiological focus :ive options.

....ui Justice Board and latterly the National Probation Service have transformed an assortment of local justice systems with, sometimes complex, local accountabilities into two, inter-related national systems with far greater accountability to the centre. This represents a significant move in the direction of a national system of youth justice, with the potential to inject a greater degree of equity into a system previously characterised by significant variations in provision, quality of service and sentencing outcomes (Audit Commission, 1996).

Although the Crime and Disorder Act 1998 hands new responsibilities to local authorities and local multi-agency partnerships, it is the Home Office, via the Youth Justice Board, which prescribes the goals they should pursue, the targets they should achieve and the time-scales within which they should achieve them. The procurement of the means whereby these goals and targets are to be achieved remains a local concern. However, the anxieties engendered by this simultaneously 'hands-on' and 'hands-off' mode of governance, leads to an unprecedented concern with implementation which, as a result, comes to be specified in ever closer detail in an attempt to minimise the scope for innovation and professional discretion. Thus, what at first sight appears to be an exercise in devolution, upon closer inspection, takes on the aspect of a franchising operation. 'Product support' is provided via a steady flow of 'evidence-based' data about 'what works' and 'pilot studies' of new administrative arrangements and modes of intervention, while 'quality control' is vouchsafed by statutory audit, and god help the laggard local authority or hapless police chief whose performance is found wanting by the Youth Justice Board auditors. Meanwhile, growing numbers of local councillors and chief executives are asking, 'whatever happened to *local* government'?

Monitoring and Evaluation

A Martian criminologist might be forgiven for assuming that the average Earthling delinquent is half a metre tall, hums and has a huge glowing face onto which harassed correctional personnel type an unending stream of rehabilitative messages. On the face of it, it is a very good idea that YOTs should collect and collate data with which to inform the development of the youth offending service and professional practice within it. However, at present, the evaluative tail appears to wagging the rehabilitative dog and professionals are devoting an inordinate amount of time to typing data into a centralised youth justice database which will neither reveal information about the impact of their interventions nor inform the strategic direction of their YOT. This problem flows directly from the attempt by the YJB to hijack data collection as a means of exerting greater managerial control over the YOTs. The problem is compounded by incompatible and incomplete data sources, and a paucity of dedicated expertise. Moreover tight YJB deadlines have meant that most YOTs experience only the costs of the evaluative endeavour rather than its benefits.

Because the YOTs data will be aggregated nationally by the YJB, the resultant analysis will not be sensitive to local variation. This centralised data-set presents formidable problems of processing and analysis. As a result, the types of data that will emerge from the final analysis will have to be refined down, and it is a fairly safe bet that the data which finally emerges from this process will hold few surprises, focussing on the individual and familial 'risk factors' said to precipitate youth offending (Farrington, 1996) on the one hand and the impact of prescribed, offence-focussed programmes, which aim to effect cognitive change and an appreciation of the consequences of offending, on the other. These are, after all, the theories and practices upon which the new youth justice is built, and experience, rather than cynicism, suggests that they will be shown, for reasons discussed in Chapter 6, to have been effective.

The Inculcation of Culture

One of the few 'big ideas' informing UK criminal justice policy at the dawn of the twenty-first century is 'cultural change'. In her consultative document *A New Choreography*, Eithne Wallis, the newly appointed director of the re-configured National Probation Service, stated that:

> Nothing short of deep-rooted culture change in the organisation can deliver these reforms and outcomes. Many probation areas have already made a good start and we will acknowledge and build on these achievements. Sometimes, however, I shall be leading the Service against the grain of its past history and traditions. As National Director, my primary strategic objective is to build the capacity of the NPS to deliver the Home Secretary's priorities and requirements. (Wallis, 2000)

In a similar vein, the unpublished Youth Offending Team *Pilot Report* (Youth Justice Board, 2001) is at pains to stress the importance of the development of 'a new, correctional, practice culture relevant to the Crime and Disorder Act' within the YOTs. Temporarily abandoning their scientific neutrality, the authors assert that this 'new culture':

> ...is not about dealing with crises or exceptional cases; about non-intervention; about keeping cases open for long periods of time nor about placing victims in a secondary

role...(it)...is about new and clear views of what managers and practitioners take for granted as routine work. The Pilot Youth Offending Teams have moved to embrace this new culture of work but much more needs to be done.

(Youth Justice Board, 2001)

Whether it is appropriate for notionally disinterested academic evaluators to specify so forcefully the nature of the new culture the Youth Offending Teams should be attempting to realise is, of course, debatable. The struggle to impose cultural homogeneity within the YOTs is rooted in the assumption that the development of a shared 'vision', ethos and mode of professional practice, which accords precisely with Home Office and YJB policy goals, is an unequivocally desirable outcome. However, the realisation of this new culture, the report suggests, has been impeded by professionals who cling to discredited, anachronistic, practices. Yet, as Roy Bailey and Brian Williams (2000) found in their study of two Midland YOTs, divergent perceptions of how Youth Offending Teams should discharge their functions were not simply a product of idiosyncratic professional histories or aberrant professional priorities. They also derived from real ambiguities within the 1998 Act, real differences of view between senior officers in the partner agencies and real problems encountered by young people and victims. For their part, the education and health professionals seconded into the YOTs couldn't see how or why they could or should develop the requisite 'offence-focus' in their work.

It may be that what the YOT evaluations actually reveal is the impossibility of imposing a homogeneous culture upon teams comprising different professionals who are required, sometimes by law, to represent the interests of different protagonists in the legal process. It seems that in its effort to construct a corporate youth justice system, the YJB has systematically confused the building of an effective multi-agency team with the eradication of professional difference and the denial of structural conflict. An effective multi-agency team makes its differences explicit and creates a forum in which these differences can be discussed intelligently and some decision reached. A further barrier to the development of the homogeneous, 'correctional', cultures prescribed by the Youth Justice Board and the Home Office is the growing clamour from young people and their advocates, emboldened by the UN Convention on the Rights of the Child and the new UK Human Rights Act, to have a voice in decisions taken about them by public bodies (Crimmens, forthcoming). However, the development of such a 'culture of critical discourse' (Habermas, 1983) which inevitably requires each protagonist to question both themselves and the assumptions which inform their practice is not what the Home Office and the YJB have in mind at all. Yet, it is hard to see how the desired cultural hegemony could ever be sustained, since a defining characteristic of a culture is its capacity for adaptation to changing circumstances. The alternative to such cultural evolution is stasis and the collapse into an even more 'target-happy', 'outcome-led' bureaucratised practice, which will almost certainly result in even less time being spent in face-to-face contact with young people in need and in trouble.

The quest for cultural change is more than a straightforward attempt to re-fashion practice in accordance with the dictates of 'what works' or 'economy, efficiency, and effectiveness'. It also marks a repudiation of a set of ideas about crime and justice which have their origins in the seismic cultural shifts which took place in the 1960s. In the sphere of criminal justice Howard Becker's *Whose Side are We On?* (1967) and David Matza's *Becoming Deviant* (1969) launched a debilitating critique of the kinds of correctionalism currently in vogue in the UK, while posing an intriguing choice to justice system professionals: whether to be part of the solution by establishing solidarity with those who had fallen foul of the law, or part of the problem by colluding with the system's spurious correctional pretensions. These were ideas which came to inform the minimalist 'delinquency management' and 'back to justice' strategies developed by youth justice professionals in the 1970s and 1980s. The problem as perceived by the Home Office and the YJB in 2001 is to prevent this potentially dissident workforce 'going native' once again, by ensuring that they remain 'on message'. This is to be achieved by instituting a cultural change, at the core of which is a far more pervasive managerial and political control.

De-professionalisation

As we have noted, New Labour's apparent ambivalence, if not antipathy, towards 'public servants' in general and youth justice professionals in particular, has its origins in the neo-conservative critique of the welfare state that gained currency in the 1980s. One way to dislodge this parasitic by-product of the welfare state is to dismantle the structures which sustain it. De-professionalisation holds many attractions for criminal justice system policy makers and senior managers with an iconoclastic and homogenising bent. Non-professionals have little or no knowledge of alternative ways of doing things, as a result the potential for disagreement with, or deviation from, prescribed method or procedures is minimised. This means, for example, that the integrity of the Home Office accredited 'offending programmes', discussed in Chapter 6, is far less likely to be subverted by the exercise of 'professional discretion'. Such training as these new recruits receive is essentially practical and any ethical issues which arise can be resolved by reference to the relevant 'values statements' or codes of practice. Over time, this recruitment strategy spawns a new division of labour in which non-professionals 'deliver' the 'programmes' and the dwindling number of professional workers become, essentially administrative, 'case managers'. If successful, this strategy would produce a cheaper, more flexible and far more manageable workforce.

Increased throughput, tight time targets, the escalating demand for information and data, burgeoning bureaucracy and 'initiative fatigue' mean that, more than ever before, face-to-face work in youth justice is being undertaken by unqualified sessional workers and volunteers (Porteous, 2001), or sub-contracted to private or voluntary sector agencies, staffed largely by unqualified workers. The annexation of the voluntary sector by government to provide mainstream criminal justice services was already evident in the 1980s (Pitts, 1988; Nellis, 1989). In the 1990s, dwindling charitable donations have increased the sector's reliance upon state funding. However, nowadays, this funding is secured via a process of competitive tendering for non-negotiable central and local government contracts. The rise of 'contract culture' has meant that voluntary sector organisations are under immense pressure to act as low-cost providers of mainstream correctional services rather than exemplars of innovative practice or advocates for young people in trouble with the law.

Narrowing the Aetiological Focus

In the contemporary discourse, aetiological theory has given way to the specification of 'risk factors'; the statistical correlates associated with youth offending. These 'risk factors' derive from the *Cambridge Study* of 411 South London boys undertaken by David Farrington and Donald West between 1961 and 1985 (West and Farrington, 1973) (and discussed in the next chapter). It is undoubtedly the case, as David Farrington (2000) asserts, that the 'risk factor prevention paradigm' has the great advantage of being 'easy to understand and to communicate, and it is readily accepted by policy makers, practitioners and the general public.' However, as he also acknowledges, it is not possible at present to distinguish between those risk factors which are causes and those which are effects. Yet, if we are unable to accord some degree of causal primacy to 'parenting', 'truancy', 'drug abuse', 'homelessness', 'low income' and the like, or theorise the ways in which these correlates interact, we are little nearer understanding the causes of youth crime and our choice of methods of intervention must remain haphazard. In the event, this, by no means insignificant, problem has been resolved by a process of political and scientific attrition.

In the Home Office consultative document *Tackling the Causes of Crime* (1996) eight key risk factors are identified: parenting, truancy, drug abuse, lack of facilities, homelessness, unemployment, low income, and economic recession. These 'risks' are similar to those cited in the Audit Commission Report *Misspent Youth* (1996) which is hardly surprising since they both derive from the findings of the Cambridge Study. However, in the Audit Commission report the risk factors are divided into 'foreground' and 'background' factors. Familial and developmental factors occupy the foreground, while factors such as family income, employment and the socio-economic status of the neighbourhood are relegated to the background. In 1997 New Labour published its *No More Excuses* White Paper. *No More Excuses* drew heavily upon the 1996 Audit Commission Report and *Crime and the*

Family, written by three New Labour insiders (Utting, Bright and Hendrickson, 1993), which was also based upon the *Cambridge Study*, and concluded that 'the tangled roots of delinquency lie, to a considerable extent, inside the family'. In consequence, *No More Excuses* reduces the multiplicity of risk factors originally identified by West and Farrington to three main groupings. Parenting, Schooling and Peers, with the key risk factors identified as 'being male', 'poor parental discipline', 'criminal parents' and 'poor school performance'.

As we have noted, in an interview with the *Observer*, Home Secretary Jack Straw narrowed the risk factors down even further, asserting that:

> *All the serious research shows that one of the biggest causes of serious juvenile delinquency is inconsistent parenting.*

> (*The Observer*, 1 February 1998)

Restricting the Rehabilitative Options

Although the risk factor prevention paradigm would not seem to point unequivocally towards any particular intervention programme, its proponents appear to be unanimous in their espousal of the transformative powers of cognitive-behavioural interventions (see for example, Farrington, (1996)) discussed in Chapter 6.

Whatever their logical fit, there can be little doubt that the risk factor prevention paradigm and cognitive-behavioural programmes are ideas whose time has come. Once again, Eithne Wallis (2000), Director of the National Probation Service, captures the spirit, pace, style and syntax of New Labour's correctional thrust perfectly when she asserts that:

> *This is the leadership challenge now facing the newly created National Probation Service for England and Wales. The scale of change and reform unleashed through the Criminal Justice and Court Services Bill is unprecedented in the Service's history and the service delivery targets are formidable. The 'What Works' portfolio of evidence-based offender programmes is ground breaking in its scale, on the fast moving world stage of correctional services.*

> (Wallis, 2000)

It is intended that these evidence-based, cognitive-behavioural, programmes, accredited by the newly formed Community Justice National Training Organisation (CJNTO) will become the 'national curriculum' of the National Probation Service by 2004 (Wallis, 2000). Their development will be paralleled by the spread of similar programmes, accredited by the H.M. Prison Service Offending Behaviour Unit, which are currently operating in 100 UK prison department establishments. In prisons, and increasingly in the probation service, sessions are video-taped and sent to the Home Office where they are evaluated. The monitors are particularly concerned with the integrity of programme implementation; that the programme should run exactly as intended by its designers. Thus, those personnel who, quite literally, deviate from the 'script' are brought to book since they may well jeopardise programme integrity, and hence the accreditation of the institution or Probation Area. We are witnessing the emergence of a 'one-size-fits-all' national (correctional) curriculum for offenders in prison and the community and, its corollary, a substantially enhanced capacity for senior managers to quantify and control the day-to-day, face-to-face, work of probation officers, prison officers and ancillary workers. With the advent of the new Intensive Supervision and Surveillance Programmes, it is more than likely that these programmes and these managerial regimes will spread to the YOTs. In accrediting a limited range of ideas and practices, and tying the allocation of resources to their successful introduction and execution, 'accreditation' effectively discredits alternative ideas and practices and prevents innovation from below. The homogenisation of correctional intervention is justified on the grounds that the programmes commended by CJNTO and the Prison Service Offending Behaviour Unit are those to which 'research points as the most thorough and best designed programmes showing the most promising results.' (Farrington, 1996). Indeed, this phrase has become a kind of official mantra amongst Home Office ministers, the YJB, senior figures in the welfare, justice and community safety industries, and the denizens of some university senior common rooms. However, the apparent confidence in these interventions, cognitive skills training (and its derivatives), restorative justice and mentoring, appears, as we discuss in Chapters 5 and 6, to be rooted in a partial reading of the research evidence and an over-estimation of their 'promise'.

Chapter 4

Locking Up Children

In the old approved school system demonstrations that the failure rates were enormous or that the institutions had a host of other difficulties were irrelevant for policy, simply because residential institutions have one enormous advantage over community care. Behind their walls the children are invisible. (Millham et al., 1977)

The Erosion of the Juvenile Jurisdiction

The 'New Youth Justice' is rooted in a repudiation of what we might call, for the sake of convenience, the 'old youth justice'. The old youth justice comprises 1960s and 1970s 'welfarism', which emphasised the central role of social inequality in the aetiology of youth offending and the need for robust state intervention to ameliorate the personal and social circumstances of young offenders, and the 'progressive minimalism' of the 1970s and 1980s which strove to divert young people from a potentially stigmatising formal involvement in the justice system. In the 'new youth justice' these apparently contradictory, although potentially complementary ideas have been supplanted by a focus upon the *deeds* rather than the *needs* of young offenders (unless these needs can be shown to have led directly to their offending), and a strategy of early, and in some cases pre-emptive, formal intervention with crime-prone and offending young people. These interventions are rooted in the belief that early exposure to the criminal justice system will have long-term deterrent and rehabilitative effects.

We should note that the 'new youth justice' is consistent with what John Pratt (1989), has described as 'Corporatism'. In the Corporatist model, all the relevant agencies and organisations enter a partnership to deal effectively and efficiently with young offenders. However Pratt was concerned with the changing organisational structures of youth justice rather than theories, ideologies or the professional practices such as 'welfarism' and 'progressive minimalism' thus enabling us to envisage a corporate 'welfarist', 'minimalist' or 'correctional' youth justice system. Indeed, the 'new youth justice' marks the advent of what we might call 'corporate correctionalism'.

In the 'new youth justice', as the title of the White Paper which preceded the Act, *No More Excuses*, suggests, the idea of youth crime as a product of poverty, social inequality or psychological disadvantage is supplanted by an emphasis on individual and family responsibility.

The Vanishing Pre-Pubescent Super-Predator

As we have noted, the belief in government that the problem of youth crime could best be attacked by inculcating a sense of responsibility into a small, often under-age, hard core of child criminals was in large part a product of furore surrounding the Bulger case (1993). In its evidence to the House of Commons Home Affairs Select Committee the Association of Chief Police Officers (ACPO) contended that between 1981 and 1991 recorded offences committed by 10 to 17-year-olds rose by 54 per cent and that a significant part of this rise was attributable to the activities of a new, *pre-pubescent super-predator*. However, in 1992, the Home Office had conducted a study in 33 of the 43 police services in the UK, of juveniles below the age of 17 who had committed 10 or more offences between April and June of that year. A total of 106 children and young people were identified, of whom 68 (66 per cent) were aged 15 or 16 and 8 (7.5 per cent) were aged 10 or 11. This left fewer than 30 12 to 14-year-olds.

In their study *Persistent Young Offenders*, commissioned by the Home Office, Ann Hagell and Tim Newburn (1994) used three different definitions of persistence. One identified children and young people with the largest number of arrests and offences over a year, one was based on the earlier Home Office definition of ten offences in three months, and one was based on the criteria for the proposed secure training order, namely that the child or young person should have committed three imprisonable offences. Hagell and Newburn found that few juveniles offended persistently for protracted periods and that persistent offending was usually relatively transient. These findings echo those of Elliott et al. (1986) in the United States.

Each of the three definitions of persistence identified a different set of young people, which led the researchers to conclude that if no distinct or discrete group of young people can be identified, 'any definition of persistence will inevitably be arbitrary' and that 'a significant degree of inequity could arise' from the legislative criteria for secure training orders. The study also showed that persistent offenders were not disproportionately involved in serious offending. Serious offences, such as grievous bodily harm, aggravated burglary, rape and sexual offences comprised less than one per cent of the offences committed by the persistent offenders, involving only 1.6 per cent of the children studied; the same proportion as in the youth offending population as a whole.

Nonetheless, the belief that younger, and sometimes under-age young offenders constituted a major problem, skewed the 1998 Crime and Disorder Act in crucial ways (see Figure 4.1), turning it into a means whereby the criminal law would penetrate the previously sacrosanct realm of childhood. Not least of the government's considerations in revamping law and policy in this way however, was the evident political popularity of similar measures introduced in the USA under Ronald Reagan in the 1980s. This endeavour continues with the impending introduction by the Youth Justice Board of *Pre-Crime Risk Panels*, in 2003, charged with surveillance and intervention with under-age 'pre-delinquents'.

Figure 4.1: The Provisions of The Crime and Disorder Act (1998)

Pre-emptive interventions
> The local child curfew
> Child Safety Order
> Parenting Order
> Anti-Social Behaviour Order
> (Pre-Crime Risk Panel 2003)

Pre-court preventive interventions
> Reprimand (once only)
> Final Warning (once only)

Non-custodial preventive disposals
> Referral Order (2001)
> Fine
> Action Plan Order
> Reparation Order
> Supervision Order
> Probation Order
> Community Service Order
> Combination Order

Incarceration
> Detention and Training Order (partially indeterminate)

Goodbye *Doli Incapax*

In the immediate aftermath of the 1997 general election, Jack Straw made great play of his decision to abandon the principle of *doli incapax*. In a speech to the Police Federation on 21 May 1997 he said:

At the heart of our new approach is the determination to reassert the recognition of personal and social responsibility. Young offenders must be made to take responsibility for their actions. At present under the archaic rule of doli incapax *the criminal law assumes that offenders aged 10–13 are incapable of differentiating between right and wrong. We will reverse that absurd assumption and make the law catch up with common sense. In general, children aged 10–13 do know the difference between right and wrong. And they ought to be treated as if they do.*

In fact, *doli incapax* does not imply, as Jack Straw suggested, that young people aged 10–13 are incapable of differentiating between right and wrong, but rather that they may, under certain circumstances, not be competent to understand the gravity or the consequences of their actions by dint of their immaturity. It is for this reason that the onus is placed upon the prosecution to demonstrate criminal intent, as distinct from knowledge that certain actions are simply right or wrong. As recently as 1990, in its White Paper *Crime, Justice and Protecting the Public* (Home Office, 1990) the Conservative Government noted that the principle of *doli incapax* should be retained because it made 'proper allowance for the fact that children's understanding, knowledge and ability to reason are still developing'. The abandonment of *doli incapax* must be viewed in the context of the UK having the lowest age of criminal responsibility in Europe (eight in Scotland and ten in England and Wales), with the exception of Eire where it remains at seven. *Doli incapax* has, in the past, served to reduce the discrepancy between the ages of criminal responsibility in the UK and mainland Europe.

As we have noted, in the recent period, nearly all US states have passed laws which restrict the jurisdiction of the juvenile courts and reallocate specified groups of offences and offenders to adult criminal jurisdictions (Feld, 1987; Szymanski, 1987; Wilson, 1994). Jeffrey Fagan's definitive study of dejuvenilisation in the USA (1991) compared two cohorts of 200 juvenile offenders, matched in terms of the seriousness of their offences and their antecedents, who passed through juvenile courts in New Jersey and the adult criminal courts in New York. The study indicates that the 'going rate' for any given offence by young people with similar antecedents was similar in both jurisdictions and the deterrent effect of the penalties imposed by the courts was also identical. In fact, as was the case in an equivalent British study undertaken by the Home Office in 1983, the adult criminal court tended to err, if anything, on the side of leniency. As such these findings constitute a significant 'own goal' for the proponents of dejuvenilisation.

But even if the US research supported the case for the erosion of a separate juvenile jurisdiction, in attempting to make sense of youth justice policy in Britain we are still left with the difficulty that the USA presents problems of youth crime which, in terms of both their nature and volume, are, as we have noted, profoundly different from the problems of youth crime in Britain. It is, therefore, difficult to divine what, practically, these new

Americanised measures, which almost certainly violate the UN Convention on the Rights of the Child, will achieve.

The other key principle which has informed juvenile and youth courts in the UK, is embodied in the Children and Young Persons Act 1933 which prohibits the identification of children and young persons involved in criminal proceedings. In Clause 42 of his Crime (Sentences) Act 1997 Michael Howard introduced an amendment to the 1933 Act which would allow convicted offenders who appear in the youth court to be publicly named if the court 'is satisfied that it is in the public interest to do so'. This provision, incorporated into the Crime and Disorder Act 1998, allows youth court magistrates to *name and shame* young offenders. Beyond the fact that such naming and shaming might well undermine any attempts at rehabilitation, 'named and shamed' youngsters would undoubtedly be hounded by the press and, in certain high-crime neighbourhoods, could be abducted and beaten senseless by local vigilantes as happens on a limited scale at present. This is probably not what Amiti Etzioni, whose ideas we discussed in the previous chapter, or those like Tony Blair and Jack Straw, who have been influenced by them, mean when they describe 'naming and shaming' as a 'legitimate community-building device'. The provisions of Michael Howard's Crime (Sentences) Act 1997 which were incorporated into the 1998 Act will, in future, allow courts to impose curfew orders with electronic tagging on 10 to 15-year-old offenders. This scheme was piloted in Norfolk and Greater Manchester in January 1998. The 1997 White Paper notes that: 'The pilots will be carefully evaluated... Already, the indications from existing schemes which test tagging on adults are that a curfew order backed by electronic monitoring can help offenders to structure their lives better, and help ensure compliance with other community penalties.'

This is, to say the least, an original interpretation of the experience of existing schemes for adults which have, at times, collapsed into farce (Mair and Mortimer, 1996). But it also raises serious questions about the relevance and applicability of regimes, which have allegedly worked with adults in their twenties and thirties, with children of ten or twelve. These anxieties are reinforced by the fact that curfew orders will not be supervised by youth justice workers. As to its likely impact, the Penal Affairs Consortium (1997) has observed that:

> *Electronic tagging is at least as likely to provoke re-offending by juveniles as to prevent it, as well as being uniquely stigmatising. The young people concerned will have to attend school with a tag attached to their wrist or ankle branding them as an offender. Some children will undoubtedly boast about their tag and wear it as a badge of honour, adopting a 'hard' image to live up to it.*

However, what really constitutes the radical edge of the government's dejuvenilising thrust is the lowering of the age to 12 (or to ten if the Home Secretary deems it politic), at which youngsters can be sentenced, as subjects of a detention and training order (DTO), to custodial confinement, in a secure training centre, or Prison Department establishments.

Pre-emptive Intervention

Wilson and Kelling's (1982) idea (that incivilities, if left unattended, will lead on to far more serious crime) combined with New Labour's concern (that the roots of the problem of crime are to be found in the misbehaviour of children and younger adolescents) both find expression in the *local child curfew*, the *child safety order* and the *anti-social behaviour order*.

The local child curfew

The local child curfew provides new powers for local authorities and the police to set up an area curfew which will prohibit children under ten from being in specified public places at specified times unless supervised by a responsible adult. This provision has hardly ever been used but in 2001 the age was raised to 16. Now, a child under 16 who is found out unaccompanied in a curfew area during curfew hours may be taken home by the police and placed in the care of a responsible person. If there is no responsible person there to look after them, the police can use their existing powers to remove the child to 'other suitable accommodation'. A breach of the order provides grounds for the imposition of further orders (the child safety order and the parenting order), breaches of which may, in turn, trigger care proceedings. As such the curfew threatens, in certain circumstances, to become a 'fast track' to residential care in its own right. Before the free-market experiment of the 1980s put most of them out of business, adventure playgrounds, play centres and detached youth workers did the job for which the child curfew order is designed, but they did it without stigmatising the children of the poor.

The child safety order

A child safety order can be granted when a local authority can show that:
- The child has done something which would constitute an offence if they were over ten.
- The child's behaviour suggests that they are 'at risk' of offending.
- The child is disruptive or harassing other residents.
- The child has breached a local curfew order.

The child safety order may be granted by a Family Proceedings Court and may require a child to be home at a certain time or stay away from certain people or places or to attend school. A child safety order may be linked with a parenting order if the court so wishes. If the requirements of a child safety order are not adhered to, the local authority may commence care proceedings. The most obvious objection to the child safety order is that it may serve to criminalise children below the age of ten, thus effectively lowering the age of criminal responsibility to zero, even if the behaviour for which the order is imposed is not, in fact, criminal. As such, this represents one of the most radical attempts to dejuvenilise and criminalise child and youth misbehaviour ever attempted in Europe.

The parenting order

The parenting order has, so the *No More Excuses* White Paper (1997) insists, been designed to 'help and support parents to control the behaviour of their children'. The advent of the parenting order must be seen against the backdrop of New Labour's high-profile commitment to the rejuvenation of the family as an effective caring and controlling social unit, and the pre-eminence of family forms characterised by '...two participating parents' (Straw, 1997). New Labour's new-found interest in the family was, apparently, triggered by a study undertaken by Utting et al. entitled *Crime and the Family* (1993). In fact, as we have noted this study leans very heavily on research undertaken by David Farrington and Donald West's Cambridge study. On the basis of their reading of Farrington and West's findings, Utting et al. conclude that 'the tangled roots of delinquency lie, to a considerable extent, inside the family'. By 1995, for New Labour, family policy had become synonymous with crime prevention. Thus, in his speech to the 1995 Labour Party Conference Tony Blair declared that 'a job and a stable family' were the best crime prevention policies.

The parenting order will be imposed upon the parents of convicted young offenders; the parents of children who are the subject of an anti-social behaviour order, a sex offender order or a child safety order; and on parents who have been convicted of failing to send their children to school. Parents will be required to attend special guidance sessions once a week for three months. If the court deems it necessary, it may impose additional conditions such as a requirement that the parent take and collect the child from school and that the parent is at home at a certain time every day. These conditions may be imposed for up to a year.

With few exceptions, professionals, managers and not a few magistrates are extremely sceptical about the parenting order, although not about work with parents per se, which both professionals and parents appear to rate positively. For its part, the National Association for Youth Justice believes that if work associated with parenting and child safety orders is to be carried out at all, it should be carried out under the auspices of children and families teams from local authority social services departments, rather than youth offending teams. They also note that many of the parents who could be made the subjects of a parenting order have already sought assistance from social services departments and voluntary sector projects, but have been refused help because these agencies are under-resourced and overworked.

All previous measures to penalise parents for offences committed by their children have been neglected by the bench because they are essentially unjust. As a result, despite the fact that magistrates are enjoined by the Act to impose parenting orders in all cases, unless they state why they are unwilling to do so, it remains unlikely that the parenting order will meet with any more success than previous measures which have attempted to inculcate a greater sense of responsibility into the parents of children in trouble with the law.

The anti-social behaviour order

An anti-social behaviour order may be sought by the police, or the local authority, from a civil court. The order can require the subject of the order to refrain from certain behaviours or activities, or from entering certain places at certain times. So, for example, if a person is suspected of loitering around schools at break times in order to supply drugs to students, an anti-social behaviour order may require them not to come within 500 metres of the school between the hours of 8.00 a.m. and 6.00 p.m. However, this provision means that quasi-criminal penalties may be imposed without recourse to judicial process and the rules of evidence.

> These are people not formally convicted of any crime, yet languishing under house arrest or curfew, not even formally suspected of any crime and yet under repeated police investigation, and possibly ending up in prison – for up to five years remember – for infringing the terms of an ASBO by playing football in the street, leaving rubbish in their garden, or going out for a pint of milk at night.
>
> (Gardner et al., 1998)

These new pre-emptive measures extend the scope of the law significantly and are likely to encounter a succession of legal challenges if courts choose to impose them. It is ironic, of course, that whereas the community safety provisions of the 1998 Act aim to civilianise crime control, the youth justice provisions strive to criminalise incivility.

Prevention

The *No More Excuses* White Paper indicated that sentencing in the new youth justice system was to be guided by the '3Rs', *restoration*, *reintegration* and *responsibility* at all points in the tariff. This neatly alliterative strategy, which was lifted from the NACRO Young Offenders Committee report, *3Rs: Responsibility, Restoration and Reintegration* (1997), was described by Norman Warner as 'long term'. It was long term, he said, because eventually the impact of the pre-court pre-emptive interventions and the non-custodial preventive disposals introduced by the Act would obviate the need for incarceration. The government was also adamant that, because these preventive measures were evidence-based and should therefore instil a sense of responsibility and a capacity for self-discipline in young offenders, there was little likelihood that, having once been the subject of a preventive measure, the young person could be sentenced to one again.

In the 1980s, the heyday of 'systems management', 'prevention' was more or less abandoned by youth justice professionals. This was a reaction against the preventive strategies of the 1960s and 1970s, in which youth service, educational and therapeutic provision were, it was claimed, pressed haphazardly into the service of an ill-defined and unquantifiable 'prevention' (Pitts, 1988). The hard-headed, short-haired, systems managers of the 1980s would have none of these wishy-washy endeavours rooted, as they saw it, in both the morbid 'needology' of traditional social work and the deluded imaginings of the partially reconstructed hippies who haunted the fringes of youth justice, 'wittering on' about 'personal growth' and 'social change'.

The new 'prevention' which emerged in the 1990s was also a product of its time, reflecting a concern with fiscal propriety, robust management and individualistic explanations of social problems which were the hallmark of the era. In consequence, preventive intervention with young offenders in the twenty-first century was designed to take place within the youth justice system. Thus preventive interventions were linked with police final warnings, referral orders (introduced in 1999) reparation orders, action plan orders and supervision orders. The ideas which informed this approach to prevention were derived from the recommendations of *Young People and Crime* (Graham and Bowling, 1995) and *Misspent Youth* (Audit Commission, 1996) which were, in turn, derived from the theories of 'delinquent development' and 'victim-offender mediation' to be discussed in Chapters 5 and 6.

Custody

As we have already noted, the Crime and Disorder Act introduced secure training centres for 12 to 14-year-olds but it also allowed the Home Secretary to extend the new detention and training order (DTO) to 10- and 11-year-olds, if he believed that circumstances required it. For 12 to 14-year-olds, the DTO, which will be served in a secure training centre, may be imposed if a child commits three 'imprisonable' offences (all of which may be committed at the same time). For 15 to 17-year-olds, the DTO is available for any imprisonable offence sufficiently serious to justify custody under the Criminal Justice Act 1991. Orders will range in length from four months to two years.

Half of the period of the DTO is spent in custody and half under community supervision, which may be reinforced by a *home detention curfew*. The custodial element of the sentence may be shortened or extended on the basis of staff assessments of the young offender's 'progress' against an agreed 'sentence plan'. This reintroduces an element of indeterminacy into custodial sentencing for young people and raises fears about the degree of power placed in the hands of the social workers and prison officers who run these custodial establishments. A young offender who breaches their supervision requirements will be liable to a fine of up to level three (currently £1,000) or may be returned to custody for three months or their remainder of the sentence, whichever is the shorter.

Youth custody has been rising since 1993 (Home Office, 1998c) and the implementation of the 1998 Act, the rationalisation of the 'secure estate', the planned expansion of secure and custodial provision and the introduction of a 'three strikes' sentencing strategy for burglary, in June 2001, have exacerbated that trend. Such an expansion has inevitably diluted further the educational and rehabilitative resources available to young prisoners. However, it has also made even harder the task of developing penal regimes which do not worsen the problems which brought the young people into custody in the first place. An immediate problem facing the government upon its election was that the rising demand for secure local authority accommodation was rapidly outstripping supply. The Home Office stated that, in the short term, the practice of remanding juveniles to Prison Department establishments should continue but that youngsters deemed 'vulnerable' should be held in local authority provision. However, a report on the remand rescue initiative at Feltham Young Offender Institution (YOI) concluded that:

> It is extremely concerning to see such a large number of children who are deemed suitable for a custodial remand, considered 'unsuitable' for secure accommodation. It would appear that increasingly restrictive definitions of vulnerability are being adopted and access to secure accommodation appears to depend upon the willingness or ability of the local authority to locate and fund a placement, rather than a proper assessment of need.

> (London Youth Justice Managers' Group, 1998)

Yet, even committing a 15-year-old who is not officially deemed to be 'vulnerable' to these institutions, automatically renders them vulnerable to violent intimidation, opiate abuse and sexual molestation as well as exposure to Dickensian living conditions, as the Chief Inspector's report on Werrington Young Offenders Institution makes clear:

> I find it quite incredible that the Prison Service should have thought it appropriate to remove tolerable although not ideal arrangements for the treatment of children in custody in favour of utterly unsuitable conditions, replacing dormitories not with small house blocks, but one, large new cellular house block, of the type being put up in adult prisons. To compound this, immediately the new accommodation was built, the

population was increased and now 192 children are confined in 96 single cells designed for adults, on four landings of one long building. But what is even worse, and for which I can only assume that the Prison Service will plead the demands of overcrowding, because it cannot possibly be claimed to be providing appropriate custodial treatment and conditions for children, senior management failed to provide sufficient or appropriate resources, to go with the increased numbers. To find children no longer eating together, but forced to take their food back to their cells, which are little more than lavatories, to eat, being limited to two evenings of association in a week, on landings where there are no chairs, so the time amounts to little more than an hour and a half standing outside rather than inside a cell, would be bad enough if found in any juvenile establishment. To find that adult prison conditions have been deliberately introduced, over-turning previous and appropriate treatment and conditions for children, is nothing short of disgraceful. (Home Office, 1998b)

So alarmed was the Chief Inspector of Prisons, Sir David Ramsbotham, by the conditions in YOIs in England and Wales that, in 1997, he recommended to the New Labour government that no child or young person under 18 should be held in Prison Department establishments.

The government recognised that there were serious managerial and logistical problems within custodial institutions for children and young people and, in 1997, it asked the Youth Justice Taskforce to report upon the state of the 'juvenile secure estate'. The taskforce considered the arrangements for detaining young offenders in YOIs run by the Prison Service, secure accommodation run by local authorities and the Glenthorne Youth Treatment Centre run by the Department of Health. Its final report concluded:

The different types of facilities for young people that constitute the secure estate are in need of major reform. Current arrangements are both inconsistent and unsatisfactory. Young offender institutions are too large. Bullying and abuse of one young offender by another occurs too often while the education offered is often poor. Some young offender institutions, notably Lancaster Farms, have made major efforts to provide good services but even in these cases there is scope for improving links between the supervision a young person receives inside the institution and the supervision provided when the young person returns to the community. (Youth Justice Board, 1998)

Yet, like governments throughout the preceding 200 years, New Labour responded to the apparent failure of imprisonment by supporting the development of a new kind of prison, the youth training centre (YTC). The YTC, the Home Office maintained, was to be robustly managed in accordance with clear goals, to be 'transparent' in its operation, to utilise only proven rehabilitative programmes within a professional regime which accorded with 'best practice' in the residential care sector.

Locking Up Children

The prototype for New Labour's new forms of custodial confinement for younger children was the Medway Secure Training Centre (STC), located, as fate would have it, just outside the village of Borstal in Kent, where the first, and highly successful, Borstal institution was established by Alexander Patterson in the 1920s. Run by Rebound ECD (Education, Care and Discipline), a subsidiary of Group 4 and Tarmac, Medway STC was designed to house up to 40 of Britain's most troublesome 12 to 14-year-olds at a cost of £2400 per head per week. On the face of it Rebound ECD did not have to try too hard to improve upon previous results:

> *The Home Office Prison Statistics for 1992 contain the latest reconviction figures for 14 to 16-year-olds released from Prison Service custody: these are for those released in 1987 and followed for four years. Eighty-one per cent of boys in this age group leaving Detention Centres and 85% of those leaving Youth Custody Centres were reconvicted within two years. The figures after four years were 90% and 92% respectively. The figures for girls aged 15 and 16 leaving Youth Custody Centres were 49% after two years and 55% after four years.* (Penal Affairs Consortium, 1994)

However, as Woody Allen once observed, 'if you want to make God laugh, tell him your plans'. Medway STC opened in spring 1998. Staff were vetted in accordance with the recommendations of the Warner Report, *Choosing with Care* (Warner, 1996). They then received 11 weeks training, which included instruction in the use of restraint techniques permitted by the Children Act (1989). Accountability was to be ensured by creating easy access for inmates to a variety of 'watchdog' organisations. Thus the site of Medway STC was festooned with posters about, and the telephone numbers of, Childline, The Samaritans and the Voice of the Child in Care, and there were plenty of telephones on which to call them. Voice of the Child in Care also provided 'independent visitors', who visited the children frequently. Moreover, the institution was monitored by both the Home Office and the Social Services Inspectorate. Medway STC represented the 'cutting edge' of 'institutional transparency'. Sue Clifton, an ex-police officer, who was first head of the centre observed, just prior to its opening in May 1998, that 'Rehabilitation is the whole emphasis. We try to play down the security systems' (*Community Care*, 7–13 May 1998). Yet, within weeks we learned that:

> *More than 30 police wearing riot equipment had to use dogs to quell the disturbance at the Medway Secure Training Centre. Three staff were injured and windows smashed as 15 children, many wielding snooker cues and balls, ran riot last night. It was an hour and a half before the incident was brought under control.*

> (*London Evening Standard*, 26 June 1998)

This was, more or less, a re-run of the scenes which had accompanied the launch of the similarly hyped DHSS Youth Treatment Centre, in Brentwood in Essex, in the mid-1970s. Like Medway, Brentwood STC had also attempted to bring some of the most difficult and disturbed children in the country together under one roof. The original Brentwood Centre was eventually burnt to the ground by inmates. As to the possibility of these regimes reducing the criminality of their inmates, Masud Hoghughi, principal of Aycliffe, a residential unit for seriously disturbed young people in the north-east of England, and Professor of Psychology at Newcastle University has observed:

Quite extensive evidence suggests that no amount of tinkering with institutional structures, programmes and procedures has any important or long-term impact on the propensity to re-offend…I would simply say that because the political and professional fashion of an era leads us to expect that a particular provision, such as a Borstal or community home is the 'right' place for processing delinquents into law-abiding citizens does not make them so. We have too many social white elephants, from the re-organisation of the National Health Service to Youth Treatment Centres and the proliferation of 'observation and assessment centres' to have much faith in fashionable wisdom. Nor have any but a small confused band of those who run institutions for delinquents ever claimed any expertise in curbing further delinquency.

(Hoghughi, 1983)

By the autumn of 1998, the 'small confused band' running Medway STC were getting very jumpy indeed as they were 'bitten, hit and headbutted' by children, some of whom were teetering on the edge of mental illness. More than 100 assaults on staff were recorded in the centre's first seven months of operation, along with £100,000 worth of damage. Over the period, 35 of the original 100 staff resigned and an increasingly perplexed and frustrated Home Office finally decided it was time to call in reinforcements. Nick Cohen writes:

The despised public-sector Prison Service has now been ordered to draw up riot control plans better suited to Strangeways or Fort Apache the Bronx. According to the latest leaked documents from the Home Office – and I don't know what morale's like in Whitehall but I'm getting more Home Office leaks than Christmas cards this season – 'prompt and effective' measures must be planned for when 'there is a major threat to overall control'. Containing the 12 year olds is so arduous a task that the most senior and hard-bitten security officers in the Prison Service, known as 'Gold' commanders, are on alert. 'Strategic command of an incident will rest with a Prison Service Gold,' the memo continues, 'who will operate from the Headquarters Control Suite.' Gold's Swat team will be authorised to use 'basic and advanced control and restraint techniques'. ('Hey, Tony, Leave Those Kids Alone', *The Observer*, 20 January 1998)

So much for the 1989 Children Act's 'restraint' guidelines. The Social Services Inspectorate submitted a damning report on Medway STC in January 1999, recommending that it be shut down and that the other four STCs under construction, at an estimated cost of £30m, should be put on hold. Paul Boateng, recently transferred from the Department of Health, where he launched the Quality Protects initiative to safeguard children in residential care, refused to be drawn on the issue of closure, referring to the Medway trainees as 'little monsters'. A leaked 'unpublished' report by the Home Office in October 2000, indicated that, in the first six weeks after release, 30 per cent of the first cohort of STC children had reoffended (Goldson and Peters, 2000).

In Spring 2002 England and Wales had more children and young people under lock and key than at any time since the youth justice system was brought into being in 1908, and more, pro rata, than any other Western European country. There were also more children, young people and parents under the supervision of youth justice personnel. Between 1995 and 1999, the numbers of children and young people sentenced to some form of custodial confinement in England and Wales (excluding those held under the Mental Health Act 1983) rose by approximately 30% from 5,863 to 8,492. These figures are the more remarkable because this period has seen a steady decline in the crime rate. Not only were more young people being held in custody; they were also being held for longer. Between 1989 and 1999 the average custodial sentence for 15 to 17-year-old boys increased from 5.6 months to 10.3 months. For girls the figures were 5.5 months to 7.1 months.

Most Young Offender Institutions (YOIs) are under-funded and overcrowded and some are badly mismanaged. Even in the better institutions, only 30% of young prisoners receive education. At Feltham YOI in 2001 only 10% of inmates were attending education classes despite the fact that in the system generally, 54% of inmates score below level one (GCSE standard) in reading ability. Sir David Ramsbotham, Chief Inspector of Prisons, found that over 50% of young prisoners on remand and 30% of those serving a sentence have a diagnosable mental health problem. These problems are compounded by widespread drug abuse, violence and intimidation. Self-harm is at record levels. In the past 10 years 22 boys aged 15 to 17 have taken their own lives in YOIs in England and Wales and one has been killed by a cell-mate. Among 18 to 20-year-olds, the figure for successful suicide attempts during the period is 65. A recent Chief Inspectors report on Feltham YOI noted that 'the boredom and isolation of spending long hours in cell was overwhelming'; the regime there was, he said, 'rotten to the core'. Michel Foucault (1977) has observed that, from its inception, the failure of the prison has always been greeted with plans to construct a 'new' prison. Spencer Millham (1973) has shown that in the UK, the failure of, or crises within, each new form of secure provision for juveniles has spawned another type of institution which promptly finds that it is heir to all the difficulties which confounded the institution it has superseded.

The Ghost of Systems Past

It is important to remind ourselves that the revamped youth justice system ushered in by the Crime and Disorder Act 1998 is a system rather than a simple conglomeration of measures which government ministers and their advisers believe to be a good idea. Systems are, by definition, characterised by the inter-relatedness and interdependence of all system elements. A systemic perspective alerts us to the reality that, when agents and agencies within a justice system effect choices about the populations with which they will intervene and the ways in which they will use their power and authority, they will have consequences for all the other parts of that system.

The youth justice system introduced by the Crime and Disorder Act 1988 has the following characteristics:

- It allows formal pre-emptive intervention with populations previously beyond the reach of the youth justice and child protection systems, thus drawing larger numbers of children, young people and their parents, into the purview of these systems.

- By utilising a mixture of civil and criminal measures, the subjects of these interventions become de facto protagonists in legal proceedings which may result in the imposition of additional penalties, sanctions or injunctions.

- The ending of police discretion in repeat cautioning and its replacement by one reprimand and one final warning, backed up by programmes of restorative justice, cognitive-behavioural change and parental education, will mean that children and young people in trouble will exhaust this option at a younger age and an earlier stage in their offending careers.

- The *Final Warning*, and the programmes which accompany it, will probably deter around 70 per cent of those inducted into the system. It is unlikely to stop the remaining 30 per cent; most of whom will come from troubled backgrounds which give them no real 'stake in conformity'. They will now enter the Youth Court at a younger age and at an earlier stage in their offending careers than would previously have been the case.

- The *Absolute and Conditional Discharge*, a disposal previously imposed in 28 per cent of the cases coming before the Court was replaced by the Referral Order from 2001. Having been found guilty of an offence, a young person is referred to a *Youth Offender Panel*, with a professional and lay membership, which will determine the nature of the penalty to be imposed and/or the type of programme a child or young person should pursue. Any prosecution flowing from a breach of the *Absolute* or *Conditional Discharge* required that a young person should re-offend, that the offence should be detected, that they should be apprehended, charged, prosecuted and found guilty. A breach of a *Referral Order*, by contrast requires only that the youngster fails to attend a session of their 'programme'. As evidence from a similar scheme operating in Denmark indicates, this will almost certainly result in a higher number of young people re-appearing in Court (Mehlbye and Walgrave, 1998) and so being made the subjects of an *Action Plan Order*, a *Reparation Order* or a *Supervision Order*. Should they breach these orders by re-offending during their currency, and over 55 per cent will probably do so (Audit Commission, 1996), or should they offend after a second community sentence, they are very likely to receive a custodial sentence or have a 'residence requirement' inserted in their supervision order. This is because the 1998 Act repeals the certified specified activity requirement which required the Youth Court to state that a supervision order was being imposed as an alternative to, and therefore the equivalent of, a custodial sentence. This caveat was designed to indicate that the young person had reached a particularly serious stage in their offending career but that the community alternative could offer a sufficient level of control and containment and a greater prospect of rehabilitation. This change will mean that the supervision order will be imposed upon 'lower tariff' offenders, thus drawing them towards the 'gates of the prison' much faster.

- The extension of the power of the Youth Courts to remand children and young people directly into secure and penal establishments, the unequivocal signals sent to magistrates by the expansion of secure and custodial provision, and the Home Secretary's observation, in spring 1998, that 'prisons are a demand-led service, if the courts want to impose custodial sentences, it is my job to provide the cells', have all fuelled the use of custodial disposals by sentencers. This process was moved up a gear in 2001 with the introduction of a 'three strikes' sentencing strategy for burglary.

- With the advent of the Secure Training Centres, the numbers of 12 to 15-year-olds sentenced to DTOs will increase substantially and quickly fill the available places. This will mean that existing YOIs will have to be redesignated, and growing numbers of 15-year-olds will be pushed up into YOIs. Norman Warner, Chair of the Youth Justice Board of England and Wales, has confirmed that this is likely to be the case in the 'short term'. There is no official word on why or when this situation is likely to change.

We Have Been Here Before...

As the Heath, Wilson and Callaghan administrations of the 1970s discovered, early intervention in a youth justice system which does not 'manage' the sentencing process, will draw youngsters further into it, and accelerate their progress through it. In 1965, 21 per cent of convicted young offenders were dealt with in attendance centres, detention centres and Borstals. The early 1970s saw a growth in early intervention by the police and social workers and an increase in the availability of secure and custodial provision for

young offenders. By 1977 the proportion of youngsters being dealt wi
custodial provision had risen to 38 per cent. As these populations gre\
and young people in these institutions became less and less problemat.
1983, Leon Brittan indicated that magistrates should feel free to impose harsh sentences
if they saw fit. Between May 1983 and May 1984 the youth custody population rose by
65 per cent. As a result of this experience, and a few others like it, it is now a firmly
established precept that if politicians hand more power to the bench, or even hint that
they wish magistrates to make greater use of their existing powers, they will. This is why,
subsequently, Home Secretaries Hurd, Waddington and Baker took to sending the bench
unequivocal messages about reducing sentence lengths and using alternatives to custody
whenever possible, in an attempt to inject some rationality and proportionality into
sentencing in the youth justice system.

The National Association for Youth Justice (1998) has calculated that the 1998 Act
will lead to a 150 per cent increase in the numbers of children and young people entering
the youth justice system. This is called 'net-widening' and it is what 'unmanaged' youth
justice systems with a rehabilitative orientation tend to do (Cohen, 1979).

The New 'New Penology'

Beginning in the 1970s in the USA and the 1980s in the UK, we saw the emergence of
what Feeley and Simon (1992) describe as a 'new penology'. The new penology marked
the convergence of two intellectual and political currents. One, dubbed 'the decline of the
rehabilitative ideal', marked the exhaustion of the belief that, through scientifically informed
professional interventions with individuals, families and groups, in institutions and in the
community, it would be possible to change the behaviour, beliefs and attitudes of children
and young people who broke the law (Preston, 1980). The other, a neo-Conservative
criminology, held that crime, like the poor, was always with us and that our best bet was
to incapacitate the most serious offenders with exemplary jail sentences and subject lesser
criminals and those on the edge of crime to cost-effective management and surveillance.

The new penology represented a merging of managerial, technical and social scientific
discourses into a new technology for the optimal disposition of adjudicated offenders.
Until 1992, the youth justice system of England and Wales, with its commitment to
diversion, normalisation, and informalism approximated to this model. However, since
1992, Conservative, and latterly Labour, Home Secretaries have committed themselves to
a far more optimistic strategy predicated upon a confidence in the deterrent effects of
early intervention and the efficacy of evidence-based correctional interventions. The youth
justice provisions of the Crime and Disorder Act 1998 are built upon two central assumptions
about the nature of youth crime. The first is that, for whatever reason, young offenders

fail to anticipate, or are unconcerned about, the impact of their crime upon their victims. The second is that young offenders have failed to develop the cognitive capacities and social skills necessary to avoid or resist involvement in crime. It follows that interventions to reduce or eradicate youth crime will strive on the one hand to confront them with the consequences of their criminal actions in order to change the ways they feel about their offending, while on the other it will get them to examine the logic of the choices they make, in order to change the ways they think about their offending. In the next chapter we shall focus upon the ways that young offenders are confronted with the consequences of their actions. In the subsequent chapter we shall consider the ways in which they are encouraged to think about their offending.

Burgeoning child and youth imprisonment notwithstanding, Home Office ministers and their advisers still appear to believe that young offenders can be 'turned around' at a relatively early stage in their criminal careers by the administration of these programmes, thus obviating the need for incarceration. The new measures will work, they argue, because they are 'evidence-based' and rooted in 'what research points to as the most thorough and best designed programmes, showing the most promising results' (Farrington, 1996). But what if they are not, and what if they don't?

Chapter 5

The Confrontation with Consequences

Anglo-Saxon liberal legalism has crushed the communitarian justice of the Celtic peoples, the Maoris, Aboriginal Australians, native Americans, and Asian ethnic groups, with an unequivocal imperial system that sacrifices diversity in problem solving strategies to the belief in equal treatment under one standard strategy.

(Braithwaite and Daly, 1994)

Defend the children of the poor and punish the wrongdoer.

(Words carved above the main entrance to the Central Criminal Court at the Old Bailey, London)

Restorative Justice

In Australasia, North America and Western Europe, the 1990s saw a growing belief among the politicians, police officers, academics, clergy, penal reformers, managers and professionals involved in youth justice that *restorative*, rather than *retributive* modes of justice offered the solution to what they saw as the worldwide crisis of youth and adult justice systems. It is, perhaps, a testimony to the impact of the restorative justice movement, that it occupies a central place in the Crime and Disorder Act, underpinning the Final Warning, the Action Plan Order and the Detention and Training Order. Moreover, restorative measures constitute the central plank of the Youth Justice and Criminal Evidence Act 1999 which introduced a Referral Order. This order requires that a convicted juvenile be referred to a panel of lay people and professionals for a decision about the most appropriate response to his or her offending (Goldson, 2000).

The Origins of 'Restorative Justice'

In May 1997, at a conference in Belgium, penal reformers and academics from Europe, North America and Australasia put their signatures to the 'Declaration of Leuven'. In this document they affirmed their belief that restorative justice was superior in virtually every respect to existing systems of retributive justice. The Declaration of Leuven has been dismissed by some critics as the utopian outpouring of a handful of politically marginal intellectuals and would-be social reformers (Haines, 1997). But this ignores the reality that, in the recent period, youth justice systems in many European states and other advanced industrial nations around the world have introduced substantial elements of restorative justice (Christie, 1977; Braithwaite, 1989; Wright, 1991; Barberan, 1997; Blatier and Poussin, 1997; Ciefu, 1997; Mika and Zehr, 1997).

What is now known as 'restorative justice' has its roots in the criminological debates about the relative merits of 'formal' and 'informal' systems of justice of the 1970s and 1980s. In these debates, formal justice was castigated for its inability to respond to the real nature of the interpersonal conflicts it clumsily identified as crime, and its consequent irrelevance to the needs of both victims and offenders. Formal justice systems, it was claimed, not only failed to reduce crime but actually worsened the problem to which they were supposed to be a solution, by deepening the antagonisms between the protagonists.

Whether, and why, restorative justice should emerge in any particular national youth justice system can only be answered by reference to national histories and contemporary political contingencies. However, there appear to be a number of supranational factors, the convergence and interplay of which have ensured that, as we enter the new millennium, restorative justice has emerged as the new 'big idea' in European youth justice.

The Failure of Retribution

The 1980s saw a marked increase in the incidence of recorded crime in Europe and the USA. In the face of the parallel increase in the numbers of recorded offences and the numbers consigned to jail and community corrections, there was a widespread recognition that the justice system was 'failing'. Alongside this came the realisation that the bulk of victims of crime were located on the social and economic margins, a predicament they shared with the perpetrators of those crimes, who often lived in the same neighbourhoods. This meant that, whatever the outcome of the legal process, victims and perpetrators were destined to have a continuing relationship (Lea and Young, 1984).

The Repudiation of Minimalism

The 1990s witnessed growing disenchantment, in the Anglophone world at least, with both the 'benign neglect' of left-wing 'radical non-intervention' and the malign indifference of the neo-liberal right, in matters of youth justice, as crime rates rose and the social and economic predicament of lower-class children and young people worsened.

The Politicisation of the Victim

In the 1990s, the victims of crime emerged as a significant political constituency in the UK, prompting Home Secretary Michael Howard to offer them a Victims' Charter. More significantly perhaps, the bereaved parents of Leah Betts and Steven Lawrence, and the wife of Philip Lawrence, the murdered headmaster, all emerged as central political actors in the law and order debate. These developments supported pressures to give victims a 'voice' in the justice process and to 'empower' local people to take back control of their neighbourhoods and in some cases, under the pre-emptive provisions of the Crime and Disorder Act 1998, their neighbours as well. The logic of these developments as Braithwaite (1989) has opined, is that, 'Sanctions imposed by relatives, friends or a personally relevant collectivity may have more effect on criminal behaviour than sanctions imposed by a remote legal authority'. Although this idea has proved less popular with the British public when applied in Saudi Arabia, the involvement of victims in the justice process has, apparently, made sense to politicians and justice system administrators and professionals around the world.

The Rise of Authoritarian Communitarianism

As we have noted, the 1990s also saw the advent of the highly influential communitarian doctrine which contends that the family, teachers and the police must work together to inculcate an appropriate morality in the young, and that crime can be thwarted if wrongdoers are made visible to their community through processes of public 'shaming'.

The Advent of Organic Justice

In contrast with the authoritarianism of certain versions of communitarianism, the 1980s and 1990s witnessed the growth of a nostalgic relativism in the social sciences and penal politics which rejected the 'grand narratives' of the dominant, Western, state justice systems in favour of forms of 'conflict resolution', or 'peace-making' justice which were local, indigenous, organic and authentic. 'Formal' justice systems, it was claimed, not only failed to reduce crime but actually worsened the problems to which they are supposed to be a solution, by deepening the antagonisms between the protagonists. Christie (1977), for example, argues that the state and the lawyers have 'stolen' the conflict from the parties and advocates a return to culturally relevant forms of conflict resolution.

Neo-Christian Moral Entrepreneurism

In the face of dwindling congregations and the widespread revision of traditional articles of faith by the clergy, the churches have sought a new, secular, terrain upon which to deploy what remains of their beliefs, values, skills and personnel. Having relinquished their claim to understand and to be able to facilitate a better relationship between 'man' and God, elements within the church have switched to the more modest project of modelling desirable social relationships. This marks a move from a metaphysical to a metaphorical role for the Christian church. Importantly, in the UK, the church entered this terrain in the early 1990s at a moment when many members of the government's front bench were making considerable play of their Christian beliefs and their desire to restore the nation to moral health.

The Idea of Restorative Justice

In their study of restorative justice programmes in North America, Mika and Zehr (1997) identify the key concepts, beliefs and principles operationalised in the restorative process:

1. Crime is a violation of individual rights and interpersonal relationships

The victims and the community have been harmed and need restoration. The primary victims are those most directly affected by the offence but others, such as family members of victims and offenders, witnesses and members of the affected community are also victims. The relationships affected (and reflected) by crime must be addressed. Victims, offenders and the affected communities are the key stakeholders in justice. A restorative justice process maximises the input and participation of these parties in the search for restoration, healing, responsibility and prevention. The state has circumscribed roles, such as investigating facts, facilitating processes and ensuring safety, but the state is not a primary victim.

2. Violations create obligations and liabilities

The offender's obligation, inasmuch as it is possible, is to make things right. Since the primary obligation is to the victim, a restorative justice process empowers victims to effectively participate in defining obligations. Offenders are offered opportunities and encouragement to understand the harm they have caused to victims and the community and to develop plans for taking appropriate responsibility. Voluntary participation by offenders is maximised and coercion and exclusion are minimised. However, offenders may be required to accept their obligations if they do not do so voluntarily. Obligations may be experienced as difficult, even painful, but are not intended as pain, vengeance or revenge. Obligations such as restitution to victims take priority over other sanctions and obligations to the state such as fines. Offenders must actively address their own needs. The community's obligations are to victims and to offenders and for the general welfare of its members. The community has a responsibility to support victims of crime and to meet their needs. It also bears a responsibility for all its members and the social conditions and relationships which promote both crime and community peace.

3. Restorative justice seeks to heal the rifts and right the wrongs

The needs of victims for information, validation, vindication, restitution, testimony, safety and support are the starting point of justice. The safety of victims is an immediate priority. The process of justice maximises opportunities for exchange of information, participation, dialogue and mutual consent between victim and offender. Face-to-face encounters are appropriate in some instances, while alternative forms of exchange will be more appropriate in others. Victims have the principal role in defining and directing the terms and conditions of the exchange. Mutual agreement takes precedence over imposed outcomes. Offenders' needs and competencies are addressed. Recognising that offenders themselves have often been harmed, healing and integration of offenders into the community are emphasised. Offenders are supported and treated respectfully in the justice process. Justice values personal change over compliant behaviour. Removal from the community is minimised. Lode Walgrave (1994) has helpfully expressed the differences between retributive, rehabilitative and restorative justice in diagrammatic form (see Table 5.1).

Table 5.1: Differences Between Retributive, Rehabilitative and Restorative Justice

	Retributive	*Rehabilitative*	*Restorative*
Reference	Offence	Criminal person	Losses
Means	Inflicting harm	Treatment	Obligation to repair
Objectives	Juridico-moral balance	Conformity	Elimination of loss
Victim's position	Secondary	Secondary	Central
Criteria for evaluation	Just desserts	Conformity	Satisfaction of parties
Societal context	State power	State welfare	State responsibility

Does Restorative Justice 'Work'?

In 1992, following the introduction of Rule 6A (Section 2) into the penal code, the youth justice system in Catalonia, Spain, placed victim-offender mediation and reparation at the centre of its youth justice system. In the following year, 40.2 per cent of all cases entering the system were dealt with in this way. In 68.5 per cent of these cases victims and offenders were able to reach agreement about the remedy. Jaime Barberan notes that:

> *A fundamental principle underlying mediation in Catalonia is that although financial or material compensation may be important, most important is the re-establishment of a dialogue between victim and perpetrator in order to restore the relationship which was fractured by the offence. Moreover, this fractured relationship may hold the key to many others in the neighbourhood and so its successful restoration may be central to the young person's successful re-integration into the neighbourhood. Indeed, 78.2 per cent of all outcomes rated successful by participants were based upon solutions which were based on such a dialogue.*   (Barberan, 1997)

In their evaluation of the first year of operation of the programme, Elejabarrieta et al. (1993) observed that it proved harder to reach agreement in cases where the perpetrator initially lodged a 'not guilty' plea and easiest in the cases of 12- and 13-year-olds. Successful outcomes were most frequent in cases involving damage to property, and least frequent in cases of interpersonal violence. Nonetheless, most victims and offenders participating in the process registered satisfaction with it. The much publicised Northants Diversion Scheme (Audit Commission 1996) contains an element of mediation, and a substantial majority of offenders and victims who have participated felt that it had been beneficial.

The Limitations of Restorative Justice

1. Methodological difficulties

There are some serious methodological problems in evaluating restorative justice, since projects are often evaluated too early because of anxieties about the cessation of funding. As a result, it tends to be the atypical fully-funded, well-resourced demonstration projects which are fully evaluated and about which we have the best information. Beyond this, restorative justice often constitutes just one element in a broader programme of intervention, and as a consequence it has proved difficult to isolate its specific effects.

2. Theoretical problems

At the core of reparation and mediation are unanswered questions about the mechanisms of change triggered by these modes of intervention. More specifically, we do not know whether young offenders can generalise identification with a particular victim they have harmed to an empathy with other potential victims. The Kirkholt study (Forrester et al., 1990) suggests that 'burglars' divide the world into legitimate and illegitimate targets, raising the possibility that even reparation and mediation programmes rated as 'successful' by both victim and offender may, at best, merely have served to de-legitimise a particular victim in the minds of the offenders.

3. Impact on offending

Like the proponents of the cognitive-behavioural programmes discussed in the next chapter, even the most enthusiastic advocates of restorative justice are only able to assert that 'outcomes in terms of recidivism seem to be positive, though further research is needed to establish this more firmly' (Bazemore et al., 1997). In his overview of restorative justice programmes undertaken for the Home Office, Tony Marshall (1999) notes that research on the relationship between participation in restorative justice programmes and re-conviction is inconclusive. This finding is echoed by Lipsey and Wilson (1998) in their meta-analysis of the ten best evaluated US 'restitutive' intervention programmes. In their analysis of several hundred evaluations of victim-offender mediation programmes in the USA, probably the largest ever undertaken, Howell et al. (1995) found that although victims and offenders often indicated a high degree of satisfaction with the process of mediation, its impact upon re-offending appeared to be minimal. Indeed, whatever its merits in terms of victim-offender satisfaction, there is little to suggest that restorative justice has a particularly positive effect on re-conviction rates (Van Hooris, 1985).

4. The educative role of law

As we have noted, restorative justice is predicated upon the belief that, wherever possible, the law should be kept at bay and that extra-judicial modes of conflict resolution are almost always superior to judicial modes. This assumes, however, that the law and the judicial process are simply a mechanism for distributing sanctions. In fact, in recent years, in its dealings with domestic violence, marital rape, 'date rape', racist offences, sexual offences, 'neighbours from hell' and, increasingly, offences previously designated as 'bullying', and hence of no concern to the law, the judicial process and the law have played a key role in redefining the rights and obligations of parties to a legal conflict. In so doing, the law has revealed its 'educative' function. It is fairly evident that these interventions have been welcomed by victims and that they are 'progressive' in both intent and effect. These legal interventions, like much legislation on race and gender, also outstrip, and contribute to the revision of, popular opinion because they give greater weight and authority to the alternative perspective. Such interventions lie beyond the scope of restorative justice which, by definition, is bounded by the pertaining, popular, view of propriety and proportionality. It is hard to see how extra-judicial forms of conflict resolution could contribute to the revision of social expectations and the construction of new moral sensibilities in the way that the judicial process, in its progressive moment, is able to do.

5. The symmetry of victim and offender

It is evident from self-report victimisation studies, that those neighbourhoods with the highest levels of crime also have the highest incidence of repeat victimisation and the lowest rates of reporting (Lea and Young, 1994; Forrester et al., 1990; Hope, 1995). Not least of the reasons for this is that in these neighbourhoods, the bulk of the crime is committed by close neighbours, and victims often know, or can guess, the identity of the perpetrators and are destined to have continuing face-to-face contact with them. It is hardly surprising that in such circumstances most people are loath to report crime, let alone initiate prosecutions, since to do so could well invite further, often violent, offences being perpetrated against them. Similarly, victims of domestic violence or marital rape are easily dissuaded. One of the major advances in the policing of such offences has been the decision, in recent years, on the part of many police forces to take an active stance and initiate prosecutions in their own right rather than at the behest of the victim. This can serve to deflect malevolent attention away from the victim and inject a countervailing power into a situation in which all the power was previously in the hands of the perpetrator. In these circumstances, it is precisely the formalisation of the legal intervention, the entry of the state as a powerful legal protagonist which, by offering the necessary protections to the victim, resolves the conflict. Beyond this, of course, there is growing support among organisations which work with both the victims and perpetrators of domestic violence and child abuse that, in many cases, only a formal legal intervention will persuade many perpetrators that what they are doing is not, in fact, 'normal' and, to that extent, such intervention maximises the safety of victims (Morran, 1996).

6. Clarity of aims

A further limitation of restorative justice as it has developed so far, is that its purpose often remains unclear. Some projects are largely victim-oriented, concerned, inasmuch as it is possible, to restore the victim to their former condition of well-being. In others, the aim appears to be to make good the damage done by the crime through financial or other forms of reparation. In other projects, the 'community' emerges as the victim, while the actual victim is effectively edited out of the script. These projects usually utilise some form of community service. Most restorative justice programmes are located in the voluntary sector and so their aims and objectives often reflect the theological or humanistic perceptions of their funders concerning the ways in which human beings should relate to one another. Aims and objectives sometimes become blurred and the conflicting interests of stakeholders are obscured. Thus, for example, a project claiming to be a resource for victims may, in fact, be acting primarily as a mechanism for diverting young offenders from custody. Because of this loose fit with the justice system, accountability is often tenuous and the criteria by which decisions are to be reached are often unclear.

7. Incorporation

The signatories to the Declaration of Leuven want to see existing systems of retributive justice replaced by restorative justice. However, youth justice in New Zealand offers the only example in the world of a system where restorative justice is offered as a straight alternative to due process of law. In North America and Europe, restorative justice has usually developed as a relatively minor component at the 'light' end of retributive justice systems. Moreover, there is a continuing tension between restorative justice as a 'bottom-up social movement' which is antagonistic to formal systems of retributive justice, and its 'top-down' incorporation into the justice system. Mika and Zehr (1997) have observed that where funding comes from a statutory source, projects are likely to retain a more retributive mandate. In England and Wales restorative justice is either offered by the police as an alternative to prosecution, or by order of the court, thus undermining much of its philosophical rationale. Moreover, it can be positioned at any point in the system: at the 'front end', as a component in programmes linked to the police final warning, in the middle as part of an action plan order, or at the 'back end' as a last resort before the imposition of a Detention and Training Order, or indeed, as a component in the post-release element of a Detention and Training Order.

8. Spreading the net

It is, as yet, unclear whether restorative justice widens the net of control, by drawing new populations of low-tariff offenders into the justice system, or pushes more serious offenders up-tariff. However, this is an ever-present tendency in such ill-defined, ambiguously positioned, yet apparently benign, interventions. In Denmark, a system of youth contracts, upon which the referral order, introduced by the Youth Justice and Criminal Evidence Act 1999 was based, was introduced in September 1991 (Mehlbye and Sommer, 1998). These contracts aimed to make first and second-time young offenders accountable to their victims and to subject them to greater surveillance. One unintended consequence of these measures has been that in a substantial minority of cases, a breach of the youth contract has led to the imposition of penalties significantly more severe than the original offence would have warranted. In this case, restorative justice, coupled with a penal sanction, has the inadvertent effect of projecting the young person deeper into a retributive justice system. There is little evidence at present that restorative justice either defends the rights of, or delivers services to, young people in trouble. Indeed, some commentators (Haines, 2000) have suggested that mediation may simply offer yet another setting in which an effectively silent young offender can be browbeaten by a roomful of adults into an agreement they do not understand.

9. Indigenous justice?

Despite the extravagant claims of its supporters, there is also little evidence that restorative justice, as currently practised, is particularly responsive to cultural differences in conflict resolution. This reservation takes on greater importance when we learn that the traditional Maori 'family group conference', which is not by definition indigenous to anywhere else, but has nonetheless been adopted throughout the world, is having problems securing the participation of Maori youth. It appears that they are opting for the security of due process within a retributive system of justice.

It is both ironic and significant that a mode of informal justice which aims to mobilise relationships of kinship and friendship within a face-to-face 'community' should emerge at a moment when both the family and the 'community' are under unprecedented stress. Moreover it seems evident that, the far more benign intentions of its professional and academic devotees notwithstanding, restorative justice is to be part and parcel of a broader initiative to restore authority and discipline to families, schools and neighbourhoods. This 'communitarian' endeavour appears to be bent upon exhuming the 'restorative' practices believed to have characterised a simpler and more harmonious age, but one in which we were even less tolerant of youthful misbehaviour than we are now. As such restorative justice, as an essentially progressive endeavour, is in grave danger of becoming implicated in the 'naming and shaming', the electronic tagging, the erosion of the distinction between adult and juvenile jurisdictions and the conflation of crime and incivility which characterise the emerging youth justice system in England and Wales (Hughes, 1996). Thus, the crucial question is not whether restorative justice is a 'good' or 'effective' option, but where it will be located in the sentencing tariff and what practical and ideological purposes it will be required to serve within an increasingly punitive youth justice system, the end point of which is the expanded, teenage prison.

Chapter 6

The Development of Discernment

They may have poor levels of ability in relation to solving problems within relationships, through being unable to predict the consequences of their behaviour. Egocentricity is common, according to Ross, and is manifested in a lack of sensitivity to the thoughts and feelings of other people. Value systems may be very limited, often to a concept of 'if it's good for me it must be good'. Finally, offenders might have trouble with critical reasoning, being irrational and illogical; they are easily influenced by others.

(Gardiner and Nesbitt, 1996)

The only advice I can offer, should you wake up vertiginously in a strange flat, with a thoroughly installed hangover, without any clothing, without any recollection of how you got there, with the police sledge hammering down the door to the accompaniment of excited dogs, while you are surrounded by bales of lavishly-produced magazines featuring children in adult acts, the only advice I can offer is try to be good humoured and polite.

(Tibar Fischer, 1994)

Cognition and Sensibility

The implicit aetiology of youth crime underpinning the Crime and Disorder Act 1998 is derived from 'developmental' theories of criminality, while most of the pre-emptive, preventive and punitive measures available under the Act involve interventions aimed at getting young offenders to 'think straight'. In this chapter we shall interrogate the ideas associated with the concept of 'delinquent development' and their fit with the cognitive-behavioural interventions they inform. These ideas are important because, together with fast-tracking and restorative justice, they will determine whether the youth justice provisions of the Crime and Disorder Act 1998 achieve their primary goal: the reduction or eradication of crime among adjudicated young offenders.

The Origins of the Theory of Delinquent Development

In Britain, the Cambridge Study of Delinquent Development is the most comprehensive longitudinal study of youth offending ever undertaken (Farrington and West, 1993). Between

1961 and 1985, a research team followed 411 South London boys, born in 1953, from the age of eight to their thirty-second year. Respondents were asked to report the nature and extent of their offending during this period and these data were compared with offending recorded by the police. Alongside this, the boys' parents and teachers and other professionals were asked to rate their abilities, attitudes and behaviour, utilising IQ tests, 'social adjustment scales' and 'personality inventories'. Importantly, the study was able to observe differences between convicted and non-convicted young people over the period. However, until recently, the aetiological theories and rehabilitative programmes associated with the theory of 'delinquent development' have been largely neglected by both mainstream criminology and policy makers in the UK. In the 1970s and the early 1980s, the methods and the objectives of studies of this kind were out of tune with the prevailing orthodoxy which held that:

> It does not seem to matter what form of treatment in the correctional system is attempted, whether vocational training or academic education; whether counselling inmates individually, in groups or not at all; whether therapy is administered by social workers or psychiatrists; whether the institutional context of the treatment is custodial or benign; whether the sentences are short or long; whether the person is placed on probation or released on parole; or whether the treatment takes place in the community or in institutions. (Wilson, 1975)

This sombre assessment, based on Martinson's (1974) survey of 231 research studies, was underscored by many subsequent investigations which drew similarly pessimistic conclusions. Indeed, it was on the basis of this evidence that, in the mid-1970s, criminologists reluctantly announced the demise of the 'rehabilitative ideal' (Preston, 1980). Over the next decade or so, a broad consensus emerged to support the view that the best we could hope for in our work with offenders was to minimise the negative impact of prosecution, imprisonment and social work intervention on their lives (Bottoms and McWilliams, 1979; Thorpe et al., 1980; Morris et al., 1980).

As we have seen, although these developments disheartened some criminologists, they offered a ready rationale for the development of pragmatic, non-interventionist, strategies, which problematised the impact of official decision-making upon the 'system careers' of cohorts of young offenders. At this point, the Cambridge study's unfashionable concern with the biological and psychological origins of youth crime and its inattention to the impact of official 'labelling', in an era when these issues were a major focus for policy, practice and research, meant that it attracted little serious attention beyond a handful of university criminology departments.

The Rehabilitation of Rehabilitation

As we have noted in Chapter 2, by the late 1980s, a rising crime rate and growing concern about violent youth crime were placing mounting pressure on the Conservative government to 'catch up with the mood of the people'. Stanley Cohen once observed that much criminology operates on a 'Midas-in-reverse' principle, i.e. 'if it's gold, criminologists will touch it'. And so, before one could say 'Lombroso lives', canny criminologists were returning to the data upon which the belief that 'nothing works' had been based and, not altogether surprisingly, they discovered that it now told a somewhat different story:

> *The outcome research of the early 1970s was capable of being interpreted in other ways than 'nothing works'... This has recently led some writers...who worked at the Home Office Research Unit in the 1970s to argue that the pessimistic conclusions drawn from this research were not necessarily justified.* (Blagg and Smith, 1989)

In this they are no doubt correct since the 'nothing works' doctrine, based as it was on a global analysis of reconviction rates, failed to pinpoint those individuals, projects and institutions whose endeavours did, in fact, 'work'. While such localised data do not undermine the thesis that, in the majority of cases, rehabilitative methods cannot be shown to have been instrumental in achieving rehabilitation, it does suggest that sometimes, with some people, in some circumstances, for some reason, some things do 'work'. However, this rehabilitation of rehabilitation was palpably political in intent. As Christopher Nutall, described by *The Independent* as the 'hard-headed' Director of Research and Statistics at the Home Office, told a meeting of Chief Probation Officers in 1992: '"Nothing Works" should be killed; not just because it's not right but because it has had a terrible effect. Let's not talk about it any more. Let's talk about what does work.'

The Justice Model

The practical consequence of these political manoeuvres was the emergence, in the late 1980s, of what came to be called the 'justice model' as the rehabilitative model of choice in both adult and youth justice systems. The justice model was sold to the key political, professional and media constituencies as a tough, confrontational, non-custodial response to offending. It was 'targeted' at 'high tariff', 'adjudicated offenders' in individualised 'offending programmes', the duration of which was endlessly elastic, determined by the length of the prison sentence to which it was to be an alternative.

The justice model's political fit was vouchsafed by the treatment's obvious re-moralising objectives and its claim to address the offender's capacity for moral discernment and rational calculation. However, its legitimacy could not be achieved by political rhetoric alone. The rehabilitative or 'correctional' technology also had to be seen to be effective or subject to the type of objective, 'scientific', evaluation which would, in due course, demonstrate its effectiveness. This opened a very wide door for a new body of theory. As New Labour's election campaign gained impetus, and the contours of its criminal justice and social policy strategy became clearer, it was evident that a set of ideas, which linked the justice model's concern with the inculcation of a sense of personal responsibility with early intervention to curb the bad behaviour and transform the attitudes of pre-adolescent offenders and their parents, was urgently needed. It was at this point that the Cambridge Study of Delinquent Development (Farrington and West, 1993) was taken down from the shelf and dusted off by Utting et al. (1993), a group of New Labour insiders, in search of evidence to link the early onset of youth crime with parental tardiness and inconsistency.

By 1995, the account of youth crime, and how it might be prevented, derived from the Cambridge study had become the 'big idea' in youth justice and crime prevention in Britain, providing the intellectual backbone for both *Young People and Crime* (Graham and Bowling, 1995) and *Misspent Youth* (Audit Commission, 1996). By 1997 the Cambridge study had become the 'serious research', adopted by Jack Straw as the intellectual bedrock upon which New Labour's policies on youth crime and the family were to be founded. The appeal of Farrington and West's study for New Labour is fairly clear. In a time when politicians are unwilling to countenance robust social and economic intervention to counter social problems, and eager to demonstrate that they are 'tough on the crime', an analysis which identifies poor child-rearing practices and weak parental control as the fundamental problem, and a strategy which targets families and classroom regimes and their capacity to inculcate self-control in unruly and disruptive children and, moreover, resonates closely with the moral sensibilities of New Labour's new constituencies in middle England, is a political godsend.

The Theory of Delinquent Development

The Cambridge study found that the early onset of offending, signalled by a first conviction, tended to presage a protracted criminal career. Thus males who were first convicted between the ages of ten and 13 tended to become the most persistent offenders 'committing an average of 8.1 offences leading to convictions in an average criminal career lasting almost exactly ten years'. The study found that the peak age of offending for convicted young people was also their point of greatest affluence, yet it also found that unemployment doubled the risk of offending. Unlike the non-convicted group, who tended to seek out less well-paid jobs with 'prospects', the convicted group tended to work in relatively well-paid, unskilled short-term jobs. The Cambridge study identified a tendency for young men to 'grow out of crime'. The nature of their offending changed over the period; from petty theft and vandalism in early adolescence, through car theft, more serious property crime and violence in later adolescence, via less easily detectable crimes, like fraud and theft from employers in their twenties, culminating in eventual desistance.

Offending and Anti-social Behaviour

For Farrington and West, the differences in the frequency and severity of offending by young people are an indicator of other, more profound, differences. Thus, they argue that 'delinquency is only one element of a much larger syndrome of anti-social behaviour'. Of the children who were convicted, 45 per cent were rated by their primary-school teachers as 'troublesome and dishonest' against 14 per cent who were not convicted. Remarkably, at 14, it appears that all the convicted offenders were rated by their teachers as 'aggressive' and 'frequent liars'. In adolescence, the convicted boys drank more beer, got drunk more often, smoked cigarettes, gambled more heavily, had tattoos, were more likely to smoke marijuana, try LSD, and engage in 'precocious' and unprotected sex. They were also more likely to have been convicted for minor motoring offences and to have driven while over the official drink-drive limit. They appeared to get on less well with their families and, in consequence, were more likely to live away from home.

Causes, Modifiable Risk Factors and Predictions

In the Cambridge study the authors frequently refer to 'predictors' of future delinquency. However, in subsequent work on the implications of the study for rehabilitative or correctional intervention (Farrington, 1996) these 'predictors' are transformed into 'modifiable risk factors'. Moreover, in their later work, the authors are at pains to stress that an awareness of these 'risk factors' will not allow us to predict the onset of criminality in any particular case. Presumably, this disclaimer represents a tacit acknowledgement that even the most elaborate predictors of individual offending devised by criminologists have always over-predicted the incidence of crime alarmingly. However, it is an important reservation because the Cambridge study has been embraced by politicians, policy wonks, 'opinion formers' and some youth justice managers and professionals, as if it offered a sure-fire predictive instrument with which to target, and then eradicate, youth crime.

The Cambridge study is rooted in a belief in 'radical differentiation', an intellectual premise which asserts that 'delinquents' are possessed of 'literally thousands of factors', many of which are not directly associated with actual offending, but which distinguish them from non-offenders. However, as we have noted David Farrington (2000) has recently acknowledged, a serious limitation of the risk-factor paradigm is that it is not possible at present to distinguish between those risk factors which are causes and those which are effects. Yet, if we are unable to accord some degree of causal primacy to these risk factors, or theorise the ways in which these correlates interact, we are little nearer understanding the causes of youth crime, and our targets for intervention must remain haphazard. Nonetheless, David Farrington (1996) deems some risk factors more significant than others:

1. Pre-natal and perinatal factors

Mothers who smoked, drank alcohol, used cocaine or sustained physical injuries during pregnancy tended to have children with a low birth weight, whose school attainment was low, who exhibited 'anti-social behaviour' at school and engaged in substance abuse and early sexual intercourse. These children were also more likely to be 'hyperactive', to achieve lower scores on IQ tests and to have speech disorders. Moreover, if the parents were young, single and on low incomes, or state benefits, when their child was aged five, the child was more likely to become a convicted offender. The presence of a father appeared to ameliorate these effects, not least perhaps, because it tended to boost family incomes.

2. Hyperactivity and impulsivity

Conviction correlated very strongly with 'hyperactivity-impulsivity attention deficit' disorder. The key characteristics of this 'syndrome' are, it appears, poor concentration, a 'poor ability to defer gratification', a 'short future-time perspective' and a heightened propensity for 'risk-taking'. In the Cambridge study, boys rated by their parents as 'risk takers' at age ten, were far more likely to have been convicted by the time they were 32. However, this medicalisation of the problem sidesteps the crucial question of whether we are confronting a cultural or a bio-genetic phenomenon, or the interplay of both and, if we are, how we might tell them apart.

3. Intelligence and attainment

In the Cambridge study, twice as many boys scoring 90 or less in non-verbal intelligence tests when they were aged between eight and ten were convicted. However, as Travis Hirschi and Michael Hindelang (1977) have convincingly demonstrated, it has proved inordinately difficult to disentangle low intelligence from poor motivation and low school attainment. Thus, as David Farrington (1996) acknowledges, the link between low intelligence and criminality remains highly speculative.

4. Parental supervision, discipline and attitude

The Cambridge study found that 'harsh or erratic parental discipline, cruel, passive or neglecting parental attitude, poor supervision and parental conflict, measured at age eight, all predicted later convictions'. Harsh discipline at eight also 'predicted' future violent offending. This led the authors to conclude that there was significant intergenerational transmission of aggressive and violent behaviour from parents to children. However, subsequent research has suggested that the link between parental violence and subsequent violent offending by their children is somewhat more tenuous. Terry Thornberry and his colleagues (1994), for example, argue that:

> *Our research has shown that no single risk factor is responsible for serious delinquency and violence. Quite the contrary: Chronic offenders have multiple risk factors in their backgrounds, including deficits in such arenas as family, school, peers and neighbourhood characteristics. Moreover, these factors tend to be cumulative and to interact with one another to produce very high levels of serious offending.* (Thornberry, 1994)

5. 'Broken homes' and separations

The study found that offending was high for boys from 'broken homes' (sic) and that the children of single teenage mothers were particularly likely to be convicted. However, convictions were significantly higher for the children who lacked maternal affection or were reared in unified homes with a high degree of parental conflict. Thus lack of affection and conflict appeared to be as significant as parental separation or single parenthood. However, it proved very difficult to disentangle the effects of low income from lone parenthood since most lone parents in the study were living in poverty.

6. Socio-economic deprivation

Low socio-economic status (SES) at ages eight to ten 'predicted' future conviction. In adolescence, the respondents offended more frequently when they were unemployed. Indeed, the more erratic their work record, the more likely they were to offend, suggesting that having a 'steady' job can lead to desistance. The study found that although SES was a good predictor of offending, poor housing and low family income was a better one.

7. Peer influences

The Cambridge researchers found it difficult to pin down the effects of peer group pressure since most of the activities in which young people engage, both legitimate and illegitimate, are undertaken in groups. They did find a correlation between lessening contact with peers and desistance from crime but because this tended to occur in later adolescence it might also be explained by a process of 'ageing out' of crime.

8. School influences

The proportion of students convicted in the schools attended by the boys varied from 0.3 to 23 per cent per annum. Attending a 'high delinquency school' proved to be a significant predictor of later convictions. However, the study appears to indicate that this was because the most troublesome eight to ten-year-olds went on to attend the highest delinquency schools, suggesting that schools with high levels of delinquency were merely a product of the 'quality' of their intake. This view is somewhat speculative however, since other research (Power et al., 1972; Rutter et al., 1978; Graham, 1988; Pitts and Smith, 1995) has indicated that the culture, atmosphere and organisational structure of a particular school may have a powerful influence upon the prevention of, and desistance from, youth crime among its students, irrespective of the problems which children bring to the school.

9. Community influences

Somewhat confusingly, the Cambridge study identifies families, peers and social norms as 'community influences', whereas this term is more commonly used to refer, for example, to interactions between residents, the degree of demographic stability in a neighbourhood and a neighbourhood's links with the local economy (cf. Reiss and Tonry, 1986). However, in the Cambridge study these factors are given little attention. For Farrington and West (1993), residence in the inner city predisposes children and young people to involvement in crime and other forms of deviance, because it is in the city that families experience greater 'adversity'. Yet there is a clear sense in the study that this 'adversity' is far less significant than the pre-existing deficiencies of the residents who are affected by it. Just as, in the Cambridge study, the problems of the school are reducible to a problem of the proclivities and deficiencies of the students who attend them, so problems in a neighbourhood are ultimately explicable in terms of the shortcomings of the neighbours. Elliott Currie (1985) refers to this type of reasoning as the 'fallacy of autonomy', the belief that what goes on inside the family can be separated analytically from the forces that affect it from the outside: the larger social context in which families are embedded for better or for worse. Indeed, a growing body of evidence suggests that the routine adversity of life in high-crime neighbourhoods may of itself be sufficient to overwhelm the best efforts of the most competent parents to protect their children from involvement in crime and criminal victimisation (McGahey, 1986; Sullivan, 1989; Sampson et al., 1997; Wikstrom and Lober, 1997; Hagan and McCarthy, 1997).

The Limitations of the Theory of Delinquent Development

The Cambridge study emerges from a school of criminological research which was extremely influential in the UK until the early 1970s. Rooted in developmental psychology, it presupposes that the origins of crime are best sought within the developmental histories of individual criminals and, more contentiously, that this search is best conducted in accordance with the protocols of the natural sciences. Not surprisingly, both the methods and the findings have attracted criticism. It is argued, for example, that the research transforms crime, a dynamic, interactive process, into a static 'effect' of developmental anomalies; that it lumps together diverse phenomena, like low birth weight, unemployment and 'anti-establishment attitudes', as if they were a single phenomenon, and then ascribes them an arbitrary numerical value. It is also accused of treating *statistical* normality as if it were an index of *social* normality, or indeed social acceptability. As to its methodology, beyond the widely accepted criticism that the methods of the natural sciences are largely inappropriate for the study of social action, this study continues to 'bang the drum' for scientific protocols and statistical methods, long since abandoned by most natural scientists and statisticians in favour of more sensitive and flexible tools. Beyond this, both its scientific neutrality and contemporary relevance are called into question when, for example, it describes divorce and unemployment as 'anti-social'. Not surprisingly, perhaps, when 'social factors' impinge upon this analysis, they have, at best, a secondary importance, simply serving to exacerbate developmental anomalies originating in the family, the first few weeks of life or, indeed, the womb.

Embeddedness

Yet the evidence presented in the Cambridge study lends itself to a quite different interpretation. Working from West and Farrington's original data, Hagan (1993) has argued that the phenomena they identify can be just as readily explained as the outcome of a process in which an initial social or developmental disadvantage, a lack of 'social capital', is gradually and cumulatively compounded and amplified, 'embedded', through interaction with peers, other adults and defining agencies:

> *Survival itself may be a struggle, and children and families must adapt to the diminished circumstances and opportunities they encounter. So while many parents who are well situated within secure and supportive social networks may be destined or driven by their capital positions and associated inclinations to endow their children with forms of social and cultural capital that make success in school and later life likely, the children of less advantageously positioned and less driven parents may more often drift or be driven into and along less promising paths of social and cultural adaptation and capital formation.*
> (Hagan and McCarthy, 1997)

Thus a poorly educated young woman in an area of high social need and youth unemployment finds no compelling reason not to become pregnant. In consequence she is re-housed in a hard-to-let flat on a high-crime estate, where she becomes the target for the depredations of local teenagers. Increasingly depressed, lonely and afraid of further victimisation she stays in her flat, drinks a little and smokes marijuana to calm her nerves. Her child is under-stimulated, frustrated and deeply anxious about his mother's distress.

At school his behaviour is erratic, his concentration is minimal and he is constantly being sent to the headmistress. Other parents stop their children playing with him. Eventually a social worker and an educational psychologist are called in – and so on. This is a familiar tale and, sadly, we know how it usually ends. But it is not simply a tale of the inevitable unfolding of a developmental deficit. It is a story about a complex interaction of social, economic, cultural and developmental factors and burgeoning negative stereotyping. For the people caught up in this spiral, their worsening predicament is paralleled by the progressive erosion of their capacity to make any impact upon that predicament. However, inasmuch as there are downward spirals of embeddedness, Robert Sampson and John Laub (1993) have presented longitudinal data which demonstrate that opportunity, stable employment and cohesive partnerships can initiate upward spirals, or pathways to conformity which lead to desistance from crime.

The Neighbourhood Effect

Hagan suggests that such 'embeddedness' is likely to be far more prevalent in neighbourhoods characterised by low socio-economic status (SES). In so saying he raises an important epistemological question concerning the relationship between individual risk factors, neighbourhood SES and the impact of social reaction. The key methodological question is whether, and to what extent, the influence of 'neighbourhood factors' on residents' offending, and within this, the phenomenon of embeddedness, can be demonstrated empirically. How, in other words, can we discover whether differences in neighbourhood offending rates result from the characteristics of the neighbourhood, or the characteristics of individuals living within that neighbourhood? Few studies have attempted to address this problem and those which have, have encountered formidable problems of measurement and methodology. The most successful has been the Pittsburgh Youth Study, *Individual Risk Factors, Neighbourhood SES, and Juvenile Offending*, conducted by Wikstrom and Loeber (1997), which explored the relationship between individual risk factors, neighbourhood characteristics and juvenile offending. Their findings, as we shall see in Chapter 7, pose a serious challenge to developmental theories rooted in a 'control theory' of human development, since they suggest that the impact of neighbourhood on the offending careers of children and young people with low SES may be decisive.

The Contemporary Relevance of the Theory of Delinquent Development

In the late 1960s, at the time the Cambridge study was in full swing, I was working as a detached (street) youth worker in the south London neighbourhoods from which the

Cambridge respondents came, though I was as unaware of the Cambridge study then as its authors or subjects were of me. A number of the young people I worked with hailed from families in which each generation of male children spent their adolescent years in residential special schools, children's homes or approved schools. Both the families and the authorities expected this would be the case, and so it usually was. Given what we now know about the impact of such institutions (see Crimmens and Pitts, 2000), it is clear that many such placements were, of themselves, criminogenic. Unsurprisingly, many of the young people ran away, and it was often while they were 'on the run' that, again not surprisingly, they clocked up most of their offences (Millham, 1978). In the late 1960s and 1970s youth incarceration was relatively commonplace. In 1977 in England and Wales, for example, there were around 21,000 youngsters in special boarding schools, 25,000 in children's homes, 7,000 in approved schools or community homes, 8,500 in young offender institutions and 7,500 in Borstals and detention centres, totalling 69,000. This compares with 35,500 in 1996/98. This being so, any study of youth crime and punishment in this period must account for the impact of 'labelling', stigma and institutionalisation on the self-conceptions and offending patterns of this population.

The Cambridge respondents were almost all 'White' and 'British', whereas 75 per cent of the youngsters who now inhabit high-crime, de-stabilised, neighbourhoods are not. A study of the differential, youth justice system careers of Black and White young people undertaken in the 1980s (Pitts, 1988), noted that the antecedents of Black and White youngsters who ended up in custody were very different. Whereas the White young people tended to come from families with many 'risk factors' and had been known to the police and welfare and justice agencies, sometimes over generations, Black youngsters were often from 'respectable', upwardly aspiring families. They had often had promising early school careers but, usually at around the age of 15, they began to get into trouble. Trouble with the law was often preceded by trouble in school. This often took the form of teachers complaining to parents that the youngsters were adopting a 'threatening', 'Black', posture. As a result, there was often conflict between the young people and their parents, who wanted them to 'knuckle down' and 'get their exams'. And then there was conflict with the police on the streets, whom, the Black young people said, were giving them 'endless pressure'. It seemed that the onset of crime among these two groups of young people was precipitated by rather different factors and that attempts to reduce their criminality would, in consequence, need to adopt a significantly different focus. Put simply, all youth crime is not of a piece, and to treat it as if it were, is likely to undermine attempts to reduce it.

The other question about the contemporary relevance of the Cambridge study concerns the historical and economic context in which youth crime emerges. Farrington and West's boys were aged eight in 1961 and 21 in 1974, when the oil crisis triggered the de-industrialisation of Western industrial societies which led, in the early 1980s, when these boys were over 30, to structural youth unemployment. In reality, of course, they grew to adulthood in an England where working-class neighbourhoods were still relatively stable, when single parenthood was still heavily stigmatised, but also at the height of the post-war boom when well-paid jobs for young people were still plentiful. If, as many commentators have argued (see Young, 1998 and Giddens, 1998), the onset of 'late modernity' has generated new, and quite unique, social and economic structures (Lea, 1998) and forms of youth and adult crime (Hobbs, 1997), we must ask whether such studies, rooted in a set of social and economic conditions which seem unlikely ever to return, can be useful to policy makers in the twenty-first century.

The Implications of the Theory of Delinquent Development for Intervention

One of the most perplexing features of the risk factor paradigm is that, despite disagreement about how risky these risk factors actually are, and despite the fact that we do not know which risk factors are causes, and which effects, and even though we lack any theory about how these risks interact, one with another, their devotees are virtually unanimous in prescribing correctional programmes which aim to develop 'cognitive social competence' as a remedy for this multiplicity of deficits. Because the logical link between the risk factor prevention paradigm and these programmes has yet to be satisfactorily explained, we are left to infer that the numerous and disparate social, economic and psychological risk factors identified by West, Farrington and others, have the single, simple, effect of undermining the young offender's capacity for self-control; the very deficiency, which, as luck would have it, cognitive behavioural programmes are designed to remedy. This simple and convenient explanation is made yet more implausible when we recognise that some of the leading aficionados of the risk-factor paradigm are also major purveyors of the, often costly, cognitive behavioural remedy (Ross, 1988; Hawkins and Catalano, 1998).

Promises, Promises

As we noted in Chapter 3, the measures incorporated into New Labour's youth justice strategy were what David Farrington (1996) has described as 'those which research points to as the most thorough and best designed programmes showing the most promising results'. But, as he points out: 'Unfortunately, few well-designed evaluation projects have been carried out in the United Kingdom, resulting in an unavoidable emphasis on innovative work in the United States.' Here, he is referring to the Maryland review of crime prevention studies undertaken by the National Institute of Justice (NIJ), a division of the US Department of Justice, in response to a mandate from the US Attorney-General and the US Congress in 1996. By 'promising' the NIJ refers to 'programmes for which the level of certainty from available evidence is too low to support generalisable conclusions, but for which there is some empirical basis for predicting that further research could support such conclusions' (Sherman et al., 1998). Programmes which the NIJ identifies as 'working' are those which 'we are reasonably certain prevent crime or reduce risk factors for crime in the kinds of social contexts in which they have been evaluated and for which findings can be generalised to similar settings in other places and times'. Given our earlier observations about American 'exceptionalism', this statement raises important questions about whether, or to what extent, the UK might qualify as an analogous social context. David Farrington's recommendations for action (1996) span both those measures deemed to 'work' by the NIJ and those they deem 'promising'.

Cognitive Skills Training

Amongst the most promising interventions commended by David Farrington are those developed by the cognitive psychologists, Robert Ross and his associates in Canada, and David Hawkins and Richard F. Catelano in the USA. Hawkins and Catelano's work has focused upon impulsivity in children which can, they suggest, be reduced by using cognitive-behavioural or interpersonal skills training. This training aims to replace impulsivity with a capacity for reason, concrete thinking with abstract thinking, low empathy with high empathy, and egocentricity with 'other-directedness'. Of their programmes Hawkins and Catelano (1998) write:

> *Our skill-based programs have helped more than 125,000 families learn to reduce risks that could contribute to the development of problem behaviours by teaching strategies to strengthen and clarify family expectations for behaviour and enhance the conditions which promote bonding in the family. For parents of children from seven to seventeen, these programs provide real solutions to today's parenting challenges. Curriculum materials are suitable for home use, work-shop settings, or for lunchtime seminars and 'brown bag' sessions in the workplace.*

(Developmental Research Programmes Inc., promotional materials)

Robert Ross and his colleagues have pioneered similar programmes in adult 'corrections' in Canada and, in the 1990s, these techniques have crossed the Atlantic in the form of the Reasoning and Rehabilitation programmes which have been extensively adopted by prison and probation services and to a somewhat lesser extent by local authority youth justice teams in England and Wales (Raynor and Vanstone, 1994).

Reasoning and Rehabilitation

The belief that these cognitive-behavioural programmes represent 'the most thorough and best designed programmes' (Farrington, 1996; Audit Commission, 1996) has become a kind of official mantra among Home Office ministers, senior personnel in the welfare, justice and community safety industries, and the denizens of many university senior common rooms. The nature of these programmes is described succinctly by David Farrington:

> *Ross attempted to teach delinquents the cognitive (thinking skills) in which they were deficient, in the expectation that this would lead to a decrease in their offending. His reviews of existing delinquency rehabilitation programmes suggested that those who succeeded in reducing offending generally tried to change the offender's thinking. He then carried out his own Reasoning and Rehabilitation programme, finding (in a randomised experiment) that it led to a significant (74 per cent) decrease in re-offending for a small sample in a short nine-month follow-up period. His training was carried out by probation officers, but he believed that it could be conducted equally well by parents or teachers. Ross' programme was designed to teach delinquents to stop and think before acting, to consider the consequences of their behaviour, to recognise alternative ways of solving their interpersonal problems and to consider the impact of their behaviour on other people. It included social skills training, logical reasoning and creative problem solving, assertiveness training (to teach non-aggressive socially appropriate ways to obtain desired outcomes) and negotiation skills.*

(Farrington, 1996)

Yet, for all its early promise, Reasoning and Rehabilitation has yet to demonstrate its efficacy in the sphere of youth offending in the UK. There are four main reasons for this:

1. Culture or cognition?

Ross et al. (1988) identify certain attitudes, beliefs and modes of thought which, they maintain, are peculiar to 'offenders' and derive from their incapacity to reason correctly. Thus, they argue that offenders are distinguished by the fact that:

● They are impulsive – they fail to think before they act.
● Their thinking is concrete rather than abstract.
● They fail to understand the reasons for rules and laws.
● They have difficulty seeing the viewpoints of other people.
● They are illogical and irrational.
● They suffer from conceptual rigidity and are inflexible and dogmatic.
● They become locked into cycles of dysfunctional behaviour.

- They have difficulty solving relationship problems.
- They are unable to predict the consequences of their behaviour.
- They are commonly egocentric
- They have low empathy for the thoughts and feelings of others.
- Their value systems are very limited; 'if it's good for me it's good'.
- They have trouble with critical reasoning.
- They are rarely self-critical.
- They are easily influenced by others.

However, this assertion is based on evidence originally gathered by Ross and his colleagues from older, 'career', offenders with substantial experience of imprisonment. Curiously, the alleged characteristics of this extraordinary group of offenders have, over time, come to be generalised by Ross and his colleagues to an ever-larger number of offenders, until in their later work they are represented as the characteristics of offenders per se. Yet, it is not at all clear that the characteristics attributed to the original group of 'old lags' studied by Ross (et al.) indicated that they were suffering from some form of cognitive malfunction. It is equally possible that, because the attitudes and beliefs, itemised above, are characteristic of those found in inmate subcultures, they were simply living in accordance with, and articulating, the core tenets of this subculture. As Saul Bellow observes:

> *This sounds like the view of the outside you'd hear from convicts. It's general opinion by now, in or out of jail, and it runs like this. 'If the facts were known, people behind bars are no guiltier than people outside, because nobody is clean, and only people inside know what's real and what's phoney.' I suppose you have to make the most of, or get what advantages you can out of, the time you served.*

(Bellow, 1997)

If Bellow's protagonist is correct, rather than focusing upon the malfunctioning cognitive machinery of prisoners, we should turn our attention to the processes of acculturation and institutionalisation fostered within penal institutions. A prison inmate cited by Donald Cressey puts it thus:

> *It is not the possibility of non-legitimate vocational training that makes the prison a man-perverting agency of great power and efficiency. It is the doleful fact that some nebulous something happens to a man between the time he checks into and checks out of a prison; some inculcation of the essence of bitterness and social antagonism, an inculcation which is not merely a veneering process but a deep inoculation. And this something spawns a man who is invariably less desirable as a citizen than he was at the time he stood before the bar of justice.*   (Cressey, 1973)

Cressey comments, 'I think the "nebulous something" which happens to an inmate is participation in a convict subculture that has developed an *espirit de corps* with crime, hustling, extortion and violation of official prison rules as common interests.'

2. Machinery or morality, a categorical error

At the core of Reasoning and Rehabilitation programmes is an assumption that offenders can be taught new cognitive skills which will enable them to anticipate the consequences of their behaviour for themselves and others, and make 'appropriate' moral choices. Thus, it is assumed that if they can think 'straight' they will go 'straight'. In so reasoning, the purveyors of reasoning and rehabilitation, like the eighteenth century classicists, conflate rational logical thinking with moral law-abiding thinking and, in so doing, commit a categorical error since they fail to distinguish between the cognitive 'machinery' which enables logical thought, and the ethical choices made possible by a capacity for logical thought. The assumption that people engage in crime because they lack a capacity for logical thought is, at least, tendentious. Some may, but in reality people often resort to crime, violence or deception because, in the circumstances in which they find themselves, it 'works' for them. Thus their involvement in crime, while morally reprehensible, is nonetheless rational.

3. Methodological muddles

The major evaluation of Ross et al.'s Reasoning and Rehabilitation programme (Robinson, 1995) reveals that prisoners who volunteered for, and completed, the programme had a far lower reconviction rate, in the 12 months following release, than prisoners who did not volunteer for the programme, 19.7 per cent against 50+ per cent. However, in addition to the group who volunteered and completed the programme and those who did not volunteer for the programme, there was a control group, which volunteered for the programme, were placed on a waiting list, but never actually undertook the programme. Whereas 19.7 per cent of programme 'completers' were reconvicted in the 12 months following release, 23 per cent of the control group were reconvicted. However, reconviction among 'programme drop outs', prisoners who were selected for, and commenced, the programme, but failed to complete it because of non-compliance with the programme ground rules or dismissal from the programme by staff, was 28.8 per cent. Some 14 per cent of programme participants dropped out during the course of the programme. By removing the 'drop outs' from the calculation of subsequent reconviction rates among the participant group, and comparing only the 'completers' with the 'control group', Ross et al. were making a false comparison. It is at least likely that, had the 'control group' engaged in the programme, a similar percentage would have dropped out. Had they done so, the reconviction rate of the 'control group' might well have mirrored that of the programme group. Were this to be the case, and it is a very plausible hypothesis, it would mean, as Pawson and Tilley (1997) have observed, that being on the 'waiting list' for the Cognitive Skills Programme had the same rehabilitative effect as being on the programme itself. This suggests that whatever it was that motivated prisoners to volunteer for the programme, rather than the programme itself, may well have enabled them to avoid reconviction upon release.

Meta-analyses of evaluations of cognitive-behavioural programmes suggest that, for the programmes to be effective, certain key elements must be present. In the case of high-risk offenders, programmes should occupy between 40 per cent and 70 per cent of the offenders time (Gendreau, 1996) and should last for at least 23 weeks (Lipsey and Wilson, 1998). In addition to matching the duration and intensity of programmes to the 'risk', 'criminogenic needs' and 'learning styles' of offenders, programme providers must attempt to match the programme to the offender's personality characteristics. 'High anxiety' offenders, for example, do not respond well to confrontation, 'egocentric' offenders show a poor appreciation of the victim's perspective, while offenders with both 'below-average' and 'above-average' intellectual ability tend to be, respectively, perplexed or under-stimulated by cognitive skills programmes (Fabiano, Porporino and Robinson, 1991). Meta-analyses also show that programmes are successful only if providers relate to juveniles in 'interpersonally sensitive' and 'constructive' ways and are trained and supervised appropriately. Moreover, in the case of more serious young offenders, 'relapse prevention' programmes' need to be employed in the community to monitor and anticipate problematic situations and train offenders to rehearse alternative behaviours (Vanstone, 2000). Alongside this, programme staff need to be active in linking young people into other services which meet their needs. However, even when all these criteria are achieved the average recidivism rate remains relatively high at around 50 per cent (Andrews et al., 1990). Similarly inconclusive results are reported by Maurice Vanstone (2000) although he reports positive, if not statistically significant, rehabilitative outcomes in some UK programmes for motivated adult offenders.

The community penalties administered by the YOTs are unlikely to offer either the levels of intensity or consistency of application necessary to effect change with many of the persistent or serious young offenders upon whom they will be imposed. Meanwhile, if these interventions mix low and high risk offenders, in for example, a drugs awareness or literacy element of the programme, they may trigger an 'interaction effect' (Clear and Hardeyman, 1990) in which offending may escalate amongst low risk groups, who are prematurely drawn into the system by the new measures introduced by the 1998 Act. The problem is not that these correctional options don't 'work' at all. Like the interventions they have supplanted, social casework, social group work, adventure education, motor projects etc., they sometimes, in some cases, help to reduce the incidence and severity of some young peoples' offending. However, far too much has been claimed for them and the suggestion, implicit within the contemporary correctional discourse, that if 'properly administered', these techniques will simply arrest the development of 'offending careers' is implausible. However, this belief has led to the creation of a youth justice system in which the number of community penalties a young person may receive is reduced to two, alternatives to custody are eliminated, custodial options are expanded and custodial sentences lengthened, in the belief that only the most intractable young offender could be unresponsive to these evidence-based interventions. It should come as no surprise then, that we are currently witnessing a youth imprisonment bonanza unsurpassed since the early 1980s (Pitts, 1988; Goldson and Peters, 2000).

As Pawson and Tilley argue, a critical component in behavioural change is the motivation and predisposition of offenders. In opposition to the implicit assumption within Reasoning and Rehabilitation that programmes work 'on' individuals, they argue that programmes work 'through' individuals:

> *Social programs involve a continual round of interactions and opportunities and decisions. Regardless of whether they are born of inspiration or ignorance, the subject's choice at each of these junctures will frame the extent and nature of change. What we are describing here is not just the moment when the subject signs up to enter a program but the entire learning process. The act of volunteering merely marks a moment in a whole evolving pattern of choice. Potential subjects will consider a program (or not), cooperate closely (or not), stay the course (or not), learn lessons (or not), apply the lessons (or not). Each one of these decisions will be internally complex and take its meaning according to the chooser's circumstances.*

(Pawson and Tilley, 1997)

4. Selective amnesia

As we have noted, Ross et al. based their Reasoning and Rehabilitation programmes on a review of existing rehabilitative programmes, and this suggested to them that the most successful programmes tried to change the way offenders thought about crime. This is not surprising. Indeed, a delinquency prevention programme which did not attempt to change the ways in which programme participants thought about crime would be very unusual indeed, and very unlikely to attract funding. Nor is it surprising that, as cognitive psychologists in search of a new and lucrative project, Ross et al. should emphasise this fact. What is more surprising is that in developing and marketing their Reasoning and Rehabilitation programmes, they chose to ignore the findings of the comprehensive meta-analyses of interventions with young offenders undertaken for the Department of Justice in the USA

(Altschuler and Armstrong, 1984; Howell et al., 1995). These analyses tell a rather different story about the characteristics of successful rehabilitative programmes, namely that:

- They are often conducted outside the justice system.
- They are holistic, dealing with many aspects of young people's lives simultaneously as needed.
- They are informed by an underlying developmental rationale.
- They offer diverse opportunities for success and the development of positive self-image.
- They build on young people's strengths rather than focusing on their deficiencies.
- They are intensive, often involving weekly or even daily contact.
- They adopt a socially grounded rather than a 'treatment' approach and emphasise reintegration.
- They involve young people in programme planning and decision making.
- They include enriched educational and vocational programmes.
- They utilise forms of counselling matched to the young person's needs, including opportunities for young people to discuss childhood problems.
- They provide opportunities for the development of links between young people in trouble and pro-social adults and institutions.
- They give frequent, timely and accurate feedback for both positive and negative behaviour.
- There are clear and consistent consequences for misconduct.
- They provide a forum in which young people are enabled to recognise and understand thought processes that rationalise negative behaviour.
- They offer opportunities to engage with problems and deficits which got the young person into trouble in the first place.

The rise to pre-eminence of Reasoning and Rehabilitation as a mode of intervention is accounted for as much, if not more, by its ideological, economic and administrative fit with the new forms of penalty emerging in US and UK justice systems in the late 1980s and 1990s (Feely and Simon, 1990) and effective entrepreneurism on the part of its proponents, as its explanatory power or rehabilitative impact.

Science and Politics

The criminological theories and correctional interventions discussed in this chapter and the previous one provide both an intellectual rationale and a 'technology' for the implementation of the youth justice and community safety provisions of the Crime and

Disorder Act 1998. While it is true that the measures advocated have, at some times, in some places, with some people, 'worked', their incorporation into policy is determined not simply by their demonstrable efficacy but by pre-scientific, ideological, imperatives. Indeed, it seems clear that it is the political project, to which these measures lend an air of scientific and technological proficiency, which is paramount, and around which the science and technology have had to fit. As C. Wright Mills reminds us, the subordination of science to governance, to produce what Jack Straw is pleased to call 'serious research', has a long pedigree. Writing in the 1950s, when the type of social science discussed here was at its zenith, he observes:

> *The New Social Science refers not only to abstracted empiricism but also to the new and illiberal practicality. The phrase refers to both method and use and quite correctly so; for the technique of abstracted empiricism and its bureaucratic use is now regularly joined. It is my contention that, so joined, they are resulting in a bureaucratic social science.*   (Mills, 1954)

Our criticism of this conflation of social science, technologies of change and governance is fivefold:

1. This is a practical concern: that in an increasingly market-oriented society, governments should not buy their technology from the same place they buy their science; it is too tempting for the scientists to suggest a closer fit between the two than the evidence warrants.

2. If there is to be a productive relationship between this science and technology and governance, the job of social science is to provide illumination rather than legitimation. And illumination is an active process, involving a critique of both policy ends and policy means. But the science and technology criticised here is overly reassuring to governments and publics, for it says that youth crime is the preserve of a small hard core who are constitutionally different from us, whose behaviour is irrational, but who may nonetheless be restored to 'normality' if we simply apply the technology. The 'unthinkable' possibility which, despite the rhetoric, nobody in, around or beholden to government appears to be prepared to think, is that some of the 111 per cent increase in recorded crime between 1981 and 1994 may have been perpetrated by 'normal' children and young people who were 'thinking straight' and acting accordingly (Young, 1999).

3. Because governments derive their legitimacy, in large part, from the connections they are able to make with the 'common-sense' beliefs of electorates, this science and technology holds no surprises. It tells us what we always suspected, that inadequate and incompetent parents produce inadequate, incompetent and sometimes dangerous children, and in doing so, it reassures us that we are doing better than them. It also

tells us that what divides us from these people is more significant than that which unites us.

4. It plays the same trick upon us as the social sciences which Mills railed against all those years ago. For it suggests that rather than being carefully tailored to contemporary political orthodoxies in order to mesh with new criminal justice policies, this science and technology emerges from a rarefied value-free realm amongst the dreaming spires of academe.

5. A science and technology which coincides with policy too neatly does so at a cost, which is counted in the silence which must be maintained about competing accounts and inconvenient features of social reality. Thus it appears to be possible to theorise the seismic shifts in crime rates in the 1980s and 1990s (described in the next chapter) without reference to the equally profound changes in the distribution of power, wealth and opportunity which paralleled these shifts. Yet, as we shall argue, unless these contextual 'factors' are included in the equation, the theory makes no sense and the technology is largely irrelevant.

Edward Said (1994) has argued that the academic and the public professional have a particular duty in this regard, because their profession offers them privileged insight into pertinent public issues. Thus, Said enjoins us to put our analyses into the public domain and 'speak the truth to power', however politically uncomfortable this might be for the powerful, or indeed for ourselves. In this perspective, citizens of democratic societies are best served if the public professional and the academic resist the temptation to serve as apologists for the ephemeral ambitions of governments, and quasi-governments, and speak out. This does not mean that they cannot contribute to the development of improved policies, procedures and practices, quite the reverse. It simply means that in doing so they should honour their responsibility to maintain a critical dialogue with government rather than becoming what Taylor Walton and Young (1973) once described as 'handmaidens of the status quo'.

Chapter 7

After the Gold Rush

The price of admission to the market economy has to be paid in the currency of social inequity, in entirely new kinds of social divisions, and in higher long-term unemployment. As is always the case in accelerated social transformation, crises get shifted onto the life histories of individuals.   (Habermas, 1994)

You cannot cheat the law of the conservation of violence: all violence is paid for, and, for example, the structural violence exerted by the financial markets, in the form of layoffs, loss of security etc., is matched sooner or later in the form of suicides, crime and delinquency, drug addiction, alcoholism, a whole host of minor and major everyday acts of violence.   (Bourdieu, 1998)

The Crime Rate Steepens

Between 1981 and 1993 recorded crime in the UK rose by 111 per cent. This was further and faster than ever before. Government ministers were momentarily heartened in 1988 when the crime rate dropped by 5 per cent, because it appeared that their investment in law and order, a real increase of 87 per cent during the Conservatives' period in office, was at last paying off. But recorded crime rose sharply again from the end of 1989; climbing by 17 per cent in 1990, a further 16 per cent in 1991, peaking at 5.8 million in 1992 from where it levelled off at around 5.3 million. From 1994, recorded crime in general began a slight and gradual decline, although crimes of violence and sexual offences continued to rise. However, some commentators have argued that different things were happening in youth justice. Barry Goldson (1997), for example, has argued that in the 1980s and early 1990s:

> *The principles of diversion, decriminalisation and decarceration steered a dynamic and effective juvenile justice practice. The numbers of prosecutions against children in court fell dramatically, there was an 80 per cent decline in the use of custody between 1980 and 1990 and there was a corresponding contraction in the number of known juvenile offenders per 100,000 of the population which dropped by 16 per cent. The demands of 'justice' appeared to be served by a policy and practice which*

avoided the unnecessary use of penal custody for children without placing the public at any increased risk; a humane and effective approach to juvenile crime with the added bonus of financial efficiency.

This argument appears to be supported by the facts. Between 1985 and 1996, the number of male young offenders found guilty or cautioned by the police fell by 36 per cent and the number of females by 16 per cent. The biggest decreases occurred between 1985 and 1989 when there was a 32 per cent fall in the number of male offenders, and a 44 per cent decrease in the number of female offenders, found guilty or cautioned by the police. On the basis of these data, the Penal Affairs Consortium, NACRO and the major UK children's charities have argued that the non-interventionist youth justice strategies of the 1980s had 'worked'.

However, these dramatic falls in the numbers of young people entering the youth justice system must be seen in the context of a 25 per cent drop in 10 to 17-year-olds in the population of England and Wales during this period, and a substantial reduction in the numbers of children and young people actually entering the system. Rigorous 'systems management' by youth justice professionals and the police, from 1984 onwards, and increased informality in the treatment of 10 to 14-year-olds by the police had the effect of diverting many young offenders away from the justice system altogether. There was also a fall in the police 'clear-up' (detection or charge) rate, partly caused by the introduction of PACE (the Police and Criminal Evidence Act) in 1984 which offered increased safeguards for the accused. In the courts, between 1981 and 1991, the number of cases withdrawn or discontinued by the Crown Prosecution Service rose from 21,300 to 108,300, while conviction rates for those cases which did 'go the distance' also dropped.

Meanwhile, as we have seen, between 1982 and 1992 recorded crime in the UK rose from 3.5m to almost 6m. The British Crime Surveys (BCS) record a similar, if slightly less dramatic rise, but as we have noted crime in England and Wales had risen faster and further during this period than at any time since records began. It is also the case that those crimes typically committed by juveniles, such as vehicle theft and domestic burglary, rose by 70 per cent (BCS 65 per cent) and 66 per cent (BCS 63 per cent) respectively during the period (Farrington, 1996). Farrington and Burrows (1993) found that although the number of children and young people recorded by the police as shoplifters fell by 59 per cent between 1985 and 1989, the numbers apprehended by the major stores and reported to the police remained more or less constant.

Importantly, the reductions in recorded youth crime, cited above, concern the numbers of young people entering the system, rather than the numbers of offences committed by them. Thus it could be the case, as the Association of Chief Police Officers (ACPO) had contended in its evidence to the House of Commons Home Affairs Select Committee, that by the mid-1990s, a smaller number of offenders were committing a larger number of offences. But, as we shall see, these developments were not, as ACPO has argued, a consequence of the emergence of a new pre-pubescent super-predator.

The Redistribution of Wealth

In Britain in the post-war period, governments have attempted to deal with the discrepancy between their egalitarian promises and real inequalities in health, wealth, opportunity and longevity, by pursuing social, economic and fiscal policies which reduced these discrepancies, or by adopting a political rhetoric which obscured them. Whether by fair means or foul, politicians across the board had to be seen to be committed to the idea of an egalitarian society. With the election of Margaret Thatcher in 1979 this strategy was abandoned. Instead, discrepancies of wealth and opportunity were fostered and paraded in the belief that they would act as a stimulant to entrepreneurism and productivity. The beliefs which informed this *volte-face* are, by now, fairly familiar and hold that:

- Capitalist societies are most successful if the hidden hand of the market is given free rein and state intervention in the social and economic spheres is minimised.
- Successful capitalist societies will also become progressively less equal, because those who seize opportunity will become richer, and those who do not seize it, being unprotected by redistributive taxation and employment and social legislation, become relatively poorer.

  As for crime:

- This inequality will serve as an incentive to many to seize the new opportunities generated by the free market and to enrich themselves legititimately, but for a small minority who lack the ability or the moral fibre to do so, they will serve as an incentive to cheat.
- Thus successful capitalist societies will also be societies in which there is pressure towards an increase in crime. The more successful they become the more crime-prone they will be.   (Pitts, 1996)

The major effect of the attempt to transform free market ideology into an economic strategy was the reversal, from 1979, of the post-war tendency towards a narrowing of the gap between rich and poor and the growth of both absolute and relative deprivation. Between 1981 and 1991 the number of workers earning half the national average wage or less (the Council of Europe poverty line), rose from 900,000 to 2.4 million. In the same period those earning over twice the national average rose from 1.8 to 3.1 million. In February 1999, the gap between the Gross Domestic Product (GDP) of the poorest and the richest regions in the UK was the widest in the European Union (EU). The richest region, Inner London, ranked against an EU average of 100, scored 222. The poorest regions like Merseyside and West Wales scored less than 75, rendering them eligible for EU 'special aid'.

The Redistribution of Crime and Victimisation

The 1992 British Crime Survey (BCS), based on interviews with randomly selected households, indicated that the unprecedented rise in recorded crime in the preceding decade accorded with the experience of the victims of crime. However, not only did the BCS reveal a substantial increase in the volume of crime and victimisation, it also showed that between 1982 and 1992 there had been significant changes in its nature and distribution (Hope, 1994). An analysis of BCS data reveals an alarming picture. The BCS divides neighbourhoods into ten categories on the basis of the intensity of the criminal victimisation of their residents. By 1992, the chances of a resident in the lowest crime neighbourhood ever being assaulted had fallen to a point where it was barely measurable. Residents in the highest crime neighbourhoods, by contrast, now risked being assaulted twice a year. This polarisation of risk is made clearer when we recognise that, by 1992, residents in the highest crime neighbourhoods experienced twice the rate of property crime and four times the rate of personal crime than those in the next worst category. These findings point to a significant redistribution of victimisation towards the poorest and most vulnerable over the intervening ten years.

> In parallel with the regional restructuring of the British economy during the 1980s, the inequality in crime risk grew amongst local communities, especially those in less advantaged 'Northern' regions of England...and local studies at the end of the 1980s registered large increases in crime victimisation over a relatively short period (Hope and Foster, 1992).
>
> (Pitts and Hope, 1998)

Neighbourhood De-stabilisation

A major factor in this redistribution of crime and victimisation was the introduction of market mechanisms into the management of public sector housing by the Thatcher administration, via the 'Right to Buy' schemes, which diminished the amount of available housing, and 'Tenant Incentive' schemes which shifted more affluent tenants into the private sector (Page, 1993; Hope, 1994, 1995; Dean, 1997). Between 1970 and 1990, owner-occupation in the UK rose from 55.3 per cent of households to 67.6 per cent. This 'secession of the successful' meant that, increasingly, it was the least 'successful' who were entering social housing. As Malcolm Dean (1997) observes: 'This happened despite the warnings of housing professionals about the problems which public housing projects generated when they were confined to the poor, the unemployed and elderly.'

A Concentration of Disadvantage

As predicted, as the 1980s progressed, relatively prosperous, middle-aged, higher-income families left social housing, to be replaced by poorer, younger, often lone-parent, families (Page, 1993). Meanwhile, reductions in income support for the payment of the mortgage interest of unemployed homeowners, and the house-price slump of the early 1990s, which forced many separating couples to hand back their keys to their mortgage lender, meant that 44,000 families moved from owner-occupation into social housing. Between 1984 and 1994 annual residential mobility in social housing increased from 4 to 7 per cent of households. Whereas in the 1980s and 1990s, 40 per cent of heads of households in social housing were aged 65 or over, 75 per cent of newly formed households entering social housing were headed by someone aged between 16 and 29. A high proportion of these new residents were unemployed, not least because they included a heavy concentration of lone parents:

> *Two quite distinct communities are emerging within the sector with quite profound differences in lifestyles and culture. At one end there are the established elderly residents, who have lived in social housing all their lives and who remember a time when having a council home was a desirable goal. At the other end are the new, younger residents, frequently suffering from multiple problems: unemployment, poverty, poor work skills and perhaps mental illness and drug abuse as well.*   (Dean, 1997)

In many inner-city areas, in addition to the 'two communities' described by Dean, there was also a residuum of 'established', White working-class families who were either unwilling or unable to leave the neighbourhood and who therefore lived in a state of uneasy coexistence with incoming Black and Asian families.

Young, Black and Estranged

In contrast to the steady upward mobility, in educational, occupational and social terms, of a substantial section of Britain's Black and Asian citizens, many other Black and Asian Britons experienced downward mobility in the slump which began in the late 1980s, finding themselves immobilised at the bottom of the social and economic structure. By 1995, 40 per cent of African-Caribbeans and 59 per cent of Pakistanis and Bangladeshis in the UK were located in the poorest fifth of the population. This contrasts with only 18 per cent of the White population (Rowntree Foundation, 1995). In London, by the mid-1990s, up to 70 per cent of the residents on the poorest housing estates were from ethnic minorities (Power and Tunstall, 1997).

Falling Incomes

At the beginning of the 1980s the average household income of council house residents was 73 per cent of the national average. At the beginning of the 1990s this had fallen to 48 per cent. By 1995, over 50 per cent of council households had no breadwinner (Rowntree

Foundation, 1995). In their report, *Swimming Against the Tide* (1995), Anne Power and Rebecca Tunstall noted that: 'In the most difficult big city areas of rented housing, levels of unemployment were more than three times the average, the concentration of lone parents was four times greater, and the proportion of children failing to obtain any GCSE passes was over four times the average.' In its report, *Bringing Britain Together*, the government's Social Exclusion Unit (1998) identified 1,370 housing estates in Britain which it characterised as 'poor neighbourhoods which have poverty, unemployment, and poor health in common, and crime usually comes high on any list of residents' concerns.'

The estates which experienced the greatest changes during the 1980s, saw growing concentrations of children, teenagers, young single adults and young single-parent families. Old social ties, constructed of kinship, friendship or familiarity, withered away to be replaced by transience, isolation and mutual suspicion. Neighbours no longer watched out for one another's property or shared amenities. Nor did they approach strangers, rowdy adolescents or naughty children, for fear of reprisals. In their study of one such estate, Tim Hope and Janet Foster (1992) discovered a fivefold increase in burglaries over a three-year period. Between 1981 and 1991 in Britain, those people most vulnerable to criminal victimisation and those most likely to victimise them were progressively thrown together on the poorest housing estates in Britain. By 1997, 25 per cent of the children and young people under 16 in the UK were living in these neighbourhoods (Burroughs, 1998).

Structural Youth Unemployment

The problems afflicting high-crime, low-income neighbourhoods in the UK in the 1980s and 1990s were, of course, compounded by the rise in youth unemployment which began in the mid-1970s. Moreover, because of the tendency for de-industrialisation to eliminate 'men's' jobs while simultaneously generating low-level opportunities in the service sector, the problem of youth unemployment was, disproportionately, a problem for young men. Whereas in previous recessions, youth unemployment had risen, only to fall again during the ensuing 'boom', the youth unemployment of the early 1980s did not work like that. The economy boomed, but youth unemployment kept on rising. Thus we found ourselves in a new era in which youth unemployment was no longer cyclical and temporary but structural and, apparently, permanent. By the late 1980s, unemployment in the 16–19 age group averaged 20 per cent (General Household Survey, 1995). In areas of high unemployment like Yorkshire and Humberside the figure was 25 per cent. However, these figures obscure the fact that in certain parts of the major cities, or on the housing estates on their periphery, youth unemployment sometimes topped 60 per cent.

This new reality was illustrated starkly by the Delors report, *Growth, Competitiveness and Employment* (1993) (see Table 7.1) which calculated the rates at which the economies of the major EU states would need to grow if youth unemployment was to be remedied. These rates of growth were, of course, unachievable, leading Delors to deliberate upon the redistribution of work in the member states, the development of new forms of employment and measures which might be taken to ameliorate the social consequences of exclusion from economic life.

Table 7.1: Growth, Competitiveness and Employment		
Country	*Unemployment rate (%)*	*Growth rate required (%)*
Eire	10.9	117
France	10.8	113
Germany	5.6	49
UK	11.4	198

The Dumbing-down of the Youth Labour Market

Until the mid-1970s, state secondary schools and universities in the UK produced more or less the right amount of the right type of labour to meet the needs of commerce, industry and the public sector. When, from time to time, youth unemployment reared its head, governments tended to account for it in terms of a mismatch between the low levels of skill and knowledge achieved by school leavers and the higher levels demanded by commerce and industry. From the mid-1970s, however, de-industrialisation, technological change and dwindling job opportunities changed all that.

Between 1988 and 1996 the proportion of pupils in poorer areas gaining five or more A–C grades at GCSE rose from 20 to 32 per cent, but these commendable improvements were not matched by improved job prospects, as traditional apprenticeships and traineeships in industrial manufacturing dwindled to nothing. In a buyers' labour market, such skilled jobs as remained now demanded higher levels of qualification, skill and experience. The rapid expansion of UK universities in the 1980s was, in part, a response to growing 'qualification inflation'. Ironically, of course, from the mid-1980s the growing residuum of perfectly able working-class young people with no prospect of permanent, skilled employment was joined by unemployed university graduates, and latterly postgraduates. Thus, an emergent 'slackatariat', having failed to secure 'graduate' employment, and wearying of the struggle for the available low-level jobs (Roberts, 1998), often settled into low-maintenance, bohemian, lifestyles in the poorer parts of the major cities, took to the road as New Age Travellers or retired to the erstwhile 'hippie' havens of Wales and the West Country to grow any number of things.

Training

So, in 1983, the Conservative government introduced the Youth Training Scheme (YTS), based on the German New Apprenticeship model, which had, it was said, fuelled the German 'economic miracle'. While YTS was presented as the ultimate solution to the 'skills deficit', little was made of the fact that de-industrialisation had precipitated a massive work deficit (the economic recession of the early 1980s eradicated 20 per cent of all manufacturing jobs). While the best of these schemes, usually those which were employer-based, absorbed trainees into their workforce, or equipped them with 'transferable' skills, there were plenty of schemes in which the 'training' involved poorly-paid drudgery. Meanwhile the Further Education Colleges, which by the late 1980s were tending to recruit the young people who had been rejected by other schemes, were to all intents and purposes simply warehousing their trainees, keeping them temporarily off the streets and out of the unemployment statistics.

In a study undertaken by the mental health charity MIND, on a housing estate in Sunderland, of the 250 young people interviewed, only 36 per cent had been on a YTS scheme. Of those, 78 per cent had failed to complete the scheme. Wilkinson (1996) notes that:

> They see training schemes as a device to fill in time until they return to the dole with no possibility of a real job at the end of the training period. This, compounded by problems of lack of choice, inadequate or non-existent training, employer abuse of the system and a pervasive sense of pointlessness, provides little in the way of positive motivation to undertake training.

The government read the decline in the take-up of training places in the late 1980s as a sign that too many able-bodied young people were refusing to join the scheme and 'sponging' off the state instead. As a result, in 1988, social security benefits were withdrawn from 16 and 17-year-olds in a bid to drive them into YTS. From that point onwards, youth unemployment officially ceased to exist. In the 1990s, the government got out of the youth training business altogether, handing their new Training and Enterprise Councils over to the employers.

Shifting the Crisis, Counting the Cost

Youth unemployment took a heavy toll. West and Sweeting (1996) followed 1000 young people between the age of 15 to 21 in the west of Scotland. They noted a significant deterioration in the mental health of those who became unemployed. They write:

> *Economic recession, unemployment, low-paid jobs and the sense of having no future*
> *are potentially all components of a social malaise that may affect the health of us all*
> *but especially the young...9 per cent of males and 7 per cent of females who were*
> *unemployed, reported attempting suicide, much higher rates than those found for*
> *those at work or in education.*

As Tony Novak (1997) has noted, the suicide rate for males aged 15–24, having remained stable at around 65 per million between 1975 and 1984, rose to 110 per million by 1990 (Wilkinson, 1994). The suicide rate for young women rose much more slowly, which Novak attributes to the relatively buoyant market for female labour, and the fact that the increase in births to young women under 20 during the period offered some of them an alternative pathway to adulthood.

Youth Crime and the Labour Market

Does unemployment cause youth crime? Home Office data (1995) indicate that only 18 per cent of convicted offenders aged 16–17 were in employment compared with 46 per cent in the general population. Graham and Bowling (1995) found that among 'persistent offenders' only one in ten 16 to 17-year-olds, one in two males in their mid-twenties and one in three females in their mid-twenties had a steady job. Yet, as Mercer Sullivan (1989) has shown, if young people are to maintain a plausible identity and a sense of self-esteem, they need to sustain a lifestyle which allows them to participate in the same kinds of social, recreational and vocational activities with the same frequency as their peers. To do this they must somehow secure an income, and to do that they must enter the labour market. But different kinds of neighbourhoods have access to different 'sectors' of the labour market.

In low-crime neighbourhoods, residents will tend to derive their incomes, identity and sense of self-esteem from one, primary sector, employment source. 'Primary sector' labour markets offer 'steady' jobs with reasonable wages and prospects for advancement. Workers in this sector tend to be older, better qualified, more reliable and better motivated, qualities which are strengthened and reinforced by the higher quality and the greater stability of their jobs. The characteristics of the primary sector workforce tend to be shaped by, and mirror, their conditions of employment.

In contrast, residents in poor, high-crime neighbourhoods will tend to derive their livelihoods within secondary sector labour markets which attract younger, less skilled, less well educated and less reliable employees. The work here is characterised by low wages and sporadic, dead-end work supplemented by 'government transfers, employment and training programmes, crime and illegal hustles' which, as McGahey (1986) has observed in his studies of young people in New York City's Bronx, 'constitute important additional sources of income, social organisation and identity for the urban poor'. Wilkinson (1994), in the UK, echoes McGahey in arguing that: 'It is often more rewarding for them to be involved in the informal economy of 'fiddle jobs' and criminality, a way of life which does at least provide some kind of status and esteem.'

McGahey's and Wilkinson's findings are, to a large extent, congruent with those of Lipsey (1995), whose meta-analysis of 400 American studies of youth crime and employment suggest that 'training' and secondary sector employment are both far less conductive to desistance from youth crime than primary sector employment since they offer youngsters little or no 'stake in conformity', while simultaneously eroding their sense of self-esteem. Primary sector employment, by contrast, because it offers benchmarks by which young people may measure their progress towards 'qualified', 'fully trained' and hence 'adult' status, offers a route for 'maturing out of crime'. However, whether or not 'lower-class' young people find primary sector employment is usually determined by whether or not they have a parent, relative or adult family friend already engaged in primary sector employment, who can 'get them in'. This is because, in working-class neighbourhoods, young people tend to be introduced to the labour market via personal contacts rather than the Careers Service or employment bureaux.

But, of course, these facilitative adults are in no position to 'bring on' the next generation if they have no access to the primary sector labour market themselves. Indeed, a key characteristic of neighbourhoods which have poor or non-existent links with primary sector labour markets is that skilled, economically mobile adult workers leave them. Their departure, because it signals the collapse of the economic infrastructure which supported, and gave demographic stability to, the neighbourhood, signals the onset of accelerated demographic de-stabilisation and deepening family poverty. Thus, McGahey (1986) argues that the quality and quantity of jobs in a neighbourhood determine the ways people form households, regulate their own, and the public behaviour of others, and use public services. The resulting neighbourhood atmosphere then helps to shape the incentives for residents to engage in legitimate employment or income-oriented crime. A high level of adult involvement in primary sector employment spawns stable households, stable families, stable social relationships and enhanced vocational opportunities for the next generation. A low level of involvement has the opposite effect. In such circumstances, neighbourhood de-stabilisation, by weakening, or severing altogether, the link between neighbourhoods and primary sector employment, is a crucial factor in the crime and employment equation.

The Unbearable Lightness of Protracted Adolescence

The youth crime and violence in destabilised urban neighbourhoods are implosive in that they are usually committed by, and against, local residents. This intra-neighbourhood crime pattern is a distinguishing characteristic of high-crime areas in Britain (Forrester et al., 1990; Hope, 1995). Its other distinguishing feature is that the young people involved in this crime appear not to grow out of it (Graham and Bowling, 1995). Adolescence is a period of transition, but how long it lasts and when it ends depends upon whether a young person has the social and economic wherewithal to proceed to the next stage in the life cycle. In his study, undertaken in the USA during the great depression, W.F. Whyte (1943) 'hung out' with a group of 'corner boys' in an Italian neighbourhood. As the book proceeds, we realise that Doc and the Nortons are not teenagers but men, some of them in their mid- to late-twenties and that they have been hanging out on the same corner for over 10 years. They have been doing this because, having no steady jobs, they have no money to pay rent, buy furniture and do all the other things one would need to do to become a 'family man' in Cornerville. They are, as a result, frozen in a state of protracted adolescence.

In East London in the early 1990s, Black youth justice workers observed that the upper age of members of the local 'posse' had risen to over 30. And so some of the older members were introducing the younger ones to more serious crime. Like Doc and the Nortons, these men could not make the transition from adolescence to higher-status adult roles because they simply did not have the means to do so. Being locked in a state of perpetual adolescence, these young people do not 'grow up'. And because 'growing up', the assumption of adult roles, rights and responsibilities, usually accompanies 'growing out of crime' (Rutherford, 1986; Sampson and Laub, 1993), they do not. So, as Graham and Bowling (1995) suggest, they continue to perpetrate 'youth crime' into their twenties and beyond. As John Hagan (1993) has observed, pre-eminent among the factors which make for higher levels of crime in de-stabilised neighbourhoods is that young people who, under other circumstances, would have grown out of crime, leaving it behind with other adolescent enthusiasms, become more deeply and more seriously embedded in a criminal way of life:

> If early employment contacts can enhance the prospects of getting a job and subsequent occupational mobility, connections into crime seem likely in a similar way to increase the probability of unemployment…operating through branching, snowballing and multiplying processes…successive criminal acts and contacts may further embed youths in criminal networks that are isolated from the personalised networks of job-seeking.
>
> (Hagan, 1993)

In these neighbourhoods, in the 1980s and 1990s, 'connections into crime' were often closely associated with connections into drugs (Pearson, 1987; Hobbs, 1993). By dint of their peculiar age structure, family poverty, relative isolation from the economic mainstream and absence of legitimate educational and vocational opportunity, these neighbourhoods generated a voracious demand for alternative sources of solace:

> ... *even within a town or a city with a major problem it will tend to be concentrated in certain neighbourhoods and virtually unknown in others. Moreover, where the problem has tended to gather together in dense pockets within our towns and cities, this will usually be in neighbourhoods which are worst affected by unemployment and wretched housing.*
>
> (Pearson, 1987)

But it was not simply that opiates offered blissful oblivion to the vulnerable and opportunity to the unscrupulous. Beyond the fact that users and sellers were, more often than not, the same people, was the reality that opiates filled a pressing existential need in de-stabilised neighbourhoods:

> *Controlled intoxicant use is more likely where a person has other valued life commitments, such as employment, which are incompatible with daily heroin use. One vitally important aspect of unemployment is the devastating impact which it makes upon an individual's time structures... involving a profound disorientation of daily routines... The compulsive logic of the heroin lifestyle: get straight – hustle for money – score drugs – get straight and hustle for more money – this effectively solves a major psychological burden of unemployed status.*
>
> (Pearson, 1993)

By the mid-1980s the numbers of registered heroin addicts in the UK had soared to 12,000, suggesting that the real number was nearer 70,000. By the late 1990s the numbers were far in excess of this figure. During this period opiate addiction migrated from Piccadilly Circus and the Fulham Road to the rest of the UK. Once there, it transformed local economies. In mining areas, in the late 1980s and early 1990s, the transition from coal to 'coke' occurred at mind-numbing speed. John Hagedorn writes of an analogous American experience (emphasis in the original):

> *One major impact of economic restructuring for poor communities has been a sharp reduction in the licit economy and the vast expansion of the illicit economy, especially the business of selling drugs... The cocaine economy in these selected parts of three neighbourhoods, at any one time, employed at least 600 people, most of them young male gang members. These young men grossed over $17 million dollars annually, if they individually made their mean of $2,400 per month. We estimate that 1,500 young men were employed in those neighbourhoods alone selling drugs in Milwaukee at some time in the early 1990s. It is likely today that drug sales is the largest single employer of young African American and Latino males in Milwaukee.*
>
> (Hagedorn, 1998)

Discreditation

Although the social processes described here are sometimes characterised as a 'breakdown of community', suggesting a loss of intimacy, in fact they often presage an intensification of intimacy, albeit unsought, among local children and young people. Employment takes fewer and fewer adults beyond the neighbourhood, while the shortages of cash engendered by unemployment confine them to their immediate locality. Lack of money also means that children and young people are seldom taken out of the neighbourhood by their parents. Moreover, the growing antipathy of residents, shopkeepers, school students and possibly teachers, in the surrounding neighbourhoods, combined with the peculiar policing styles often reserved for such 'areas of disrepute' serves to force these youngsters into ever closer association one with another. Detlef Baum, writing about Turkish young people living on a run-down housing estate outside Koblenz in Germany's Rhineland notes:

> *Young people sense this discreditation in their own environment, in school or in the cultural or leisure establishments. Through this they experience stigmatisation of their difference, of their actions, and the perceived incompetence of the people they live among. The options for action are limited and possibilities of gaining status-enhancing resources are made more difficult. At some stage the process becomes a self-fulfilling prophecy; young people and adults come to think that 'there must be something in it' when their characteristics and ways of behaving are stigmatised, and some become confirmed in this uncertainty. One is no longer in control of defining oneself, one is defined by others.* (Baum, 1996)

This experience discourages movement beyond the neighbourhood. Meanwhile the neighbourhood itself, because it lacks a sufficiently developed urban infrastructure of shops, commercial and public leisure facilities, pubs, clubs and cafes, fails to equip youngsters with the cultural sophistication and the skills in self-presentation, negotiation and conflict resolution that enable them to know what to do in other urban contexts:

> *One needs to overcome these distances and that requires resources of time and money. One has to weigh up whether it is worth it, whether the experience will justify the investment of time and money. Over time, more and younger people in the Brennpunkt (neighbourhood) stop going to town.* (Baum, 1996)

And because they 'stop going to town', such status and reputation as they will earn, must be acquired in the miniaturised arena of the neighbourhood, where there is always a stage, and an enthusiastic audience, for anybody willing to make a name for themselves. As was recognised over 40 years ago:

> *Those adolescents in disorganised urban areas, who are oriented towards achieving higher position but are cut off from institutionalised channels, criminal as well as*

legitimate, must rely upon their own resources for solving the problem of adjustment. Under these conditions tendencies towards aberrant behaviour become intensified and magnified.
(Cloward and Ohlin, 1960)

It is against the backdrop of this expanding pool of economically marginal, reluctant adolescents that the intensification of crime and public disorder, which characterises de-stabilised neighbourhoods throughout Britain, must be understood. These young people are condemned by poverty and unemployment to inhabit overcrowded, under-resourced, high-crime neighbourhoods, while the labour market and the dominant culture determine that they are to be less than whole people, trapped in a limbo world, somewhere between childhood and adulthood, long after the developmental tasks of adolescence have been completed. Moreover, they are also fixed ideologically, destined to provide the screen upon which the fears and fantasies of those at the social centre are projected.

The Rolling Back of the State

The plight of the young people in these neighbourhoods was compounded from the mid-1980s by cutbacks in local government expenditure which resulted in the withdrawal of many of the services and resources which had previously contributed to the quality of communal life and social cohesion in their neighbourhoods. However, it is not simply that there was greater need and fewer organisations and individuals available to respond to that need. In the 1980s, the very nature of public services changed.

The 1980s witnessed swingeing cuts in local authority budgets, a substantial redistribution of political power from local to central government and the parallel introduction of market mechanisms into public services (Jenkins, 1995; Hutton, 1995). In this period, decisions about the goals to which public services should strive, their spending priorities and the day-to-day conduct of their staff were increasingly taken by central government or the government's appointees in the burgeoning, and largely unaccountable, 'quangocracy' which progressively annexed public services in the 1980s.

De-institutionalisation

With central government exerting increasing control over local government expenditure, local authorities turned their attention to the children's homes and residential schools which were consuming a large share of their education and welfare budgets. The timely emergence of a political and theoretical critique, 'progressive minimalism', which rejected the total institution as both psychologically harmful and criminogenic (Thorpe et al., 1980), and the fallout from successive institutional abuse scandals, offered a scientific and humanitarian rationale for radical change. In consequence, from the early 1980s, many local authorities simply closed their residential children's institutions. A few remained, but these were 'outsourced' to the private and voluntary sector. Many of their erstwhile residents, although still in the 'care' of the local authority, were placed back in their own homes 'on trial'. These developments prompted some local authorities to develop imaginative adolescent fostering initiatives, and many children and young people, previously resident in children's homes, were placed with foster families. But the wholesale decanting of youngsters in care into their own, or substitute families was not without its problems. Cliffe (1990), writing about Warwickshire, a local authority which closed all its children's homes in 1986, observes:

> *Most children were offered only one choice of foster placement and obviously, no residential placement – in other words, no choice at all. Secondly, although Warwickshire has shown that more difficult children can be fostered than was previously thought, there is still a small group – mostly adolescent boys – who need residential placements.*

> (Cliffe, 1990)

Running Out of Care

Need and want! As David Crimmens (1991), Director of the first 'safe house' for runaway children, noted:

> *One major problem presented by young runaways from Care is the breakdown of foster placements. These young people often state quite clearly that they do not want to live in a family. They have families of their own which they may, or may not, return to. They do not want the pressures of family life, other adults 'pretending to be your mum and dad', or simply to live in a situation in which they feel they have failed. What they want is a 'good children's home'.*

Confronted with this Hobson's choice, many youngsters opted for homelessness. A survey by the youth homelessness charity Centrepoint (1995) revealed that in 1994/5, 28 per cent of young people entering their night shelter had previously been in care. Of these, 51 per cent had run away before they were 16. In a subsequent study of 39 care leavers, Centrepoint found that over half had been homeless immediately after leaving care, that nearly all of them had 'slept rough' and that 30 per cent had become homeless when social work help was withdrawn. In his study of 1,158 first admissions to the 'safe house' referred to above, Matthew Pitts (1992) noted that 36 per cent of first admissions had run from a local authority with 75 per cent of 17-year-olds having 'run' at least once before. The Centrepoint study of care leavers estimated that within six weeks, most young people living on the street would resort to crime, drugs or prostitution as a survival strategy.

Home on Trial

However, the majority of young people decanted from care were placed 'at home on trial'. This meant that they were often placed in erratic families in de-stabilised neighbourhoods where the likelihood of further abuse was relatively high. Research indicates that child abuse, in the forms of sexual violation and violence is, for the most part, perpetrated by men, and occurs throughout the social structure. However, recent scholarship (Messerschmidt, 1993; Segal, 1990; Campbell, 1993; Mooney, 1993) suggests that rather than being randomly distributed, crimes against women and children tend to be concentrated in the poorest neighbourhoods. Elliott Currie (1996) attributes this, in part at least, to the progressive drain upon parenting capacities which life in de-stabilised neighbourhoods imposes. In addition, however, we should note that this violence is most prevalent among men who experience the greatest discrepancy between what they have become and what they believe, as men, they are supposed to be. If, as many commentators argue, the violent sexual abuse of women and children is essentially about power rather than sex, its concentration in de-stabilised neighbourhoods should not surprise us (Segal, 1990). In response to these developments Currie (1996) has advocated 'a wide range of supports for parents in coping with real world stresses in their communities'; however, as we have noted, the political changes of the 1980s and 1990s served only to erode these services. As a result, many youngsters placed 'at home on trial' were soon to swell the ranks of the young homeless care leavers discussed above.

A study undertaken by Hugh Shriane in Luton (1995) revealed that 46 per cent of the young people who ran away, and stayed away from home, came from the poorest public housing estate with the highest crime rate and lowest levels of youth employment and political participation in the borough. Graham and Bowling (1995), in their study of young people and crime, found a strong correlation between running away, family poverty, strained family relationships and a family's capacity to supervise its children. Of the young people entering the Centrepoint night shelter in 1994/5, 18 per cent had been told to leave the parental home or were evicted, 25 per cent had left as a result of family arguments, 13 per cent had left as a result of 'relationship breakdown', while eight per cent cited physical violence and two per cent sexual violence.

The initial vulnerability of these young people was compounded in 1988 by the Social Security Act which withdrew state benefits from under-18s, living away from the parental home. This confronted many of them with a choice between returning to the hazards of an abusive or neglectful parental home or moving on to the streets. A survey conducted by Centrepoint in the eight months following the implementation of the 1988 Social Security Act found that the numbers of 16 to 19-year-olds without proper accommodation in London had increased by 35 per cent. Their predicament was made even worse by major changes to the board and lodgings regulations in 1989, and changes in the funding arrangements for housing association hostels in the Housing Act 1989. Of the young people entering the Centrepoint night shelter in 1994/5, 41 per cent had no source of income and 43 per cent were receiving no state benefits.

The Rise and Fall of Day Care

Confronted with these difficulties, in the early 1980s, many local authorities channelled a proportion of the savings from the closure of children's homes into day care provision for youngsters who were in care but 'home on trial', and those who were subject to a 'criminal' supervision order. In London, most local authorities re-designated one or two local children's homes as 'Intermediate Treatment (IT) centres' where children and young people would attend daily, and sometimes at weekends as well, to receive their education and pursue recreational activities. Alongside the IT centres which, in the late 1970s and early 1980s, were working with around 2,000 youngsters, off-site units run by education authorities for children and young people confronting similar neighbourhood and family difficulties were catering for a further 5,000 or so on a full-time basis.

As the 1980s proceeded, further cuts in public spending and the continuing influence of a particularly simplistic reading of 'progressive minimalism', which now rejected day care as well as residential care, because it widened the 'net of control', meant that most IT centres and off-site units were eventually axed. At a stroke, their young clientele was 'normalised', their contact was reduced to once a week at best and they were redirected to mainstream, youth service, play and educational provision.

Goodbye to All That

Unfortunately, however, alongside the closure of IT centres and off-site units came the collapse of literally thousands of adventure playgrounds and play centres, which had often served as an unofficial 'safe haven' for troubled children and young people who were not surviving in mainstream education or at home. By the late 1980s, detached youth workers, who often had contact with more difficult and damaged young people, were disappearing from the streets, while drop-in advice centres were evaporating at the same rate. Meanwhile, the remaining youth clubs which, by the late 1980s, represented the core of youth service provision, were pursuing a new 'national curriculum' which had little space for these newly normalised youngsters from the social margins. And then there were the schools.

De-stabilising Schools

The demographic changes occurring in these neighbourhoods were replicated in the classroom. In an Inner London school, where the present author and his colleagues undertook a study of student violence, the transience of the housing estates which fed the school was reflected in a 50 per cent turnover in the school roll between years 7 and 11. By 1999, as a result of conflicts in Ethiopia, Eritrea and the Balkans, 17 per cent of the school's students had refugee status and many of these were 'unaccompanied' minors in the care of an older brother, sister or cousin. Because the nature of the changes in the neighbourhood had been to replace more prosperous residents with less prosperous ones, by 1997 over 50 per cent of school students qualified for free school meals, the key indicator of social deprivation.

Because poverty and transience generate educational disadvantage in children, and erode the capacity of adults to offer consistent parenting, schools in these neighbourhoods must absorb a higher proportion of children with special educational and behavioural needs. Thus, 43 per cent of the students attending the London school had been assessed as having special educational needs; this was twice the borough average. As a result, behaviour in the playground and the corridors had deteriorated. The impact of the resultant atmosphere could be measured in increased truancy and lateness among students who were previously seen to pose no attendance or behavioural problems.

Absorbing Trouble

A further consequence of rapid student turnover is that schools in de-stabilised neighbourhoods carry a large number of vacancies. In an economic climate in which local education authorities are striving to reduce surplus capacity, these schools are under constant pressure to absorb students who wish to transfer in from other schools in the authority. In the London school, 64 per cent of year 10 and 40 per cent of year 11 students had previously attended another secondary school. However, beyond the de-stabilising effect of this steady influx of transferring students, was the fact that many of them brought additional academic and behavioural problems which, in some cases, had caused them to be excluded from other schools.

> *Exclusion, whether 'constructive' or formal is one mechanism for passing the buck, often leading to cost-shunting within and between un-coordinated agencies. The strategy means that under-subscribed schools, which are forced to accept as casual admissions pupils excluded from other schools, are faced with having to support disproportionate numbers of socially and educationally vulnerable children without the resources necessary to do it properly.* (Gewisty et al., 1995)

One consequence of this has been an increase in the numbers of serious fights, particularly inter-racial ones. These fights, which may have started in the school or in the neighbourhood, would quickly attract older adolescents and young adults from the surrounding area who, having nothing better to do, would get 'stuck in'. This violence contributed significantly to the risks faced by school students who were not directly involved in the violence.

Student Victimisation

In the London school, between September 1996 and April 1997, 41 per cent of year 11 students were assaulted, with 30 per cent of these assaults occurring in the vicinity of the school or on the way home from school, in the hour or so following the end of the school day; 80 per cent of the perpetrators were male, 48 per cent were either strangers or students from another school and 24 per cent of respondents reported being threatened or assaulted with a weapon. In a similar study undertaken in a similar neighbourhood in another part of London (Pitts and Smith, 1995), over 30 per cent of victimised students identified their assailant as being older than them and, in some cases, as an adult. It is, of course, ironic that schools in de-stabilised neighbourhoods, confronting formidable social problems, are nonetheless required to import further problems of disruption, crime and violence from other neighbourhoods. But it does not stop there.

Taking Flight

Seeing the writing on the wall, some parents seek to transfer their children, further de-stabilising the school. This has the effect of reducing the proportion of parents who have effected a positive choice in favour of the school and increasing the proportion who were either unwilling, or unable, to effect such a choice. In their study of the operation of market models in state education, Gewisty et al. (1995) identified three groups of 'choosers' among the parents they interviewed: privileged or skilled choosers, semi-skilled choosers and disconnected choosers. The parents of the children at secondary schools in de-stabilised neighbourhoods tend to fall into the third category.

Disconnected choosers are primarily oriented towards the local comprehensive schools, partly as a result of positive attachment to the locality and to going to school with friends and family. In addition, school has to be 'fitted into' a set of constraints and expectations related to the demands of work and household organisation. For low-income families on time-constrained budgets, the limitations of private and public transport play a key role in decision-making. Such choosers have limited capacity for participation in the education market but they are making active and positive choices. However, these are not made in ways that reflect the primary values of competitive consumerism which are embedded in the English market complex.

These are not neglectful parents. Some of them, like the refugees from Eritrea, Ethiopia and the Balkans, speak little English and many of them have been traumatised by the experience of violence, change and loss. The parents who seek a transfer tend to be more prosperous and articulate and are often active in fund raising and the PTA. They are also the parents who are most likely to reinforce the school's espoused ethos at home. Their departure is a double blow for the school, diminishing both its material and moral resources.

Staff Morale

Not surprisingly, these changes undermine staff morale, and so the turnover in the student group is mirrored in a rapid turnover of teachers. In 1997 in the London school, one-third of the teachers left. Some of these teachers had been promoted and others were simply moving out of London for 'family reasons', as many London teachers do. Nonetheless, these seismic staff changes are far more common in schools in de-stabilised neighbourhoods. As a result, more classes in 'de-stabilised schools' are covered by probationary teachers and supply teachers and, as a result of the transfer of teacher education to the schools, student teachers. This is particularly ironic since the teachers we interviewed in two large London secondary schools were unanimous that their students did not like too many 'new faces', took time to trust people, and needed to gain experience in forming and sustaining positive relationships with adults.

Government Lends a Hand

Roy Hattersley has observed that:

> Between 1958 and 1979 the ratio of teachers to pupils fell steadily throughout Europe. In Britain it improved from 1:26 to 1:19. Then the position changed. The rest of Europe continued the improvement. But, seizing on the reduction of the school population, the Thatcher government cut the British teaching force by 50,000 in 10 years. Now Britain employs fewer teachers per pupil than any other developed country.

> (*The Guardian*, 26 August 1997)

In addition to real staff cuts inflicted by central government, which in the London school meant that school governors were faced with a choice between maintaining pastoral services for socially disadvantaged students and teacher redundancies, schools in de-stabilised neighbourhoods have had to devote additional energy to the implementation of the national curriculum, government league tables and the local management of schools (LMS). Severe cuts in ancillary services – the Education Social Work Service, school counselling, pastoral care, home-school liaison, home tuition, off-site units, child and family guidance clinics, the youth service and those parts of the voluntary sector not undertaking statutory youth justice and child protection work – have exacerbated these difficulties. These changes have steadily eroded the ability of schools to deal with the problems presented by their students. In consequence, the additional work generated for teachers by problematic students – meetings with their parents, social welfare and criminal justice agencies, the production of reports for, and attendance at, case conferences, court hearings, etc. – has burgeoned.

In *Learning from Failure* (1997) Kathryn Riley and David Rowles studied 15 schools designated by OFSTED as 'failing'. They found that 'failing schools were serving communities with high levels of deprivation (unemployment, single-parent families, and a high uptake of free school meals)'. They also noted that the schools were usually housed in poor buildings and their intake represented a residuum of children that grant-maintained or grammar schools had not selected. This finding is echoed in OFSTED's own report on 'failing schools', *From Failure to Success*, and in the report of the Catholic Education Service, *A Struggle for Excellence: Catholic Secondary Schools in Urban Poverty Areas*. A report by the Local Government Management Board (LGMB) found that better-off pupils are increasingly congregating in the same schools, leaving other schools with a disproportionate number of 'poor' and 'difficult' pupils. Ironically, the 'additional needs' formula used by the Conservative government to help the least prosperous local authorities, benefited Harrow more than Barnsley, and Westminster more than Birmingham or Liverpool. The LGMB study found that most failing schools were located in the poorest areas, served by local authorities with the most limited resources.

When wholly legitimate pressures from below to render schools safer and more manageable places for teachers and students to work and study in, met pressures from above to improve school league-table rankings, something had to give. Between 1992 and 1997 formal permanent and fixed term exclusions from schools in England and Wales rose from almost 4,000 to 150,000 (Parsons, 1996; Smith, 1998). In London and other large metropolitan authorities, the predicament of the de-stabilised school has been compounded by the disappearance of an overarching education authority, like the Inner London Education Authority, whose banding policies once distributed children with special needs more equally between schools and contributed to the social and demographic mix of the school. A toxic combination of regressive taxation, council-house sales, under-funding and 'parental choice' continue to push many schools in de-stabilised neighbourhoods into a downward spiral which, despite their best efforts, school staff are powerless to reverse.

Riots

In 1991 and 1992 there were several riots in which young people attacked and, in some cases, destroyed, houses, shops and community facilities. Latterly they fought with police to retain control of these neighbourhoods. It is widely accepted that the inner-city riots of a decade before were triggered by 'racist policing' (Scarman, 1982). The riots of the early 1990s, by contrast, apparently 'just happened'; on 13 low-income, out-of-town, 'slum clearance' estates, with heavy concentrations of children and young people, and three times the national average level of youth unemployment and poor reputations. They were preceded by:

> ... 'rumbling riots'. The police and community had tolerated, or were forced to put up with, unusual levels of violence and lawbreaking by young men prior to the riots. Disorder had gradually mounted and there was weak social control, serious intimidation, an unwillingness by residents to act as witnesses and irregular policing.

> (Power and Tunstall, 1999)

The rioters attacked community facilities 'built up with the involvement of dedicated and active local leaders':

> In fact, in some areas local activists suggested that these programmes were directly provocative, since most government resources went on physical buildings rather than jobs, on large outside contractors rather than small local businesses, on short-term improvements including short-term training, rather than long-term commitments to the development of the local social and economic infrastructure. The character of the areas and their problems were more complex and far more deep-set than the programmes. Most externally-funded programmes were driven by outside constraints and did very little to change the prospects for young men or their stake in what happened. For this reason, they appeared to have little compunction about destroying quickly what had often been hard won and built up over a long period.   (ibid.)

Clearly, Power and Tunstall are telling us about the inadequacies of piecemeal, supply-side social reform, and Ann Power, as a key contributor to New Labour's social exclusion strategy, knows more about this than most. But are they also telling us about the end point of the types of social processes set in train by the political and economic changes of the 1980s and 1990s? Beatrix Campbell, writing of the Meadowell estate which experienced one of the most severe riots, is in no doubt that this is where the social, economic and cultural processes outlined in this chapter lead:

> Crime was part of the economy, and part of what it put up with. It endured an epidemic of poverty. Every one of the children at one of the estate's primary schools depended on clothing grants and three quarters depended on free school meals. A quarter of young men up to the age of twenty four were unemployed and long-term unemployment among males was the highest in the North East. Thirty years before the riots of 1991, nearly eighty-five per cent of all crime in the borough occurred in this one housing estate. In the period between the Sixties and the Nineties the region lost most of its staple jobs for men in the shipyards. In the year before the riots, it had the highest crime rate in the country.

> (Campbell, 1993)

Explaining Neighbourhood De-stabilisation

Anglo-American criminology has offered two quite distinct explanations of neighbourhood de-stabilisation. One, which we might call the deficit model emphasises the central role of the family in the inculcation of self-control in their children, while the other, which we might call the opportunity model places the onus on socio-economic factors. The deficit model holds that the problems in these neighbourhoods are largely attributable to the personal characteristics, the values, and beliefs, modes of thought or bad habits, of the residents. The proponents of this position tend to adopt a culturalist (Murray, 1994) or psychological, often cognitive-behavioural, approach to problems of crime (Ross et al., 1988; Gottfreidson and Hirschi , 1990; Hawkins and Catalano, 1998; Farrington and West, 1993; Farrington, 1996). The opportunity model holds that the problems afflicting these neighbourhoods are, in the first instance at least, visited upon them from the outside in the form of poor housing, unemployment, exclusion from educational opportunity, benefit cuts, social stigma, the drugs trade and discriminatory policing. Not surprisingly, perhaps, those who espouse the opportunity model tend to favour a sociological or socio-political perspective (Cloward and Ohlin, 1960; McGahey, 1986; Sullivan, 1989; Wilson, 1987; Currie, 1991; Sampson and Laub, 1993; Hope, 1994; Wikstrom and Loeber, 1997; Sampson et al., 1997; Pitts and Hope, 1997).

Thus far, few theorists have made a sustained attempt to bridge these two levels of explanation: the personal or biographical, and the socio-political; yet this is, perhaps, the most urgent task confronting a social science that wishes to be politically relevant in the new millennium. In Chapter 5 we noted that Wikstrom and Loeber's Pittsburgh youth study (1997), marks an important breakthrough in the 'deficit-opportunity' debate, in that they were able to measure the relationship between individual risk factors, neighbourhood characteristics and juvenile offending. The individual risk factors they measured were:

- hyperactivity-impulsivity-attention problems
- lack of guilt
- social situations
- poor parental monitoring
- poor school motivation
- peer delinquency
- positive attitude towards delinquency

These factors correspond closely with the risk factors deemed by Farrington and West (1993) and latterly Utting et al. (1993), Graham and Bowling (1995) and the Audit Commission (1996) to be most closely associated with the onset of youth offending.

Wikstrom and Loeber divided the neighbourhoods in which their research subjects lived into high, medium and low socio-economic status (SES) areas. They then devised an inventory of serious offences including car theft, breaking and entering, 'strong-arming', 'attack to seriously hurt or kill', 'forced sex' and 'selling drugs'. They found that for subjects with no, or very low, risk factors, there was a clear neighbourhood effect upon offending, with serious offending by children and young people with the lowest individual risk factors occurring significantly more frequently in the lowest SES neighbourhoods (see Table 7.2). It is evident from these findings that neighbourhood of residence is a more important influence on serious offending among children and young people with the lowest risk factors than for others, and that the relation between risk factors and serious offending 'breaks down' for those living in the most disadvantaged communities. These findings suggest that the causal significance of neighbourhood SES has been seriously underestimated in both mainstream criminological theory and contemporary criminal justice policy.

Table 7.2: Percentage of boys in Pittsburgh having committed acts of serious delinquency by neighbourhood type and number of risk factors

Number of risk factors	Neighbourhood SES			
	High	Medium	Low	Low
	(Non-public housing areas)		(Public housing areas)	
0	3.4	13.7	13.6	51.3
1–2	32.8	37.5	38.1	53.1
3–6	56.3	60.3	72.9	83.9

Risk defined as belonging to the upper quartile of the distribution of the measure of the risk factor in question. For instance, having a score of 6 on the index of risk factors means that the subject belongs to the upper quartile of all six individual risk measures (data weighted to correct for oversampling of boys known for antisocial behaviour).

Source: Data from the combined middle and oldest sample of the Pittsburgh Youth Study. Adapted from Wikstrom and Loeber (1997).

Collective Efficacy

However, while it is clear that low-neighbourhood SES has a profound impact upon youth crime, it is also the case that some multiply deprived neighbourhoods suffer much lower levels of crime and victimisation than others (McGahey 1986). Sampson et al.'s (1997) study attempted to establish why these differences occurred. They found that rates of violence were lower in urban neighbourhoods characterised by what they describe as 'collective efficacy'. Collective efficacy refers to 'mutual trust among neighbours, combined with willingness to intervene on behalf of the common good, specifically to supervise children and maintain public order'. This finding is important because it challenges the taken-for-granted assumptions that crime is a straightforward product of poverty, unemployment, and the predominance of single-parent households or the concentration of certain minority groups. These factors, the researchers argue, may have a bearing upon a neighbourhood's capacity to develop collective efficacy, but they do not, of themselves, generate crime. The researchers observe that, contrary to popular stereotypes, some Chicago neighbourhoods which are populated largely by poor Black people have low crime rates. In these neighbourhoods, the researchers found that collective efficacy was the most powerful influence keeping violent crime at bay.

The research, conducted in Chicago neighbourhoods between 1990 and 1997, aimed to investigate child and adolescent development in the city's neighbourhoods, and the antecedents of criminality, substance abuse and violence for individual children and young people. A principal aim was to understand the impact of neighbourhood characteristics, changes in social services and the influence of the family and peer relationships on the behaviour of children and young people, as well as the personal characteristics of individuals.

Sampson and his research team divided Chicago into 343 'neighbourhood clusters', housing about 8,000 people, defined by geographic boundaries and characterised by homogeneity in terms of the characteristics of the populations and the resources available to them. Over the period, 8,782 Chicago residents representing all 343 areas were interviewed. This makes the study one of the most comprehensive ever undertaken. The questions asked of residents were intended to elicit their views of how much informal social control, social cohesion, trust and violence existed in their neighbourhoods. They were asked about the likelihood of their neighbours intervening in a number of situations, particularly to discipline neighbourhood children if, for example, they were painting graffiti or truanting. Respondents were also asked how well they thought several statements about social cohesion and trust described their neighbourhood. Examples of the statements were: 'People around here are willing to help their neighbours', 'This is a close-knit neighbourhood' and 'People in this neighbourhood can be trusted'. Neighbourhood violence was calculated by asking residents about both their perceptions and their actual victimisation, and by reviewing data in police homicide reports. In each neighbourhood, the average homicide rate for the period 1988–90 was included in the calculation to adjust for previous levels of violence. Finally, 1990 census data on several demographic characteristics were combined to create a multidimensional picture of social composition, comprising measures of disadvantage, ethnic or immigrant concentration and residential stability.

The Key Findings

Previous research has identified links between neighbourhood social composition and crime. Sampson et al. (1997) found that in neighbourhoods scoring high on collective efficacy, crime rates were 40 per cent below those in lower-scoring neighbourhoods. This difference supported the researchers' basic premise that crime rates are not solely attributable to the characteristics of the individuals in neighbourhoods. Instead, they found that a neighbourhood's crime rates were determined in large part by its social and organisational characteristics.

In neighbourhoods where concentrated poverty was high, collective efficacy tended to be low. Ethnicity, immigration and transience were important factors, and it appears that ethnic and linguistic heterogeneity may impair a neighbourhood's capacity to realise 'common values'. Neighbourhoods where residential stability was strong, by contrast, tended to have high levels of collective efficacy. The researchers concluded that 'collective efficacy, not race or poverty, was the largest single predictor of the overall violent crime rate'.

As we have noted, Anglo-American criminology has, in the form of the opportunity and deficit models, offered two quite distinct explanations for the concentration of crime in multiply-deprived neighbourhoods. While offering strong support for the opportunity model, Sampson et al.'s study (1997) also builds a bridge between socio-political and psychological perspectives, by locating child development within its socio-political and micro-social context. At the same time, it compliments the arguments of Sampson and Lamb (1992), and Hagan (1993); arguments which concern the potential of neighbourhoods to generate forms of social capital, which enhance the capabilities and prospects of children and adults in those neighbourhoods, by embedding them in virtuous upward spirals.

The Political Implications of the Collective Efficacy Thesis

Sampson et al.'s (1997) research tells us that some sense of local connectedness, and a willingness and ability to act in ways which further the interests of fellow residents, can set in train a 'virtuous circle' of mutually reinforcing social and personal effects. This will, of course, be music to the ears of New Labour's policy advisers who are wedded to the idea that it is possible to 'build' the 'capacity' of informal local 'networks' to generate the kinds of 'social capital', of which collective efficacy is the example par excellence. The strangely influential 'thinktank' DEMOS, and latterly the Conservative opposition under Ian Duncan Smith, have argued that such networks represent both an inexpensive source of informal social control and social support and a third way between the state and the market. However, it is evident from Richard McGahey's research that effective neighbourhood networks cannot be brought into being by political will alone. He has shown that effective networks are dependent upon demographic stability, the availability of appropriate housing, and the quality and strength of schools, social services and family support. These factors give residents an investment in the neighbourhood which leads to enhanced participation in neighbourhood social and political organisations. This, in turn, enriches and reinforces interpersonal and inter-group relationships in the neighbourhood. Participation in social and political organisations then enhances a neighbourhood's capacity to exert control over crime and victimisation. Such 'horizontal integration', people getting together to identify shared concerns, is also a precondition for greater vertical integration in which neighbourhood representatives come to act as advocates for their neighbourhoods in an attempt to extract resources from those political groupings, state bureaucracies and social agencies with formal responsibility for the problem of crime. It is not that these 'social' factors are more important than economic forces in shaping the destinies of neighbourhoods but, rather, that over time they are transformed into an economic factor, and a precondition for the closer integration of a neighbourhood with its economic environment. This leads McGahey to conclude that:

> *The relative abilities of different neighbourhood economies and social organisations to cope with urban, regional and national economic transformations may help explain why some neighbourhoods turn into persistently high crime communities and others do not. By viewing urban crime in relation to particular neighbourhood economies and the broader urban labour market, we may be better able to understand crime's generation and persistence and to devise more effective policies for its control and reduction.* (McGahey, 1986)

It is evident from this analysis, that any attempt by central or local government to mobilise indigenous 'networks' against crime, without considering the social and economic conditions which generate collective efficacy, is likely to fail. Conversely, an understanding of these conditions may offer the key to the development of a coherent community safety strategy which is able to address the complex, interrelated problems of urban regeneration, social exclusion, welfare dependency, school failure and youth crime.

Chapter 8

The Erosion of Solidarity

Today industrial labour – or what is left of it – is very much within the majority class of those who have an interest in preserving the status quo. The underclass on the contrary is a mere category, a victim. It is unlikely to organise and defend the many similar yet not really common interests of its members. They are, if the cruelty of the statement is pardonable, not needed. The rest could and would quite like to live without them.

(Dahrendorf, 1994)

Now look at them yoyos, that's the way you do it,
You play the guitar on the MTV,
That ain't working, that's the way you do it,
Money for nothing and chicks for free.

(Mark Knopfler and Sting, *Money for Nothing*, 1985)

Crime, Change and Social Cohesion

Since the late 1970s, the idea that the market, unmolested by governments, would bring forth a fairer and more prosperous society has had a significant impact upon the social and economic policies of Western governments (Glennester and Midgley, 1991; Bourdieu, 1998). However, as we have noted, the free market proved to have a particularly acute downside; generating social and economic divisions, undermining social cohesion, destabilising families, deepening poverty and promoting criminality. The Blair administration of 1997 has the distinction of being the first European government elected, specifically, to repair the damage done to the economy, the social fabric and popular morality by neo-liberalism. Yet while many of the problems inherited by the Blair government can be laid at the door of what Denis Healey has called 'sado-monetarism', the story of the erosion of social solidarity in Britain begins a long time before Mrs Thatcher embraced neo-liberalism.

From the mid-1950s, despite unprecedented economic growth and increasing material well-being, recorded crime in Britain rose steadily. In the 1980s, its trajectory steepened. In marked contrast, the early decades of the twentieth century saw a steady decline in 'ordinary' crime, theft, burglary, assault, despite what we would now regard as intolerable levels of poverty. This fall in crime, as John Lea (1998) has observed, paralleled the rise of the Labour Party and the trade union movement, which transformed an inchoate urban proletariat into a powerful political and moral force. As a result, the first half of the twentieth century saw the emergence of a relatively secure, unionised, industrial workforce whose social well-being was underpinned by the progressive expansion of rights to healthcare, housing, education and material security. These developments produced reliable workers, stable families and 'respectable' working-class neighbourhoods. It is not that crime, once believed to be a ubiquitous feature of lower-class life, disappeared during this period, but rather, that in popular perception, and to a considerable extent in fact, working-class crime came to be concentrated on the 'social margins', among those who had not been incorporated into what eventually came to be called 'the post-war settlement'.

In the 30 years after the Second World War, the central motif of British politics was 'progress', to be achieved through government intervention in the 'market', the redistribution of wealth via progressive taxation and welfare transfers, and the development of social and educational policies which expanded legitimate opportunity for the least well off. In the 1960s, rapidly increasing incomes, heightened material aspirations and the rise of 'consumerism' obscured, for a time, the reality that those at the very bottom of the social structure, single-parent families, the poor single elderly, etc. were not making any progress (Abel-Smith and Townsend 1964).

By the early 1980s as de-industrialisation began to drive unemployment to unprecedented levels, the post-war trend towards an overall narrowing of income inequalities was reversed. In the new '30-40-30 society' of the 1980s (Hutton 1995), it was skilled industrial and clerical workers who were forced to the social and economic margins, not just the 'poor'. Now, a Conservative government, wrestling with the burgeoning costs of unemployment, began hurriedly revising the terms of the 'post-war settlement'. Maintaining that the amelioration of the deleterious effects of 'globalisation' upon business and industry would represent a market imperfection, the Conservatives cut industry adrift to weather the 'icy blasts' of international competition alone. Meanwhile, 'deregulated' capital was 'freed' to roam the world in search of the highest interest rates and the richest dividends. Unsurprisingly these developments generated a pervasive sense of insecurity and disaffection, not only among the unemployed but among the employed and their employers as well.

> *The mood of the unemployed is not self-blame but system-blaming. Relative deprivation persists but is transformed. It no longer involves comparison across the serried ranks of the incorporated, it becomes comparison across the divisions of the labour market and between those in the market and those excluded.* (Young, 1998)

By the mid-1980s the world of 'steady', status-conferring, primary sector employment, underpinned by an interventionist state, was a fading memory for millions of British adults, and a fairy story for their children.

The Advent of Market Society

The 'rolling back' of the state, in the 1980s, paralleled the emergence of a new political phenomenon, 'market society':

> *By market society I mean a society in which the pursuit of private gain increasingly becomes the organising principle for all areas of social life, not simply a mechanism which we use to accomplish certain circumscribed economic ends. The balance between private and public shifts dramatically, so that the public retreats to a miniscule and disempowered part of social and economic life and the idea of common purposes and common responsibilities steadily withers as an important social value.*

(Currie, 1991)

Its arrival signalled the demise of an earlier solidaristic politics and the fragmentation of the political constituency, in the labour movement, Parliament, welfare, education and the academy, which had championed the idea of 'progress'. But this was not the inadvertent political by-product of the quest for efficiency as it was sometimes portrayed. The wholesale 'de-politicisation' of local government in the 1980s was central to the neo-conservative project. As Milton Friedman (1962) the economics guru who inspired, among others, Sir Keith Joseph, Lady Margaret Thatcher and General Augusto Pinochet (see Borutsky, 1991) once observed:

> *The widespread use of the market reduces the strain on the social fabric by rendering conformity unnecessary with respect to any activities it encompasses. The wider the range of activities covered by the market, the fewer are the issues on which explicitly political decisions are required and hence on which it is necessary to achieve agreement. In turn, the fewer the issues on which agreement is necessary, the greater the likelihood of getting agreement while maintaining a free society.*

The public services were the site where the struggle to neutralise the threat posed to social harmony by political participation was most intense during the 1980s. In the process, 'publics', an aggregation of citizens with shared interests, and the potentiality for common political purpose, were reduced to 'markets' of atomised purchasers, who expressed their choices through the 'pound' in their own, or their institutional proxy's, 'pocket'.

Thus within a few years, political, administrative and academic discourse was effectively purged of references to 'social justice', 'social class', 'poverty' and 'inequality', and new languages, which reflected the analyses and imperatives of newly powerful intellectual, political and professional elites emerged in the academy, politics and the public services.

Lyotard and Emotional: Retreatist Social Theory and the Problematisation of 'Progress'

Upon its publication in 1979, Jean-Francois Lyotard's *The Post-Modern Condition*, with its rejection of the 'grand narratives' of 'modernism' in general, and those of his erstwhile exemplar Karl Marx in particular, was seized upon by many left-of-centre academics and intellectuals as a source of hope and renewal in the wake of the collapse of the political and intellectual consensus which had supported the post-war settlement. Post-modernism, with its emphasis upon the ubiquity of power, the fluidity of identity and the subversive potential of language, appeared to offer an intellectual vantage point from which to 'disrupt' the 'discourse' of an ascendant neo-liberalism and exploit the values of an ever more nihilistic capitalism to radical cultural ends. However, whatever radical potential post-modernism possesses is effectively negated by its uncompromising relativism. In the world of post-modernism, there is slippage in both the sense of 'reality' and the sense of the 'self' as agent. In post-modernism the 'self' is 'deconstructed', becoming a more or less passive vehicle for transient styles and free-floating discourses. The idea that identity is forged by our experience of an inequitable social order and our struggle to change it, a process in which we 'make', rather than 'make up', our own history, is abandoned for, in post-modernism, 'all that is solid melts into air' (Marx and Engels, 1888).

At the core of post-modernism is the idea that the 'grand narratives' of modernism, with their discredited ideas of human progress, have gone the way of the dinosaur. Yet, as Terry Eagleton (1991) has observed, having stopped believing in the old story about the inexorable forward march of the proletariat, many leftward-leaning social scientists and political activists in the 1980s and 1990s seemed prepared to swallow any old story. In rejecting the 'progressive triumphalism' of vulgar Marxism, as discerning thinkers on the left always have, post-modernists, unaccountably, rejected the idea of progress or causality per se; the belief, at the core of all social theory, that socio-historical events generate determinate socio-historical effects and, by extension, that sometimes things will get better, and at others they will get worse.

But, of course, the grand narrative did not die in the 1980s. It was only the 'progressive' grand narratives of the left which ran out of track. On the political right the 'anti-progressive' grand narrative was alive, well and influential almost everywhere. In its neo-liberal moment, exemplified in the early, Hegelian-flavoured work of Francis Fukyama (1992), it celebrated the triumph of free-market capitalism as the culmination of human history. In its more traditional Conservative guise it fused the deteriorationist belief which held that nothing had been the same since the death of Queen Victoria, the First World War, the 1950s, etc. with a vision of life as one long struggle against dark urges in oneself, one's Range Rover and one's village. This latter perspective, being predicated on the idea that the problems besetting the world had their origins in a 'fall from grace', was, quite understandably, implacably opposed to the idea that 'social progress' should, or ever could, be achieved through human agency. Thatcherism straddled both strands of thought, adopting a laissez-faire stance on matters social and economic and a deeply censorious and prescriptive one on questions of sexual orientation and personal morality, while eschewing the very possibility of 'social', as opposed to individual, progress. Having terminally problematised the idea of 'social progress' as either pathetically nostalgic or hopelessly utopian, post-modernism posed no threat whatsoever to Thatcherism. What a relief it was then, some 20 years on, when Jean-François Lyotard at last came clean: 'I made up stories, I referred to a quantity of books I'd never read, apparently it impressed people' he said (Bromwich, 1999).

The Managerial Turn

For welfare professionals, the advent of 'market society' in the 1980s signalled the collapse of the political and theoretical paradigm which, up to that point, had ascribed meaning to their endeavours. These were the people by whose professional efforts the post-war dream of a well educated, 'open', egalitarian, social democratic society was to be realised. These were the people, the social workers, the counsellors, the youth workers, the schoolteachers who, as Bourdieu (1998) has observed, represented 'the left hand of the state' – 'the trace of the social struggles of the past'. Theirs was a project predicated on the materialist premise that inequitable social structures generated aberrant behaviour, the remedy for which consisted in an empathetic professional intervention, backed up by the progressive reordering of the social arrangements which had given rise to those behaviours in the first place. This was a paradigm which, although almost always in tension with social and political reality, gave coherence and purpose to the efforts of the professionals who worked within the welfare state.

In the 1980s these people found themselves in a bitter struggle with 'the right hand of the state', the total quality managers, the downsizers, the outsourcers, the auditors and the target-setters who, being in the political ascendant, found little need to disguise their distaste, indeed contempt, for the values and social practices to which the representatives of the left hand of the state had devoted their lives. The right hand of the state won, and in consequence, in the 1980s, social problems were reformulated as administrative anomalies; and professionals whose job it had been to devise solutions to social problems were eased to one side by a culture of managerialism in which the primary task was the 'delivery' of 'tightly targeted', 'cost-effective', 'packages' to 'service-users'.

Managerialism narrows the focus of reform. Turning away from sociological abstractions like social structure and social justice, it concerns itself with the detail of policy, practice, beliefs and values in an organisation, a school or a local authority. Eschewing broader political objectives, it intends that organisations should put their own houses in order. It is concerned not with a service to a 'public', but with the responses of an organisation to its 'service users' and this concern extends neither beyond that 'service user's' contractual involvement with the organisation nor to similarly afflicted individuals with no such involvement. The breathtaking modesty of the managerialist project is obscured in part by its obfuscatory language. Just as, in post-modernism, the text stands in for 'reality', so in the new managerialism a simplified and arbitrary 'target' stands in for complex social phenomena – real people, in real difficulty, who must be understood, engaged and worked with constructively.

Robust management – the establishment and maintenance of efficient administrative machinery, high professional standards and their effective scrutiny and evaluation – is central to the achievement of the political and professional goals of public services. In the 1980s, however, 'management', the mechanism, was supplanted by 'managerialism', the cult, which eclipsed the political and professional goals of local public services to become a pre-eminent goal in its own right. This transformation eroded an earlier politics in which, to a limited extent, local citizens could negotiate local needs and their alleviation with local politicians and public officials. As the 1980s progressed, the structural connections between local public services and local social problems became ever more tenuous as they strove to achieve the bureaucratic 'targets' prescribed by central government (Clarke et al., 1994; Le Grand, 1995; Crawford, 1998). And, in the process, public services relinquished any potential they had as a medium whereby private troubles could be translated into public issues (Mills, 1959). Managerialism is concerned with 'service delivery', rather than social progress. It therefore tends to be responsive to those intra- and extra-systemic contingencies which threaten its political and economic viability rather than 'publics'.

The thorny question of race, crime and justice, and the ways in which public agencies should handle it, offers a useful example of how a highly contentious public issue is transformed into a depoliticised managerial agenda item. Racial oppression may be real, morally repugnant, and pervasive, but when the new managerialism takes it on, it becomes little more than a dysfunctional organisational residue amenable to the kinds of administrative techniques developed to solve many other kinds of 'human resource' problems. Whereas an earlier politics saw racism, in part at least, as a product of structural inequality, the new managerialism sees structural inequality as a product of racism, and attitude change, brought about by administrative *fiat*, as the process whereby such inequality will be eradicated. As a result, by the late 1980s most state agencies had, or were in the process of developing, anti-racist statements, anti-racist policies, anti-racist strategies, anti-racist codes of practice and graduated sanctions for breaches of same. Despite a pervasive vagueness about what it actually was, the enthusiasm for anti-racism of the Home Office, the Probation Service, the Central Council for Education and Training in Social Work and a multiplicity of other public sector organisations and agencies was unabated. For anti-racism appeared to offer a relatively uncontentious and inexpensive strategy. As a managerially led 'negative' reform (Mathiesen, 1974), it needed only slight changes in attitudes and behaviour, and the modest reorganisation of existing resources, for its realisation. It required neither a reprioritisation of resources nor a realignment of power relations.

> *The sign on the wall of the probation waiting room says that the Service will not tolerate racist language; it is their policy. Yet where is the policy which addresses the factors which ensure that the waiting room is filling up with poor, unemployed, badly educated young people – black and white.*
>
> (Pitts, 1995)

Whereas the political programme which emerged from an earlier class analysis required, for good or ill, the transfer of the means of production, distribution and exchange to public ownership for its realisation, in the final analysis, anti-racism merely enjoins us to change our minds.

Managing Youth Justice

As we have noted, the triumph of managerialism was nowhere more evident than in the youth justice system of the 1980s where an earlier 'needology' (Thorpe et al., 1980) was swept aside by the new orthodoxy of 'delinquency management' which shifted the focus from particular children and young people, their culpability, needs and problems to categories of 'young offenders' whose progress through, or diversion from, the system was to be directed by a new breed of 'system managers':

> *If the period from the mid-1960s to the early 1970s – can be characterised as the era of professionalism, the period from the late 1970s…could be characterised as the era of managerialism. In this period, 'being on the side', or acting in the interests of, young people came increasingly to be defined in terms of the minimisation of professional intervention in their lives. The development of professional practice came gradually to take second place to the development of policy, and social imperatives were increasingly subordinated to fiscal ones. As a result, interventions by managers which aimed to limit the involvement of welfare professionals in people's lives came to assume the mantle of radicalism while practitioners who insisted upon seeking out new 'needs' were portrayed as reactionaries.*
>
> (Pitts, 1991)

Yet, as Clarke et al. observe, the managerial annexation of welfare professionalism marked the transformation rather than the demise of 'bureau professionalism':

Thus we would argue that the survival of bureau-professionalism in a variety of organisational settings is not just an idiosyncratic hangover from the old regime; nor does it always constitute residual pockets of countervailing power. It is a necessary component of the new; what is at stake is not the eradication of bureau-professionalism but the degree to which relevant clusters of skills and values can be subordinated to, and accommodated within, the new political and organisational logics embodied in managerialism. (Clarke et al., 1994)

Yet, even as their professional authority and autonomy were eroded by systems management, the power shifts and re-designation of roles occasioned by the Criminal Justice Act 1991 placed youth justice social workers in England and Wales at the heart of the youth justice process. Now a professional group which, in the 1980s, had been implacably opposed to the custodial confinement of children and young people, was handed new administrative powers, untempered by professional discretion, to prosecute breaches of community penalties, supervise through care, deliberate upon the appropriateness of parole and undertake post-release supervision. This was, of course, the period which saw the final demise of 'preventive work', bemoaned in the Audit Commission report (1996). By the early 1990s, the discourses of social need and social suffering had fallen silent. Needs assessments were ousted by risk assessments; interpersonal skills were pressed into the service of evidence gathering, the 'client' was re-designated an 'offender' while the magistracy, as representative of the 'community', now became the 'client' (Home Office, 1990). Meanwhile, multi-agency partnerships, designed to offer a simpler, more accessible and less stigmatising administrative alternative to the judicial process, were incorporated as a kind of tariff before the tariff, an ante-room to the judicial process, where the strength of cases was tested and evidence rehearsed (Pratt, 1989).

Legal Annexation

The managerial annexation of youth justice social work in the early 1990s required, and was paralleled by, a process of legal annexation. By the early 1990s youth justice social workers had been effectively transformed into agents of the legal system, preoccupied with questions of 'risk', 'evidence' and 'proof', rather than 'motivation', 'need' and 'suffering'. Traditionally, the role of law has been to organise social expectations. It strives to render the world more predictable, manageable and therefore amenable to hard and fast judgements. The traditional role of social work, by contrast, has been to respond to unpredictable, messy and invariably complex, human situations. The law generates certainties while the stock in trade of social work is, or should be, uncertainty. Thus a core task of youth justice systems throughout the world has been to provide a space where these two discourses, one concerning the establishment and reaffirmation of social expectations, rights and responsibilities, and the other concerning responses to, and the management of, a complex and sometimes chaotic social reality, can become a single dialogue: a place where the competing claims of rules and needs, guilt and suffering, justice and welfare can be squared.

However, in 1993, the bold decarcerating objectives of the Criminal Justice Act 1991 were abandoned, leaving youth justice workers with a new responsibility to be both complainant and prosecutor in breach proceedings against youngsters who failed to comply with the conditions of their court order. The will to 'partnership' articulated by the Children Act 1989 and its requirement that the child in trouble be treated as a 'child in need' were lost in the welter of justice-oriented government guidelines which ensued. Observing these developments, Michael King (1991) pointed to 'the law's propensity to "enslave" other discourses or produce hybrid or bastard discourses of dubious validity'.

First-wave new managerialism, characterised by gung-ho managerial authoritarianism, and an almost paranoid suspicion of public professionalism, fell foul of its own rigidity. By minimising professional discretion and reducing dramatically the scope for individual initiative, what was done, by an increasingly disgruntled and de-professionalised workforce, tended to be what was measured. Thus, the generation of more and more measurable, 'output'-based 'performance indicators', often paralleled a real deterioration in the quality of public services.

Second-wave new managerialism emerged in the 1990s as an attempt to correct the failures of the authoritarian 1980s 'output' culture of first wave new managerialism. It offered a somewhat different approach to management which emphasised the importance of participation and partnership in the achievement of managerially determined 'outcomes'. Whereas first-wave new managerialism had been atomistic, second-wave new managerialism was 'corporatist'. It commended 'multi-agency partnerships' to devise 'holistic', 'joined-up', 'evidence-based', 'sustainable' solutions. These solutions aimed to set in train 'virtuous spirals', as opposed to the vicious circles into which so many first-wave initiatives had been lured.

New Labour, New Managerialism

New Labour was quick to appropriate both the language and the technology of second-wave new managerialism. Its emphasis upon the rationality of 'what works', 'joined-up solutions' and 'empowerment' fitted well with New Labour's avowed commitment to rational public policy and the devolution of power to 'local people'. But the central appeal of the new managerialism was that it offered a template for the new, more restricted, role for government, a 'third way' which, New Labour believed, was necessitated by the unmanageability of the global economy and the privatisation of personal life precipitated by the radical changes in the class structure of Britain of the preceding 30 years (Giddens, 1998).

> *The state of affairs described here arises largely where government has vacated territory which it once organised, resourced, nurtured and presided over with political authority – even if contested authority – but for which it nevertheless will not or cannot abandon all responsibility. Where once it willed the means, now it tends to prescribe the ends while others are left to supply the means; and as with all instrumentally oriented practices, the logic governing the attainment of ends is the logic of rules. In short, where government was, now audit regulation and management is. And so, inevitably, this social ego is pervaded by obsessional anxieties and behaviours about the loss of control.*
> (Cooper and Lousada, 2000)

Thus, the Crime and Disorder Act 1998, in handing new responsibilities to local authorities and local multi-agency partnerships, prescribes the goals they should pursue, the targets they should achieve and the timescales in which they should achieve them, but not, in any direct way, the means for their achievement. However, as Cooper and Lousada suggest, the anxieties about their political legitimacy and electoral credibility engendered by this new form of 'hands-off' governance, lead to an unprecedented concern with the 'micro-management' of policy implementation. This anxiety also finds expression in an inability to tolerate the inevitable conflicts which justice systems must embrace. Thus, New Labour's youth justice strategy presents the political, legal, managerial and professional imperatives of the agencies and professional groupings in the youth justice system as if they are simply components of a complex whole which, when fitted together properly, by a competent management, will 'deliver' in an unproblematic and uncontentious way. Once, of course, there was criminal justice policy (which was the domain of central government), theories about crime (which were largely the domain of academic criminologists), administrative structures (which were the domain of the relevant public sector agencies and their managers), and professional practice, professional wisdom and 'practice theory' (which were the domain of the social workers, youth justice workers, youth workers and probation officers who did the face-to-face work). Then, of course, there was law enforcement (which was the domain of the police), and legal arbitration and disposal (which was the domain of the courts). There were, inevitably, tensions between these agencies because they pursued different, and sometimes incompatible, goals, carried different formal responsibilities and, importantly, represented different interests. However, New Labour finds such conflict uncomfortable and threatening and it therefore strives to characterise the new youth justice system it has brought into being as one in which such conflict has been 'designed out'. Thus it appears that the potentially incompatible interests of the protagonists within the system have been subsumed within a new, consensual, apolitical, popular, 'evidence-based' and hence self-evidently sensible, system which is, as a result, beyond all criticism.

Those who continue to criticise, like the heads of the large voluntary child care agencies who refused to tender for the contracts to administer the government's secure training centres on the grounds that they were ill-considered, ill-conceived, politically inspired and inimical to the interests, and a threat to the well-being, of the troubled younger offenders for whom they were designed, get particularly short shrift. Indeed, a senior figure associated with the Youth Justice Board of England and Wales, a confidante of Home Secretary Jack Straw, on hearing their response, opined loudly that these people should 'grow up' and get to grips with the political realities of what New Labour had taken to calling 'the real world'. Ironically, as a result of the anxiety which pervades its ranks, New Labour's new finely tuned, 'evidence-based' structures can be subverted at a stroke if the opinion polls indicate that the party, or its leader, is no longer regarded by the electorate as 'the fairest of them all'. Having snatched the issue of law and order from the Tories, New Labour is desperate not to be shunted back into the political ghetto of penal reform, where it languished for two decades. When the spin doctors demand a burst of vote-catching toughness from government ministers, managerialism goes temporarily out the window. Thus in 1999, the Home Secretary suddenly introduced Michael Howard's 'three strikes and out' sentencing policy for juvenile burglars, notwithstanding that it had, evidently, been a spectacular failure in the USA. For all the talk of radicalism and newness, the default setting of New Labour's new youth justice system is 'discipline', and faced with political pressure, social anxiety or ministerial uncertainty, it is to discipline that it reverts.

New Labour's community safety strategy similarly devotes an inordinate amount of time and energy to the detail of its day-to-day management and implementation – the development of partnerships, crime audits, monitoring systems, etc. – but little to any analysis of the origins and nature of the problem – crime – to which these elaborate, joined-up solutions are to be applied. In the 115-page Audit Commission report, *Safety in Numbers* (1999), for example, only half a page is devoted to the origins of crime. Here, Farrington and West's, by now familiar, 'risk factors' are rehearsed and the usual caveats are entered: 'Risk factors are not causes of crime as such, but the likelihood of criminality increases as their intensity or clustering increases', and so on. The origin of these phenomena, or why they are 'clustered' in the ways that they are, is apparently, of little interest. And so, in the inexhaustible spirit of 'what works' *Safety in Numbers* passes swiftly on to 'promising approaches to promoting community safety' where we learn that 'investment approaches' and 'learning approaches' may be applied by 'accountable and delivery focused partnerships' bent upon 'the integration of community safety into the mainstream'.

An alternative approach to the origins of crime in the community safety literature involves meticulously detailed, albeit tautological, analyses of the blindingly obvious. The potential offender must be ready, willing, able and equipped for crime:

● Having a predisposition for crime (criminality).

● Lacking resources to avoid crime (such as ability to restrain impulses, exercise social skills and gain a legitimate living).

● Being currently ready to offend (e.g. motivated by boredom, shortage of money or need for drugs, being in a conflictual relationship, being in a particular emotional state).

● Having the resources for crime (skills, inside knowledge, criminal contacts, tools, weapons etc.).

● Anticipating that risk and effort are minimal enough and reward sufficient to decide to act.

● Being present in the situation or otherwise able to influence it (e.g. obscene telephone call or hacking computer via internet).

● Crime preventers must be absent, incapable, or at least not credible as a threat.

(Home Office, 1998a)

The core message of the government's community safety initiative is that local partnerships, working in consultation with local people, given responsibility, legal authority and central government back-up, will manage the crime problem in their locality. Nowhere is there a suggestion that the problems afflicting high-crime neighbourhoods might have their origins beyond those neighbourhoods and that, for this reason, they may not be amenable to local solutions.

Joined-up Solutions

In the view of the government, the 'joined-upness' of solutions to youth crime and community safety consists in the simultaneous management of those 'risk factors' associated with the onset of crime and delinquency, and the application of 'evidence-based' technologies for the correction of familial, cognitive or behavioural deficiencies which lead to persistence. Alongside this, systemic anomalies are eradicated by rigorous audit and the imposition, by central government, of financial penalties upon local government, the police and the Crown Prosecution Service. Thus, central government is able to set reconviction targets for a final warning or an action plan order which make no reference to whether the subject of that disposal lives in an area of high or low crime or high or low unemployment, whether or not the economy is in recession or whether the values of the broader society are intact or crumbling – all factors closely associated with fluctuations in crime rates. This imbues the strategy with an astonishing sense of weightlessness because these joined-up solutions bear little relation to the joined-up problems out in the real world.

Joined-up Problems

A genuinely joined-up or holistic analysis of the disparate phenomena lumped under the heading 'youth crime' poor parenting, shoplifting, bullying, school exclusion, mugging, etc. – will tend to focus upon the historical, political, social and economic circumstances which precipitate and sustain them. In doing so, it will inevitably problematise commonsense understandings of these phenomena, recontextualise them, and so transform these 'private troubles' into 'public issues'. Such an analysis will, of course, pose considerable problems to a government wedded to a stance which combines the radical scepticism of 1980s new penology (Feely and Simon, 1992), concerning the futility of attempts to eradicate the 'ultimate' social causes of youth crime, what New Labour thinkers describe as 'background factors', with the optimistic pragmatism of 1990s developmental criminology, which suggests that we might nonetheless intervene effectively to modify or ameliorate those personal and familial factors which correlate most closely with protracted or serious involvement in youth crime, and that we might do so within the youth justice system. This analysis, rooted in a mélange of Fabian optimism and neo-liberal nihilism, sees criminality as a marginal activity perpetrated by poorly socialised people on the social periphery. It appears to be unable to countenance the possibility that, with the acceleration of structural youth unemployment, burgeoning income inequality and the 'rolling back of the state', crime is moving back from the social margins to the social mainstream (Young, 1999) where it is helping to fill the growing social, economic and cultural void at the core of 'post-industrial society', posing new, quite different, and increasingly costly, problems of control. As John Lea (1998) notes:

> ... crime will be most easy to control when it is a purely and simply negative, disruptive affair and the criminal offender is a fairly weak and socially marginalised individual. By contrast, control will be hardest when crime, irrespective of its harmful and destructive effects on victims, fulfils important functions – the generation of income and livelihood, political and personal power, control and even prestige and status – for significant groups of people in society who engage in it.

Crime and Social Exclusion

Yet, New Labour might well object that its deliberations on crime and justice have paid due attention to 'background' socio-structural factors and that it is precisely these factors which its social exclusion strategy is designed to address. Indeed, in *Bringing Britain Together*, a *National Strategy for Neighbourhood Renewal*, a report of the government's Social Exclusion Unit, there is a clear acknowledgement of the structural origins, and the inter-relation, of crime, poverty and inequality:

> *Over the last generation, this has become a more divided country. While most areas have benefited from rising living standards, the poorest neighbourhoods have tended to become rundown, more prone to crime, and more cut off from the labour market. The national picture conceals pockets of intense deprivation where the problems of unemployment and crime are acute and hopelessly tangled up with poor health, housing and education. They have become no-go areas for some and no-exit zones for others.*

(Social Exclusion Unit, 1998)

Of earlier, failed, initiatives it notes: 'There have been many reasons for failure. They include the absence of effective national policies to deal with the structural causes of decline.' However, rather than launching into an analysis of the relationship between structural socio-economic inequality and neighbourhood decline, and its implications for economic, fiscal and social policy, the report tells us that:

> *Above all, a joined-up problem has never been addressed in a joined-up way. Problems have fallen through the cracks between Whitehall Departments or central and local government. And at neighbourhood level, there has been no one in charge of pulling together all the things that need to go right at the same time.*

(Social Exclusion Unit, 1998)

Suddenly, the problem is reduced from one of social structure to one of social administration. Like the victim of an obsessional neurosis, incapacitated in the face of real problems, they revert to an obsessive preoccupation with the detail of that which they can control.

New Labour's national social exclusion strategy is constituted from localised strategies which are reliant upon local initiative, local leadership and a charismatic figure, employed by these local partnerships, who will endeavour to get the relevant central and local government departments 'singing from the same song sheet'. *Bringing Britain Together* pinpoints 44 neighbourhoods selected from 1,370 identified by Price Waterhouse as containing 'clusters of deprived households', where experimental, joined-up interventions will be mounted. These interventions involve job training, the development of 'more flexible' benefits, improved housing management, measures to 'tackle' anti-social neighbours, youth crime and drugs, youth work, improved local services and initiatives to get central government departments working more closely together.

This strategy may strive to tackle 'alienation' among the young, but it will not intervene to refurbish the structural links between impoverished, de-stabilised neighbourhoods and local and regional labour markets, nor will it offer the financial incentives and tax breaks to the businesses and industries which would 'kick-start' moribund local economies into life. While the strategy may, for its duration, alleviate the more acute manifestations of poverty in the chosen neighbourhoods, it is unlikely to make a significant dent upon the problem of social exclusion because, as Graham Room (1995) observes, '...the notion of poverty is primarily focused upon distributional issues: the lack of resources at the disposal of an individual or household. In contrast, notions such as social exclusion focus primarily on relational issues, in other words, inadequate social participation, lack of social integration and lack of power.' The structural economic and political problems at the heart of social exclusion in contemporary Britain are not, in the end, susceptible to a strategy which offers only the more efficacious manipulation of the apparatus of government.

Inevitably, perhaps, *Bringing Britain Together* carries echoes of the Home Office Community Development Projects and the Department of Education early-1970s programmes for Educational Priority Areas, in which analogous measures were directed at analogous neighbourhoods. Then, the conclusions drawn about the appropriateness of 'area deprivation policies' to the problem of 'social inequality', and their impact upon it, were fairly pessimistic, suggesting that the selected neighbourhoods were merely a localised manifestation of national, and indeed, international political and economic problems which fostered the persistence of 'poverty amidst plenty' and deepening social injustice:

> *We can no longer accept that the problems of Hillfields can be satisfactorily explained primarily as a result of:*
>
> *(i) inadequacy, pathology, deviancy or any other personal characteristic of its residents;*
>
> *(ii) apathy or failure to participate in community activity;*
>
> *(iii) low take-up of personal support services or poor communication between fieldworkers and residents; or*
>
> *(iv) technical incompetence or failures in planning management or administration of local government.*
>
> *Few of the problems (except redevelopment) experienced by individuals in Hillfields are different in kind from those experienced by large sections of the working class in other parts of the city, or indeed the country as a whole (e.g. precarious incomes, insecure housing, etc.) They must be treated therefore as part of a class, not as a separate minority sub-group.*
>
> (Bennington et al., 1975)

A Politics of Immobility

It is not that New Labour is unaware of the realities of crime and social exclusion nor, one suspects, are they indifferent to the plight of the poor and the unemployed. When Tony

Blair claims to be placing his 'personal stamp' upon the struggle against social exclusion or child poverty one senses a ring of authenticity. Yet, despite a huge parliamentary majority, a chronically divided opposition and for most of both their terms in government the highest, consistent opinion poll ratings ever achieved by any British political party, New Labour often appears immobilised, torn between a residual 'progressive' sentiment on these issues, and its political commitments to a partly imaginary 'Middle England'; a managerialist commitment to 'good governance', a predatory mass media and the City of London. These commitments, expressed through its policies on taxation, public expenditure, 'law and order' and 'the family', are central to New Labour's otherwise nebulous political identity and, in its estimation, its future electoral chances.

The Secession of the Successful

Yet, ironically, the social and economic forces which are progressively excluding the disaffected poor are generating disaffiliation at other points in the social structure and a demand for the very policies upon which New Labour appears to be too timorous to embark. As we noted in Chapter 7, as the 1980s progressed, those people with the means to do so progressively bought themselves out of deteriorating high-crime neighbourhoods. Yet, having achieved the enhanced status and greater sense of security which such distance engenders, they discovered that the public services which they had, in an earlier era, taken for granted, had also become 'ghettoised' in that, more and more, they represented a residual service serving a socially marginal population. Thus, as Prime Minister Tony Blair was to discover in Islington, while the neighbourhood may be fine, the schools may not. In the USA, where the residualisation of public services is much further advanced:

> ...in the area of social services, the word 'public' is often pejorative. Public hospitals are institutions of last resort, sites not of solidarity but of stigma. Public schools, once considered 'cradles of citizenship', are often so inferior to their 'private' (commodified) counterparts as to fit the larger pattern of 'private wealth, public squalor'.
>
> (Fraser and Gordon, 1994)

The deterioration of state education in the 1990s presented those parents who could afford it with a choice between moving to a neighbourhood in the catchment area of one of the 'better' state schools or shifting their children into private education. Both strategies usually involved considerable extra costs. This was happening, moreover, in a period when the jobs which yielded the salaries necessary to pay for these luxurious necessities were becoming less and less secure.

The true costs of the erosion of solidarity become apparent as 'Middle England' struggles to buy itself out of a deteriorating city and residualised public services. Of course, they resent the ghetto 'underclass', which appears to have forced these fateful choices upon them. Yet, they also resent a 'superclass' which, having enriched itself massively at the expense of small savers and investors like themselves during the 1980s, retires to the apparent safety of the 'country' or, indeed, another country. But some of them are also beginning to resent a government which has failed to recognise that an insecure Middle England, forced into deepening debt in order to maintain the standards they believed they shared with that government, is no longer mesmerised by the 1980s doctrine of 'choice', and needs, more than ever before, the high-quality, universal public services, free at the point of access, which they believe they have paid for with their taxes.

This is no roadside conversion to collectivism; Middle England is up against it, and, as always, they want their money's worth. Yet, paradoxically, this gives them a direct material interest in a more solidaristic politics than that currently on offer. Yet, as has been suggested, if this new kind of solidaristic politics is to work, the top third of earners:

> ...need to get enough out of the system directly in terms of provision and indirectly in terms of social cohesion to make them support the principle of universal welfare to which they are disproportionately heavy contributors. That requires well-designed and high quality welfare services that meet their needs as well. On the other hand, acceptance of such a settlement assumes that there is a wider public morality, which insists that universal participation is the only moral basis upon which welfare systems and society as a whole can be constructed.
>
> (Hutton, 1995)

Riches

Thus the problem is not simply that, since the 1980s, more and more families in Britain have either fallen out of the bottom of the social structure and into poverty, or been rendered insecure and debt-ridden by the de-stabilisation of traditional middle-class career structures:

> In looking at the process of social exclusion we have to realise that it is not just caused by extreme poverty, it is also a product of extreme wealth. In societies of growing inequality, social exclusion occurs at both ends of the spectrum. Self exclusion at one end and involuntary exclusion at the other.
>
> (Lea, 1998)

Whereas the industrialists of the first half of the twentieth century were dependent upon, and therefore had a direct material interest in, the well-being of the working classes, the peculiar structure of the contemporary British economy, with its over-reliance upon the City of London (Hutton, 1995), means that those with the greatest economic power now owe their primary allegiance to whomsoever is paying the highest dividends, wherever that may be. This creates a profound political problem, because nothing is more likely to trigger the voluntary self-exclusion of this 'superclass' and its money, or bring down its media-orchestrated ire upon governments, than the threat of progressive income redistribution or the regulation of the financial services industry and the financial markets. New Labour's anxiety about this means that, having initially 'burnt its fingers' with a brief outburst against 'fat-cat salaries', it now gives the City of London a wide berth.

Barely an Echo of Gordon Gekko

Any dispassionate assessment of the problem of crime in the mid- to late-1990s, particularly if it calculates the proceeds from that crime, would probably conclude that it was neither the depredations of the 'twockers', 'ram-raiders' and 'rat boys' of the early 1990s nor the mobile 'phone thieves of the early twenty-first century which posed the greatest threat to 'law and order'. Indeed, they might well suggest that it was governmental complacency in the face of greed, corruption, fraud and hypocrisy, in its own ranks and in the City of London, which posed the greater threat.

It was always clear that de-regulation of the London Stock Exchange in 1986 would give rise to an increase in corporate crime. Among the more memorable frauds triggered by de-regulation were those affecting The Bank of Commerce and Credit, Barlow Clowes and the Guinness takeover debacle. Yet these legendary cases were the tip of a growing iceberg:

New figures produced this week by management consultants KPMG show that in the first four months of this year alone, some £571 million of new financial fraud was reported. This compares with £671 million in the whole of 1992. The new wave of financial fraudsters...are at the very top of their professions – company directors or chief executives – and drawn from the high achievement age group, 41–50 year olds.

(*The Guardian*, 1 July 1993)

Recent revelations of widespread insider dealing, most notably in the case of Enron, and the illegalities perpetrated in the highest echelons of the multi-national accountancy firm Arthur Andersen, which effectively de-stabilised the economies of all the advanced industrial societies, remind us that this is a problem which is not going away. In opposition, the Labour Party was vociferous in its condemnation of deregulated financial markets. Leading for the opposition in the debate on the Barlow Clowes affair, Tony Blair castigated the Conservative government for 'years of gullibility and incompetence' (*Hansard*, 13 June 1988). Reporting on Blair's encounter with Margaret Thatcher on this matter, the *Financial Times*, with uncharacteristic forthrightness, referred to 'a financial and human catastrophe which rightly called into question the values and competence of the Thatcher government'. With the public and the press behind them, the Labour Party pledged that, when elected, it would introduce forms of financial regulation akin to those operating in the USA. Yet, since being elected, it has remained more or less silent on the question of regulation.

In fact, the law relating to these matters was considered in 1998 by the Law Commission, an independent body charged with codifying existing law, and rendering it more intelligible and workable. Their deliberations were subsequently presented, in the form of a discussion paper, to an interdepartmental governmental working group in the spring of 1999. However, this was an essentially legal and administrative exercise. Evidently New Labour judged that now, corporate crime and the regulation of the City of London merited neither the profile nor the priority it had accorded youth crime.

Towards a Joined-up Morality

For Emile Durkheim (1964), a shared morality was the precondition for the achievement of social solidarity, social cohesion and social harmony. In Durkheim's work, this shared morality, the *conscience collective*, emerges from a social order in which a 'spontaneous division of labour' has distributed work roles on the basis of ability rather than, birth, rank or privilege, and the rewards for this work are proportional and allow people to fulfil their legitimate aspirations. Thus, in Durkheim's world, the state has a role in regulating the means, the volume and nature of available legitimate opportunity, and the ends, the socially valued goals to which citizens may aspire. Should the means be unavailable, or the ends vastly at odds with the abilities and merits of those who achieve them, Durkheim argues, we should expect a state of anomie to ensue, in which the conscience collective would weaken as a source of social control, egoism and self-interest would burgeon, and crime would escalate.

The, now forgotten, gesture of the incoming Blair government towards curbing the excessive, 'tax-effective' bonuses and 'salary packages' of top earners in the City of London, might have lessened the cynicism of the many disaffected citizens who, in the wake of Thatcherism, have come to believe, not wholly unreasonably, that in Britain there is one law, and one scale of values, for the rich and another, quite different one, for the poor; what Jock Young (1999) has referred to as the 'chaos of reward'. Such a modest, but no doubt extremely popular, intervention would have gone some way towards reintroducing a crucial sense of fairness and proportionality into economic life.

This would have been important because the 'superclass' are a crucial force in setting the level of material aspiration within a society, and in doing so, they serve to maximise the frustration, and not infrequently, the indebtedness of those who lack the means to compete. Moreover, having achieved iconic status by dint of their wealth, and the televisual exposure to which it gives rise, their perceived moral, material and social values have an inordinate effect upon popular morality and popular values. Thus, at the other end of the social structure, the aura created by the apparently effortless acquisition of wealth through widely reported, and widely revered, acts of corporate ruthlessness and cunning, finds powerful resonances among the young men who 'hang out' in de-stabilised urban neighbourhoods. This moral damage is, of course, in large part the legacy of Thatcherite deregulation and the culture of greed it fostered.

Clearly, social democratic governments in their attempts to effect social progress must come to terms with business and industry. But if New Labour is to stand a chance of repairing this damage, and this was, after all, a central plank of its original electoral platform, it must one day confront its new-found friends in Worcester, Wapping and the City of London with some of the fiscal and economic home truths which it is, at present, unwilling to countenance. This would inevitably require New Labour to reconsider the kind of relationship the state should maintain with the new super-rich who have been the major beneficiaries of market society and its erstwhile friends and allies, many of whom have been driven to the social margins of that society. In short, it requires them to clarify the nature of citizenship in an era of late modernity (Young, 1999).

Citizenship

The question of citizenship poses serious problems for the Blair administration, faced as it is with accelerating technological change and continuing economic polarisation. Firstly, it poses the problem that any discussion of the rights and responsibilities of citizenship must necessarily call into question the legitimacy of the, often chaotic, distribution of wealth and opportunity which serves to inhibit both the exercise of rights and the discharge of responsibilities (Young, 1999). As we noted in Chapter 7, this 'citizenship deficit' is highly concentrated, with 40 per cent of African-Caribbeans and 59 per cent of Pakistanis and Bangladeshis in the UK located in the poorest fifth of the population (Rowntree Foundation, 1995).

Secondly, any discussion of citizenship must raise questions about its boundaries. Even before the air war in Kosovo began in 1999, there were over 10,000 Kosovan refugees living in London alone (*The Guardian*, 18 April 1999). Customs and Excise estimate that each year around 8,000 illegal migrants, mainly from Eastern Europe, enter the UK in the backs of cars and lorries (*The Guardian*, 18 April 1999). This westward drift has been discernible throughout north-western Europe for several years. Now it is accelerating. With closer economic and political integration within the EU, its enlargement into Eastern Europe, and a 'new world order' in which Britain seems prepared to intervene in, and make commitments to the citizens of, countries locked in civil strife, this influx seems destined to accelerate. Thus European governments must decide who, in these radically changed circumstances, is now a citizen; what geographical and political entity they are citizens of and what this form of citizenship offers the same rights and obligations to newcomers as it has, traditionally, to the 'host' population? These questions are particularly difficult for UK governments since, unlike France and Germany, Britain has no hard and fast rules governing citizenship, having previously pursued a strategy informed more by the imperatives of the labour market than loyalty to Commonwealth citizens (Hiro, 1992; Miles, 1993; van Steenbergen, 1994).

Not only do these changes require us to re-examine our present, essentially 'post-colonial', conceptions of cultural identity, nationhood and citizenship, they also confront us with the prospect of even more rapid economic polarisation, and growing social inequality. These new 'citizens', like the African-Caribbean and South Asian peoples who preceded them, will be young and poor and they will enter British society at the bottom end of the social and economic structure. But, like previous migrant groups, they will be ambitious for themselves and for their children. However, their great expectations are destined, in many cases, to be met by limited access to the legitimate opportunities which would enable them to fulfil their ambitions. Moreover, because of the stigma which attaches to the poor, and the neighbourhoods in which they live, particularly if they are Black or Asian, interventions by the police will be more robust, with a consequent amplification of the criminality of some young people (Becker, 1963) or, indeed, the criminalisation of innocent subjects on the basis of colour or culture alone (Cicourel, 1968; Smith, 1984; Pitts, 1988; Muncie, 1999; Marlow, 1999). This tendency has been fuelled in the 1990s by police 'performance culture', a consequence of the new managerialism, which has led to a stop and search 'explosion' in certain police forces (Young, 1999; Marlow, 1999; Loveday and Marlow, 2000). But youth crime will also probably increase because the pressures towards criminality in the types of de-stabilised neighbourhoods, discussed in Chapter 7, will intensify. As a result of both of these factors, the present over-representation of Black African-Caribbean children and young people, and the growing representation of Asian children and young people in the youth justice system is likely to be paralleled by a rise in the numbers of the children of these new immigrants.

In the 1980s, the proportion of foreign nationals in European prisons rose by 297 per cent in Spain and 118 per cent in Portugal. In Belgium, France, Switzerland and Luxembourg more than a quarter of the prison population is now composed of foreign nationals, many of whom are detained for breaches of immigration laws. In France, 85.5 per cent of newly arrested prisoners are charged with public order offences, of which about half concern infringements of immigration laws. In the recent period, economic migrants and foreign nationals found to be in breach of immigration laws and regulations have made a disproportionate contribution to the increases in imprisonment in Europe.

The size, nature and pace of the changes described here, suggest that if there was ever a need to develop a positive, inclusive, conception of citizenship which embraces the growing band of children and young people currently destined for the social margins, and beyond, it is now. It is our shared citizenship which connects us, defines who 'we' are (Dean, 1999), specifies our rights and obligations in relation to the state and one another and, ultimately, delineates the nature of the relationship we should maintain with, and the respect we should grant, each other.

Citizenship, Race and Crime

Commentators have observed that the advent of the politics of the Third Way marks the demise of the 'solidarity project' (Garland, 2000), marking a further step towards an 'exclusive society' (Young, 1999). This is because it is a politics which inverts earlier, social democratic, accounts of the relationship between the individual and society and the citizen and the state. Thus, cultural change becomes the prerequisite of structural change and the responsibility of the state to its citizens is de-emphasised in favour of the duties owed by citizens to the state. In these circumstances, the state effectively eschews responsibility for creating the social and economic pre-conditions for effective citizenship while seeking a mandate to act robustly to discipline and contain those unable to meet their civic and economic obligations (Bordieu, 1998).

As we have observed, this re-formulation of the centre-left project draws heavily upon 'culturalist' accounts of the 'underclass' which in the US have served as the cornerstone of attempts by the political right to racialise the issues of welfare and crime (Murray, 1984; Wilson and Herrnstein, 1985; Herrnstein and Murray, 1994). Indeed, in their hands, the term 'underclass' has, more often than not, been employed as a scarcely coded reference to the purported deficiencies of ethnic minorities. Yet, whereas Margaret Thatcher had mercilessly exploited fears of 'cultural swamping' and 'Black street crime' in the run-up to the 1979 general election, New Labour studiously avoided any discussion of immigration, race and crime, referring only to the need to extend equality of opportunity and to protect ethnic minorities from racial victimisation. New Labour made much of the fact that the 1997 election had brought unprecedented numbers of Black and Asian MPs into parliament, most of them on the Labour benches, and has been eager to present itself as a multi-cultural, rainbow alliance of reasonable people. Even though it was evident that New Labour's proposed policies on crime and welfare were destined to bear disproportionately upon young Black and Asian people, no reference was made to the fact that much of the newly discovered 'underclass' was non-white.

This ambiguity was reflected in one of New Labour's 1997 pre-election TV ads. which elaborated a vision of the world which would be brought into being by its youth justice and community safety strategies. The vision was of a 1950s municipal housing estate where fully-employed, skilled, solvent, (mono-racial) working class artisans took care of their families and kept their children under control. This municipal idyll was juxtaposed with images of irredeemable, 'hollowed-out', urban ghettos, populated, incidentally, by people of many races, and accompanied by grim warnings that this was the future we might expect if we were foolish enough not to vote New Labour. Here was an implicit promise that, if elected, New Labour would turn the clock back by instilling a new sense of order and discipline into those dwellers in 'social housing', which were the instigators of urban decline, and their perfidious offspring. However, turning the clock back to the 1950s, a period which only the middle-aged and older voters the campaign was targeting would remember, would mean returning to a more or less mono-racial society. It is unlikely that this was the intended message but it appeared to betray New Labour's ambivalence about these issues.

During most of its first term in office, the issues of race and crime were only linked politically by the high-profile enquiry into the murder of Black teenager Stephen Lawrence. Then, on 17 April 2001, a Hindu wedding in Bradford erupted into inter-racial street fighting in which three 'pubs' and a pharmacy were wrecked and eight cars set on fire. The conflict was, according to some Muslim commentators, the result of a racist attack by members of the neo-fascist National Front which has an office on a neighbouring estate. On 3 May 2001 the Home Secretary, Jack Straw, imposed a ban on a proposed National Front March in Oldham, 40 miles away, in protest at the alleged creation by Asian youths of 'no-go' areas for Whites. In Oldham on 27 May an estimated 500 Asian youths marched to protest at violent National Front incursions into their neighbourhoods and the failure of the police to protect them. Then in Bradford on 8 July 1,000 Asian youths battled with members of the National Front and subsequently with police on the streets. Burnley also experienced similar disturbances. Disclaiming responsibility for the disturbances, Steve Smith the British National Party's (BNP's) deputy regional organiser rejected claims that his party was responsible for the unrest, blaming the undemocratic policies of Westminster politicians saying: 'This unrest is a direct consequence of enforced multi-culturalism.' Like Jean-Marie Le Pen in France, Smith was at pains to link the issues of immigration and crime and present the BNP as a party of 'law and order'. Meanwhile hundreds of Asian young men, who had been arrested as a result of confrontations with the police following the disturbances, were being held on remand in northern gaols.

But this was election time, and the ensuing political debate, conducted against the backdrop of the rise of the radical, right-wing, anti-immigration parties in mainland Europe and a small surge in support for the National Front in the UK, was immediately, subsumed within a longer-running debate between the government, the opposition and the right-wing press which hinged on the latter's assertion that the government was 'soft' on migrants and asylum seekers. As a result, the emergent common sense had it that more asylum seekers would simply lead to more violent inter-racial incidents of the type seen in Bradford, Burnley and Oldham.

The fact that between 1995 and 1999, 80 per cent of migrants to the UK were from the developed world, the overwhelming majority being White, that the non-white protagonists in these disturbances were, in fact, second and third generation British Asians rather than asylum seekers and that the White protagonists were supporters of the neo-fascist BNP was lost in the heat of political battle. Even when the BNP polled 12,000 votes in Oldham in the June general election, securing third place in two constituencies, no government spokesperson appeared willing to address the fact that this might be worrying for local Asian citizens.

Lord Ouseley, a Labour Peer and former chair of the Commission for Racial Equality, was asked by the City of Bradford to produce a report on the disturbances. Ouseley's report bemoaned the development of 'communities which were fragmenting along racial, cultural and faith lines'. Key factors, he said, were 'segregation in schools', a 'gang culture', 'drugs', 'white flight', 'political correctness', 'weak political leadership' and 'Islamophobia'. What did not feature in the report was the fact that throughout the UK racial segregation in schools has developed as a defensive strategy on the part of Asian communities subject to racial harassment and racist violence. The report did suggest that the disorders were the inevitable result of deteriorating relations amongst an 'underclass of relatively poor white people and visible ethnic minorities', many of whom 'feel that their needs are neglected because they regard minority ethnic communities as being prioritised for more favourable public assistance'. That such disturbances had never occurred in these areas before, that they were almost certainly orchestrated by the National Front or that inter-racial mixing amongst children and young people in these areas was in fact commonplace (Webster, 1995), were barely touched upon.

In the government's subsequent Cantle Report (2002) *Violent Community Disorders in Bradford, Burnley and Oldham*, the Home Secretary, David Blunkett, enjoined the Asian community to integrate with its White neighbours, and condemned certain cultural practices, like enforced marriages (sic) which had no place in contemporary Britain. He spoke positively of US-style nationality and language tests and the notion of the 'melting pot'. Cantle echoed Lord Ouseley's findings precisely, indicating that, in future, the needs of the socially excluded White community must be given equal priority with the needs of Black and Asian minorities. We may yet look back to this moment as the point at which poor Whites on the social margins became an 'ethnic minority'. The Commission for Racial Equality promptly announced new initiatives to address the plight of socially excluded White minorities and junior Home Office minister, John Denham, announced yet another role for youth workers, that of fostering racial integration amongst White and Asian young people in the Northern cities.

Nowhere was there a recognition that the problems experienced by both the White and Asian communities were, in large part, a product of de-industrialisation exacerbated by the policies of radical non-interventionist neo-liberal governments, market de-regulation, the erosion of worker's rights through trades union reforms, housing 'reforms', reductions in state benefits and the 'rolling-back' of state services. Nowhere was there an explicit condemnation of the violence instigated by the BNP. Neither was there a proposal to strengthen the law, or its enforcement, in order to prevent future occurrences. Nor was there any acknowledgement that Asian citizens might have anything to fear from a newly confident radical right wing if their painstakingly constructed defences against victimisation were pulled down.

Doing the Right Thing

These developments signalled a significant shift away from New Labour's earlier, implicit, multi-culturalism towards an assimilationist posture which resonated with many of the key demands of the radical right. Indeed in an article entitled *The Far Right is the Enemy*, the Home Secretary responded to those who had criticised his apparent repudiation of multi-culturalism and his implicit support for the 'rights for whites' lobby by arguing that unless centre-left parties acted firmly on immigration and race relations, electoral support for the far right would grow:

> *The real battle for the left must be against the far right and against racism, not between ourselves. In Britain, the British National Party is preparing for next month's local elections with relish, sensing that it can exploit problems with illegal immigration and asylum pressures in ways that have been successful elsewhere. It is a vital challenge for all mainstream parties to ensure legitimate debates about asylum, immigration, race and community relations are separated from divisive, inflammatory exploitation of fears which the fascists seize on.*
> (*The Guardian*, 11 April 2002)

The rhetoric of multi-culturalism was eclipsed by a new assimilationist rhetoric in which the 'Asian community', frequently conflated with 'Asylum Seekers', stood accused of placing an undue burden on state resources, perpetrating violent disorder and courting victimisation by its rejection of the values and practices of the socio-cultural mainstream. As Peter Hain, erstwhile founder member of the 1970s *Anti-Nazi League*, Minister for Europe and acknowledged mouthpiece for the more radical thoughts of the Prime Minister Blair, subsequently observed:

> *They (Muslims) are welcome here. But there is a tendency amongst a minority to isolate themselves and that leaves them vulnerable to either exploitation by Osama Bin Laden-type extremists and fanatics on the one hand, or targeting by racists and Nazis on the other.*
> (*The Guardian*, 13 May 2002)

In 2002, the post-modern politics of the Third Way confronted a decidedly pre-modern political threat. The disturbances in the Northern cities and the asylum-seekers debate, exacerbated by the anxieties surrounding September 11th and its aftermath, breathed new life into both 'respectable' and 'disreputable' elements on the political right. This confronted New Labour with a choice, to stand firm, defend cultural diversity and racial tolerance and try to inject some rationality and sense of proportion into the debate, or attempt to retain the political initiative by beating the radical right at its own game. However, as we have noted, above all else, New Labour is a vehicle for the acquisition and retention of political power and, in its own estimation, the key to its electoral success has been its ability to dominate the media agenda and never allow itself to be outflanked on the political right.

Another key axiom of Third Way politics is 'what counts is what works' and New Labour strategists concluded that what would work this time was a swerve to the right. And, although it was destined to give comfort to racists large and small, compound the fears of Britain's Black and Asian citizens and reinforce their growing sense of disaffiliation from the cultural and political mainstream, this strategem nevertheless served to restore New Labour's flagging opinion poll ratings.

New Labour's second term has seen the introduction of a new, more restrictive, Asylum Bill and, alongside this, an attempt to fashion a new, post-Bradford, Oldham and Burnley and post-September 11th multi-cultural community. But this new community is unlikely to be a place where the authentic voices, beliefs and attitudes of the multiplicity of people who live within it can celebrate diversity and disagreement in an atmosphere of mutual tolerance. Rather, it will be a space in which New Labour's new assimilationist vision will set the parameters of tolerance, and political deviation and cultural success will be 'policed' by a new alliance of 'community leaders', local authorities and the police, acting responsibly for the common good.

With the shelving of multi-culturalism it appears that New Labour still hankers after a monocultural world in which a disciplined, fully employed, skilled and solvent working-class looked after their families and kept themselves to themselves. This image is, in turn, overlaid upon another, far older, vision which, as we have noted, celebrates a White, male, Christian 'England', 'simultaneously held together and held apart by fine gradations of deference and patronage, and kept in place by the rule of law', which is almost always depicted as under threat and in need of restoration. Yet, as Edward Said has observed, similar appeals to socio-cultural roots by politicians in the United States have evoked a vociferous backlash as:

> *...An expanding number of recently arrived immigrants...have added their testimony to those of women, African Americans and the sexual minorities, in order to challenge the tradition that for two centuries has been derived from the New England puritans and the southern slave and plantation owners. Responding to all this has been a resurgence of appeals to a tradition, to patriotism and basic, or family, values ... all of them associated with a past that is no longer recoverable except by denying or somehow downgrading the lived experience of those who, in Aime Cesaire's great phrase, want a place at the rendezvous of history.*

(Said, 1994)

Not least of the ironies of the New Labour project has been that, while it presents itself as the party of the 'future', it finds its precedents for future action in the past. The preoccupation with 'roots', although usually attributed to Black and Asian citizens has, in reality, been a defining feature of British political life since at least 1979. Faced with future uncertainty, the contemporary political reflex is to turn to the past for a template. However:

> *Everything that is remembered about the past is washed, and often drowned, in nostalgia, pride, illusions and passions of all kinds. Indeed few people can extract solutions to their problems from their roots. The past no longer speaks with a clear voice; nobody seems agreed any more about what the lessons of history are. The old-fashioned sort of root could feed humanity only so long as differing opinions were treated like weeds, gouged out or poisoned.*
> (Zeldin, 1994)

A concern with the past, a willingness to learn from it, and a commitment to preserve that which is true and beautiful about it, is utterly commendable. However, the seismic social and cultural shifts through which we are living pose crucial questions about how we are to absorb a rising generation of children and young people whose marginality vis-a-vis the social and economic mainstream, may be paralleled by their marginality to a parental culture which cannot equip them for survival in the radically changed world they have been forced to enter.

Optimists of a post-modern persuasion have argued that, as a result of these social, economic and cultural changes we stand on the threshold of new freedoms wherein the young will be able to create new identities for themselves and put together hybrid lifestyles of their own choosing:

> *Once identities were frozen in aspic…(but now)…people can pick and choose in new ways, they can be one thing in one situation and quite another somewhere else. You may not be able to afford the lifestyle of a pop star, but you can afford a holiday in Mustique.*
> (Martin Jacques, 1998)

This may be true for some, more privileged, young people. However, out on the social margins, other young people experience the changes in their lives as loss and, ironically, like the governments which deplore their behaviour, sometimes search for solace in the spurious certainties of a largely imagined racial and cultural past.

More than ever before, and perhaps more than anything else, we need to counter both the flippant relativism of the post-modern vision and the regressive recapitulation of the brutalities of an imagined past with a source of identity which offers children and young people on the social margins a political status and some control over their destinies; a stake in, and a hand in, shaping their futures; and a standard against which to measure their progress in these areas. Founded upon the principles of inclusivity, appreciation, tolerance and a positive indifference to difference, such an approach to children and young people on the social margins, backed by economic, social, criminal justice and employment policies which also embody these values, would quickly prove superior to New Labour's nostalgic attempt to recover an imagined past in which there were only good and bad children and commonsensical ways of making the bad ones behave themselves.

Real Citizenship

In 1999, the then Education Secretary, David Blunkett, announced that schools were to devote one and a half hours a week to the teaching of citizenship. However, the version of citizenship commended to schools placed an inordinate emphasis upon the obligations of children and young people, to their parents, their school and their 'community' and was primarily concerned with attitudes rather than entitlements; civility rather than civil rights and sociability rather than social entitlements. This 'asymmetric' reading of citizenship, represented not its coming of age, but its exhaustion, and the abandonment of the idea of citizenship as a symmetrical relationship founded on open legal, civil and welfare entitlements, mutual respect and interdependence (Marshall, 1950).

This latter form of citizenship and is active, promoting a critical engagement in public life which goes beyond the periodic re-election of governments, on the one hand, or a few hours' voluntary work on the other. It would encompass an active engagement with, and a concern for, the well-being of one's self, one's peers, one's family and one's neighbours and an effective voice in the institutions which bear upon young people's lives. This would suggest that a key to engendering a sense of citizenship in school students would be the democratisation of schools, colleges and other relevant public agencies through the enfranchisement of students in their governance. Citizens have a political voice and a political stake. They are governed, but through their participation in political life they also have a hand, and an interest, in government. As van Gunterstein (1994) suggests, to be a citizen is to assume an 'office' and it is therefore incumbent on governments to create structural links, which tie these 'office-holders' into the political process in significant ways. As we note in the next chapter, in many areas of France in the 1980s and 1990s youth councils, comprising children and young people aged 10-18 with the power to call politicians and officers to account on relevant matters were established by local councils. In Bologna, Italy, in the 1990s the local authority operated a 'dual key' system wherein substantial parts of departmental budgets could only be spent if the young people's committee, comprising representative children and young people, turned their key in the lock as well. In this way, consultation and debate with young people, supported by adults, became unavoidable. In these examples, young people were included as a resource, whereby local authorities could develop a more sensitive response to their various constituencies, rather than as a problem to be dealt with. If young citizens participate in this way they will learn, as a matter of course, that wielding responsibility also means that, from time to time, they must be prepared to subordinate their own interests to the general good.

Citizens must develop a capacity for 'autonomy, judgement and loyalty' (van Gunterstein, 1994) and while this may be developed through political participation, it must also be nurtured and supported by teachers, youth workers or youth justice workers and local politicians. This task is made no easier by the fact that these values are in tension with a culture which prizes individualism above collective endeavour and rewards egotism disproportionately.

Citizens are not the passive subjects of historical and cultural processes. They are actively involved in shaping their histories and reshaping their cultures. Michel Foucault (1986) observes that the birth of contemporary citizenship, in France in 1789, compelled human beings to face the task of 'producing themselves'. This capacity for self-creation and self-renewal is, of course, essential in a society characterised by rapid socio-economic change, ever more complex ethnicities and cultural fusion. But, sadly, positive self-reinvention tends to be a characteristic of those who believe that change will offer new opportunities and a better life, and who have the personal and institutional resources to cope with uncertainty. Those who experience change as loss are far more likely to hark back to, an often imaginary, lost past, and far more willing to try to restore that past by force. Education can equip young people with the knowledge and discernment to enable these processes to occur, but it must be matched by an experience which confirms that what they end up with is worth more than what they have to go through to get it. And this is achieved when citizens are productive because, in contributing to the common wealth through economic activity, they are included in a future-oriented process. Thus it is a central task for 'solidaristic' governments to ensure that the skills and abilities of citizens are used to the full for the common good, as is the case in Sweden's Active Labour Market strategy (Esping Andersen, 1990; Ginsberg, 1992). Citizens consume. Consumerism is here to stay because it powers modern economies. Moreover, the consumer is a key stakeholder in the productive process and political citizenship consists, in part, in becoming a discerning consumer, able to use the power of consumption to shape the behaviour of powerful producers and retailers. Consumption is particularly important to children and young people whose struggle to establish a plausible social identity, and to feel included, is often predicated upon having access to the same kinds of clothes, sports equipment or music as their peers. To that extent, consumption is social inclusion.

Citizens are engaged in a relationship of mutuality, one with another, and it is upon this intricate and infinitely complex network of mutual obligation that social cohesion and social solidarity are founded. As such, the citizenship of the majority is diminished if the rights and obligations of citizenship are denied to a minority. While the citizen has an obligation to uphold the law, the state has a reciprocal duty to protect the property and person of citizens. Indeed, for those of the radical right, this is the sole justification for the existence of the state. Within this, the state has a further obligation to ensure, in the name of distributive justice, that no citizen, by dint of their neighbourhood, race, culture, social class, gender or age, is subject to excessive victimisation. At present, as we have noted, there is a profound imbalance between the risks encountered by children and young people, particularly if they are working-class Black and Asian, and the crime control and community safety programmes which target these risks.

Real citizenship confronts governments with a choice between a solidaristic and a disciplinary response to the problems of youth crime and neighbourhood decline. It asks them to decide whether the problems of youth and adult crime can best be accounted for by a weakening of discipline, or a failure of solidarity. This, they believed, was the choice confronting Francois Mitterrand and his advisers when, amidst urban youth riots, he assumed the presidency of France in 1981.

Chapter 9

Discipline or Solidarity: A Tale of Two Housing Estates

Nonetheless, I am not convinced that the social and economic changes sweeping through Western Europe will necessarily result in sharply reduced commitments to social rights… Efforts to cut back on these programmes in the face of growing joblessness have met with firm resistance. Moreover, except for England under the Thatcher government, official and scholarly explanations of the new poverty in Europe have tended to focus much more on the changes and inequities in the broader society, rather than on individual deficiencies and behaviour, and therefore lend much greater support to the ideology of equal social worth for all citizens. (Wilson, W.J., 1994)

In the 1990s my colleagues and I undertook a study of political, administrative and professional responses to child abuse and neglect, and youth crime and disorder in parts of Greater London, the Ile-de-France and Oise in Picardy. We wanted, in particular, to understand how ethnicity, racism and violence were 'handled' in the 'child protection' and 'youth justice' systems of the two countries. (France does not have separate systems of 'child protection' and 'youth justice', and the system it does have is not described in these terms.) In this chapter I shall explore the role of what the French call *solidarité*, in reducing inter-racial youth violence, and youth crime and disorder in poor neighbourhoods.

Fog in the Channel

But before we get started on this tale I want to explore why UK audiences have found this and other similar stories so hard to hear. I think there are three main reasons:

1. An absence of irony

It is evident that different intellectual traditions generate culturally specific epistemologies and meta-perspectives which inform perceptions of, and attempts to gain knowledge about, social phenomena. In comparative, trans-national research, therefore, a central task, and a precondition for understanding what we are seeing, is to transcend our own 'meta-perspectives', our ontological and epistemological ghettos, in order to gain an appreciation of what 'our' world might look like from the inside of somebody else's world.

This is by no means easy because these meta-perspectives, or ontologies, are constructed from historical, political and socio-cultural elements which structure our inner and outer worlds and constitute our identities and ethnicities. Thus they are not concepts but 'ethnocentric' categories of thought which structure our conceptual universe; what Richard Rorty describes as our 'final vocabularies':

> *It is final in the sense that if doubt is cast on the worth of these words their user has no non-circular argumentative recourse...no option but to keep reiterating their faith in 'Christ', 'England', 'professional standards', 'decency', 'kindness', 'the Revolution', 'the church', 'progressive', 'rigorous', 'creative'. The more parochial terms do most of the work.*
> (Rorty, 1989)

While acknowledging the inevitability of ethnocentricity, Rorty asks whether it is also inescapable. His answer to this question suggests an approach to trans-national comparison which can enable us to transcend our ethnocentricity. In our dealings with other cultures, he suggests, we should adopt an attitude of 'irony'. Here, he uses 'irony' in the same sense as the character in Joseph Conrad's *Under Western Eyes* (1896) who says: 'Irony irritates, not because it mocks or attacks, but because it denies us our certainties by unmasking the world as an ambiguity.' Thus, Rorty argues, borrowing a phrase from E.M. Forster, that if we are ever to 'see the world whole' we must become *ironists*. Rorty's ironists have the following three characteristics:

1. They have serious doubts about the capacity of their own final vocabulary to make sense of the experience of people with a different final vocabulary.
2. They realise that arguments phrased in their own final vocabulary can neither support nor dissolve these doubts.
3. They do not believe that their final vocabulary offers them a chance of gaining a better grasp of reality or that it constitutes some peculiar hotline to the truth.

> *I call these people ironists because...their renunciation of the attempt to formulate criteria of choice between final vocabularies puts them in the position which Sartre called 'meta-stable': never quite able to take themselves seriously because always aware that the terms in which they describe themselves are subject to change, always aware of the contingency and fragility of their final vocabularies.*
> (Rorty, 1989)

However, Rorty's ironical stance, far from presaging a collapse into nihilism or relativism is, arguably, a crucial prerequisite for effective trans-national social research or, indeed, social intervention in the multi-national, multi-racial, multi-cultural, post-traditional world of contemporary Europe. This stance is notably absent from most Anglo-American trans-national research, which appears to be bent upon a quest for categorical equivalence.

2. The quest for categorical equivalence

Trans-national social research is usually predicated upon beliefs about, and dedicated to the pursuit of, *categorical equivalence*.

> *In order to study crime comparatively, three conditions need to be met. There must be sources of material and data with which to make comparisons: crime statistics, victim surveys, research studies. Second, translatable concepts have to be available to make possible the collecting, ordering and analysis of such data. Finally, some kind of framework, part universe of discourse, part set of common concerns must exist.*
>
> (Heidensohn, 1990)

This is not an unreasonable shopping list, if all we want to do is compare domestic data, sorted into domestic categories, with foreign data which can also be sorted into our domestic categories. However, for obvious reasons, there is a paucity of such data. This quest for categorical equivalence therefore places severe limits on the range of trans-national phenomena we are able to investigate.

> *Terminological difficulties, therefore, are co-extensive with and revealing of political assumptions that should not be pushed under the rug but brought out into the open. Cross-national comparison compounds this difficulty because the terms proper to each country are also excerpted from different semantic spaces and traditions. The fact that, very roughly put, Europeans have emphasised a language of class, labour, and citizenship when considering urban hardship, while American discourse has been framed by 'supply-side' views of poverty anchored in the vocabularies of family, race and individual (moral and behavioural) deficiency, makes the question of terminology even more touchy. It would be not only naive but dangerous to make such differences disappear with the sleight of hand of translation...* (Wacquant, 1996)

A great deal of comparative criminological research is rooted in the assumption that categorical equivalence does, or should, exist, and that its pursuit will offer us a broader understanding of domestic phenomena. Yet, if this is true, as Wacquant suggests, we would appear to need only a decent translator rather than trans-national comparative research, since this approach would offer little more than a familiar foray into the territory of Anglo-American 'abstract empiricism' plus a few bolt-on Euro-datasets with which to vindicate our pre-existing categories and suppositions.

One way out of the limitations placed upon comparative trans-national research by the quest for categorical equivalence is to search instead for structural and functional equivalence. Thus, in the early stages of our research we focused our analyses upon such categories as 'system structure', 'system function', 'professional ideology', 'welfare discourse', 'legal discourse' and 'legal culture' in an attempt to ensnare these phenomena.

This proved to be more fruitful, and yielded some interesting data on the division of labour, power and responsibility between the legal and administrative spheres, and the degree of anxiety experienced by actors at different points in different national systems. However, once again, we ran into the problem that our understanding was limited by the fact that the practices we observed were embedded in implicit, culturally given, final vocabularies to which we had little or no access.

The tendency for UK researchers to seek categorical equivalence is, in part at least, a function of a colonial legacy in which trans-national anglophone scholarship in the spheres of justice and welfare developed within shared assumptions about the relationship between the law, the state and civil society which were rooted in a common history and analogous legal and administrative structures. This legacy has generated a remarkable intellectual hegemony, spanning two-thirds of the globe. These tendencies have, despite subsequent post-colonial and anti-colonial resistance (see Hesse et al., 1990 and Braithwaite and Daly, 1994), been constantly reinforced by the remarkable mobility of anglophone scholars and justice system professionals. Some trans-national researchers have strayed beyond the anglophone world. Yet, because the 'final vocabulary' which informs these endeavours is steeped in the anglophone tradition, such forays into 'elsewhere' often have a somewhat piratical air. Setting forth for foreign parts, they hope to return with new, exotic, foreign solutions to old and intractable domestic problems.

3. The empirical obsession

However, when actually 'threatened' with evidence from 'abroad', the rather threadbare canon of Anglo-American abstract empiricism is re-presented by its defenders as a profoundly rich treasure trove of unparalleled, albeit measured, wisdom, against which, unfortunately, foreign data must almost inevitably be found wanting. Yet, even though the canon of Anglo-American empirical criminology can offer little to which the averagely well-disposed broadsheet reader would not say 'so what?', it still rejects any data which have not been reshaped, and hence reduced in their significance, to a form which is measurable in Anglo-American terms with Anglo-American instruments.

How, for example, might we investigate the key differences between Sweden (with the highest GDP and the lowest income differentials in the EU, which, between 1987 and 1994, had the second lowest annual rise in its crime rate) and England and Wales (with the second lowest GDP, the highest income differentials and the second highest annual rise in its crime rate; 4.4 per cent against Sweden's 0.4 per cent)? This is surely one of the most intriguing criminological 'facts' in the modern era, but it is a fact which is apparently beyond the investigative capacity of conventional Anglo-American criminology.

Methodology

In our initial pilot study, we set out to compare the roles of *juges pour enfants* with magistrates, and *assistants sociaux* with social workers in cases of child abuse and neglect, and youth offending. We planned to utilise a series of vignettes as an unfolding case study involving a family with both child abuse and youth crime problems. We intended that these vignettes should be based on a real case from one or other of the countries. And here we fell foul of the quest for categorical equivalence, because the two systems were so different that the development of any case in one system quickly assumed features which rendered it unrecognisable in the other. In the end, we settled for a contrived case which was, as far as possible, neutral with respect to both systems. This was an important lesson, learnt by attempting to apply a familiar, tried and tested, domestic methodology, and finding it inadequate to the complex task of investigating trans-national difference. A vignette study, to paraphrase Rorty, attempts to 'hold a mirror up to nature'; to imitate, to simulate. 'In its own country, while it may not be the 'real thing' it will reflect reality faithfully enough. Across a national frontier where 'nature' is different, the mirror distorts' (Cooper et al., 1995).

The Double Take

The research participants in each country read the vignettes and then discussed them with one another. These discussions were videotaped, dubbed into the other language and transported across the Channel. Here participants commented on the ways that they, and their other nation counterparts, thought about the case. In the process, participants began to dissect not only the values and assumptions articulated by their French or English counterparts but their own as well: 'They didn't discuss evidence at all, I wonder what that says about their system…we spoke about it most of the time, I wonder what that says about ours' (Cooper et al., 1995). Instead of seeing only categorical equivalence or its absence, they saw a tantalising difference which raised previously unconsidered questions about their taken-for-granted worlds. They had become 'ironists'. In the ensuing study of professional responses to child abuse and neglect, we paired French *assistants sociaux* with English social workers who shadowed two or three of each other's cases for a year. Each pair met at two seminars, one conference and on five other occasions through the year. Following each meeting they were debriefed by researchers who attempted to clarify the multi-layered nature of the differences they were encountering. Through this intensive and extensive exposure to cultural, historical and intellectual differences, and what they meant for the children and families with whom they worked and the professionals involved with them, we began to understand the key elements of another final vocabulary. And having understood this, we were better able to interrogate, and excavate the cultural and historical origins, of our own.

In essence then, this approach to trans-national research attempts to do five things:

1. It strives to render unfamiliar the familiar via a process of cultural decentring.

2. It aims to promote a heightened perception of the multi-layered nature of trans-national difference and an understanding of these differences in their socio-historical and cultural specificity.

3. It encourages us to suspend our pre-existing, ethnocentric categories and to come to terms with the loss of categorical equivalence as the paramount paradigm of trans-national comparative research.

4. It promotes a capacity for ontological reflection, thinking about thinking, and the trans-national negotiation and adaptation of second-order constructs with which to encapsulate the conceptual differences we encounter.

5. It asserts that trans-national difference cannot be learned about by simply e-mailing data or reading books. Some degree of openness to, and immersion in, difference is crucial.

It was this trans-national 'double take' which suggested itself when, in another strand of our research, we were attempting to generate new thinking about responses to violence in and around the Charles Dickens secondary school on the Dickens estate, a high-crime neighbourhood in East London. This project was a product of an earlier, apparently unsuccessful, piece of action research, undertaken in the early 1990s, in which we investigated, and set up an intervention programme to reduce, the violent victimisation of students in two primary and two secondary schools in East London and Merseyside. This involved a process of whole-school consultation in which members of the project team worked with teachers, students and ancillary staff to devise and implement policies and strategies aimed at reducing violent victimisation. The initiative had a significant impact in the Merseyside schools and the London primary school, but the Charles Dickens secondary school on the Dickens estate remained largely resistant to our efforts to effect change (Pitts, 1993; Pitts and Smith, 1995). We attributed this failure to the inability of the school, unaided by other agencies, organisations and individuals, to deal with the violent racist, and inter-racial, conflict spilling over from the surrounding neighbourhood.

As a result, in the next phase of the research we aimed to identify those agencies, organisations, groups and individuals which constituted the 'minimum sufficient network' necessary to effect a reduction in the violent victimisation of school students in the Charles Dickens school and in the neighbourhood. We also wanted to know how those politicians and professionals with formal responsibility for the problem, and a professional commitment to its resolution, mediated the 'private troubles' of local residents and school students, with the 'public issues' which found expression in social and criminal justice policies emanating from central and local government. As part of this process, we organised a series of visits and exchanges which aimed to expose school students, teachers, magistrates, police officers, social workers and housing officials to the different 'final vocabularies' of their counterparts in analogous neighbourhoods in the Ile-de-France and Oise. And at one point, we put them all on a bus and took them to the Flaubert estate in Monet, an industrial suburb to the west of Paris, to investigate the ways in which their French counterparts had thought about, and responded to, problems of youth crime and disorder, violence and racial conflict (Pearce, 1995; Wallis, 1995).

This comparison suggested itself because both neighbourhoods were located in 'world cities', in areas which had experienced extensive de-industrialisation, economic disarticulation, high levels of structural youth unemployment, radical changes in their spatial and social organisation and patterns of production and consumption, at a time when new, non-White, populations were establishing themselves. At issue was the question of the ways in which, and the extent to which, local politicians and professionals had been able to intervene to ameliorate or reverse the negative impact and the social consequences of these changes upon the local populace.

The Dickens Estate

The Dickens estate, with a population of roughly 3,000 people, is remarkably isolated. Bordered by an arterial road to the south, a railway to the west, a canal to the north and a motorway to the east, there is only one road in and out of it. This has fostered what David Downes (1990) has described as 'a strong feeling of defensive territoriality'.

The estate is relatively close to London's Isle of Dogs where, during the course of our research, a neo-fascist British National Party (BNP) councillor, Derek Bacon, was elected and subsequently defeated. It was evident that much of the violent conflict in the Charles Dickens School had its origins in the hostility which was directed towards the Bangladeshi community in East London by influential elements within the White community (Pitts and Smith, 1995; Sampson and Phillips, 1995). This hostility was actively cultivated by the BNP, but it also gained sustenance from the relative quiescence of other political parties in the area, anxious not to alienate the White vote. In 1985 there had been a 'riot' on the Dickens estate involving 40 or so White young men who were trying to drive out the eight Bengali families living there. The families were promptly transferred off the estate by the local authority Housing Department. In the late 1980s, the Housing Department began once again to move homeless Bengali families on to the estate. By 1992, 30 Bengali and two Somali families, constituting 0.04 per cent of the 940 dwellings on the estate, were living there. However, their arrival was paralleled by a significant increase in the numbers of Bangladeshi and refugee children and young people entering the Charles Dickens secondary school so that by 1993, on what was still a largely mono-racial, White, housing estate, approximately 45 per cent of the students in the Charles Dickens school were of Bangladeshi origin, five per cent Somali, eight per cent African-Caribbean and a further five per cent or so were Greek or Turkish Cypriot, Chinese, Vietnamese and other races.

At the same time, the Housing Department, in its attempt to deal with the problem of diminishing housing stock occasioned by the Right to Buy and Tenant Incentive schemes, and the 'freeze' on local authority housing starts, was re-housing 'disruptive' tenants, those who failed to pay their rent regularly, homeless, often young, single-parent families, and a smattering of refugees, in the three, hard-to-let 'high-rise' blocks on the estate.

These changes were paralleled by an escalation of violence. By 1990 Bangladeshi families constituted 40 per cent of the victims of the 82 assaults on the estate recorded by the police. A subsequent victimisation survey put the actual number of assaults on Bangladeshi families at 136 (Sampson and Phillips, 1995), though this figure did not include Bangladeshi children and young people violently victimised at school. The suspects almost always attacked in groups. They were young; 19 per cent were under 12 and 64 per cent were aged between 13 and 18. They were both Black and White; 54 per cent were described as Caucasian and 30 per cent African-Caribbean; 84 per cent of them were male and 12 per cent female, and most attacks coincided with the Charles Dickens School's break times and the end of the school day. Hostility to Bangladeshi families would frequently spill over into the school where Bangladeshi children would be set upon by White children. On the other hand, conflicts which began in the school often spilled over into the neighbourhood where they quickly escalated into violent clashes between older Bangladeshi and White adolescents and young adults armed with pieces of wood and baseball bats. Attacks upon Bangladeshi school students on their way home from school were not infrequent and two thirds of the violent incidents which the school students rated as 'most serious' occurred outside the school, often perpetrated by older people (Pitts and Smith, 1995).

Economic Decline and Social Change

From the 1960s the East End of London has been in decline. It was then that the docks, the raison d'être of the East End, moved downriver to Tilbury, taking the core of the economically active population with them. Those unable or unwilling to leave, often poor young families and the elderly, saw the accommodation vacated by high-earning White Dockers occupied by low-earning Bangladeshi piece workers who found employment in the garment industries around Brick Lane in Whitechapel. By the 1990s the borough had the second highest level of youth unemployment in London and the South-East. The demise of the docks presaged the demise of the traditional extended family networks and the elaborate family-based criminal subculture, which had characterised the old East End (Hobbs, 1988). In its place there emerged what Hobbs (1993) has described as 'post-traditional' crime in which local, familial, criminal networks have given way to anonymous networks concerned with the sale and distribution of drugs. By the 1990s the 'organised', familial, criminal networks concerned primarily with instrumental property crime, fraud and extortion had all but disappeared, to be replaced by lower-level drugs-based networks, particularly in neighbouring Hackney, and racist attacks and inter-racial youth violence. In a prescient passage, written about youth crime and social change on the Lower East Side of New York in the late 1950s, Richard Cloward and Lloyd Ohlin (1960) observe that:

> *The old forms of social organisation begin to break down, and with them opportunities for upward mobility diminish. Indeed a new ethnic or nationality group may be invading the community, encroaching upon the old structures, and establishing a claim to dominance of the principal avenues of mobility, both legitimate and illegitimate. Thus a new cycle of community integration and deterioration is initiated. Once again the young find themselves both cut off from avenues to higher status and free from external restraint. This is a period, then, in which we should expect a resurgence of violent modes of delinquent adaptation. In the last stage of assimilation, the conflict adaptation may once again become the principal form of delinquency.*

> (Cloward and Ohlin, 1960)

The East End of London may never have been the melting pot of American popular mythology, but it has from time to time served as what Shaw and McKay (1942) have described as a zone of transition through which a succession of racial and cultural groups have passed. One of the things which happen in a zone of transition is acculturation, the process whereby the younger members of an incoming group take on some of the values, styles and survival techniques of the incumbent population while simultaneously developing modes of resistance to their hostility and violence. In the American dream, over the next couple of generations, the new racial or cultural group moves upward through the economic structure and outwards to the relative prosperity of the suburbs and eventual social assimilation.

For most of the residents in the de-stabilised neighbourhoods of the East End at the turn of the century, however, social and geographical mobility appears to have been indefinitely postponed. The 'melting pot', inasmuch as it ever existed, has become a 'pressure cooker' in which children and young people are compelled by the demands of survival to make a cultural accommodation. And so the struggle for racial and cultural succession becomes a struggle for social space which is articulated most forcefully in the victimisation of Bangladeshi families, and Bangladeshi children and young people in their homes and on the streets, and in the inter-racial youth violence which has become a regular feature of life in and around these neighbourhoods.

The Flaubert Estate

The Flaubert estate is a large public housing development on the outskirts of the medieval town of Monet in a prosperous region in the Seine valley. In 1995, the residents of the Flaubert estate constituted 63 per cent of Monet's 45,254 inhabitants (for the purposes of our research we concentrated primarily on only one of the nine *quartiers* in the Flaubert estate with a population of approximately 3,300 people). Le Gales (1994) has observed that Monet offers us a fine example of the French 'outer city crisis'. The region around Monet is an industrial enclave where the aerospace industry, car manufacturing and cement production relocated in the post-war period. In the 1960s, the Flaubert estate, a vast, modernist, high-rise development, was constructed to house skilled manual and clerical workers in these industries. In the 1970s, this predominantly White population vacated the estate in favour of private housing in the surrounding countryside and Flaubert began to fill up with unskilled manual workers recruited from North Africa, Central Africa, Turkey and, latterly, Portugal, to work in the nearby Peugeot and Renault factories. In the late 1970s these industries began to shed labour; Renault, for example, reduced its workforce from 17,000 to 9,000. This sudden hike in unemployment coincided with the second generation leaving school. The Flaubert estate, the French 'unemployed ghetto' par excellence, was in the forefront of both the 1981 and 1991 riots. However, the Flaubert estate has also been, as its mayor, Paul Picard (1995), has observed, a *ville laboratoire* in which extensive social innovation and experimentation have taken place.

One of the results of this experimentation has been that the rate of recorded youth crime and violence on the estate, which was among the highest in France at the end of the 1970s has, since the mid-1980s, declined to a level around, and sometimes slightly below, the national average (Centre National de Formation et d'Études de la Protection Judiciaire de la Jeunesse, 1995; Jazouli, 1995). (By contrast, in 1993, the Dickens estate achieved the dubious distinction of having the highest level of recorded racial attacks in a traditionally high crime London Borough).

The Social Prevention Initiative

Upon its election in 1981 the Socialist administration of Francois Mitterrand faced nationwide riots in the multi-racial *banlieue*. Fearing that they might reach the proportions they had attained in Britain in that year, Mitterrand instituted the *été jeunes*, a 100,000-strong, national, summer play scheme and established a commission of town mayors chaired by Henri Bonnemaison. The Bonnemaison Commission, which brought together both Gaullist and Socialist mayors to devise a national strategy, produced its report *Face à la Délinquence: Prévention, Répression, Solidarité*, in 1983. The report asserted that if effective action against the causes of crime was to be taken, a policy which was flexible, adapted to local circumstances, and structurally connected with the activities of government departments and local authorities, the judiciary, the voluntary sector and the needs and wishes of citizens, was needed (Bonnemaison, 1983; Dubet et al., 1985). However, as Francis Ballieau (1998) has argued: '. . . the police, the *gendarmerie* and the legal system did not lose their pre-eminence. They still remained central to the enactment of the new policy, in some cases acting as a major obstacle preventing change in the definition of public order and the conception and strategic management of public order.'

On the face of it, Bonnemaison was concerned with the effects of 'social exclusion' and the development of techniques of 'social prevention'. However, the commission was the central prop of a broader political initiative which aimed to revitalise a sense of 'citizenship' through the democratisation of those parts of the Republic where this sense was perceived to be most tenuous. This, Wieviorka (1994) notes, was deemed politically necessary because French society was perceived by the Socialists to have undergone *une grande mutation* in the previous two decades. This mutation was characterised by the dissipation of industrial society and the working-class movement, the supplanting of collectivism by individualism and subjectivism, mass unemployment and racial conflict. It was also evident to the Mitterrand administration that the multi-racial *banlieue*, the site of the 1981 riots, was the place, *par excellence*, where this sense of citizenship was at its weakest. The Bonnemaison Commission was not, therefore, solely concerned with the prevention of crime, but with the prevention of those forms of social marginalisation, or exclusion which threatened social cohesion and social order and, hence, the political legitimacy of the Republic (Donzelot and Roman, 1991). Thus, in its report, the commission argued that if youth crime and disorder in the *banlieue* were to be curbed, the solution must lie in a process of political incorporation, an expression of *solidarité* with the people who lived there (King, 1989).

The Structure of the Social Prevention Initiative (SPI)

At a national level, the National Council for the Prevention of Delinquency, chaired by the Prime Minister and attended by the majority of town mayors and representatives from the relevant government ministries, was established in June 1983. At regional level, Councils for the Prevention of Crime chaired by the chief civil servant (the *Commissaire de la République*) with the chief judicial officer (the *Procureur de la République*) as the vice-chair were established. At local level Communal Councils for the Prevention of Crime, chaired by the town mayors, were established. Communal Councils monitored local youth crime patterns, established special working groups to deal with particular problems and targeted central government funds on these problems. Their 'arms and legs' were *animateurs sociaux* from the Specialised Prevention service (see below) and the *Direction de la Protection Judiciaire et de la Jeunesse* (DPJJ, see below), who worked at face-to-face level with local young people, and latterly adults, to devise local solutions to local problems.

> *The main aim of the Communal Council is to reduce crime through improving the urban environment, reducing unemployment among the young, improving facilities for education and training, combating racial discrimination and encouraging the assimilation and integration of marginalised groups, particularly alienated youngsters and immigrants. To facilitate this process, a national network of Youth Centres, known as* Missions Locales *has been set up in more than 100 towns and cities. These centres try to bridge the transition between school and work for the unemployed and the unqualified (aged 16–25) by offering youth training and advice and assistance on matters such as improving literacy, managing financial affairs and finding accommodation. They also encourage young people, particularly the unemployed, to set up and run their own projects.* (Graham, 1993)

This structure maximised information exchange, enabled the horizontal co-ordination of neighbourhoods and local agencies and the vertical coordination of neighbourhoods with central government agencies and departments (De Liege, 1991). Importantly, it also ensured that political 'feedback loops' were created between the poorest neighbourhoods and the office of the Prime Minister.

What set the Mitterrand SPI apart from previous initiatives in France and elsewhere, was the precision with which neighbourhoods and young people were targeted for intervention:

> *…with the new government, specific practices were identified and roles apportioned within the local communities and their municipal or district representatives. Within these local contexts, an initial phase of consultation was expected to deliver a 'security diagnosis'. This preliminary joint exercise had the purpose of assessing the needs and problems of specific areas.* (Gallo, 1995)

However, unlike many of the local crime audits undertaken in the UK in the wake of the Crime and Disorder Act 1998, in which the hurried 'consultation' phase consisted of a few, normally poorly attended, public meetings, these security diagnoses were informed by the experience of the specialised prevention teams (see below) which had had a strong presence, and maintained extensive contacts, within many of the high crime *banlieues* which were targeted for intervention.

De-centralisation and De-concentration

The structure of the initiative was developed in tandem with a dual strategy of de-centralisation, the creation of new regional and departmental bodies headed by elected officials, and de-concentration, in which departmental and regional prefects, and other local officials of central government, were granted much greater autonomy, and a *politique de la ville* which was gradually developed through the 1980s (Le Gales, 1994; Lemierre, 1994). In Britain during the same period, local democracy was being progressively weakened by the transfer of power, responsibilities and resources from local authorities to central government (Hutton, 1995; Jenkins, 1995). Although the election in France, in 1986, of a government of the political right signalled reductions in the scale of the SPI, the new government affirmed its commitment to the programme. In 1988, by a unanimous vote of Parliament, a national guaranteed minimum income plan, *Revenue Minimum d'Insertion*, and increased expenditure on employment and training for young people and the long-term unemployed were introduced. Ironically, of course, 1988 was also the year in which state unemployment benefits were withdrawn from youngsters under the age of 18 by the Thatcher government.

Following the 1990 riots in Lyon and Paris, the Rocard administration created the Ministry of Urban Affairs, and responsibility for crime prevention was handed to the newly created Minister of State for Cities. The new Ministry responded to this 'unrest' in the *banlieues*, and the concurrent rise of Jean-Marie Le Pen's National Front, by expanding the existing SPIs in impoverished city-centre quartiers and the *banlieues*. This involved a comprehensive programme of improvement in housing, education, crime prevention, job training, youth activities and 'beefed-up' public services in the 400 most 'sensitive neighbourhoods' across the country.

This led to a sharpening of the focus upon urban and suburban crime and an attempt to involve the private sector in crime prevention to a far greater degree. The Praedrie Report, *Enterprises and Neighbourhoods* (1991), observed that if the *banlieues* were to be successfully drawn into the economic mainstream, they would require much greater involvement with, and much more investment from, the business community, and far better communication between those in need of employment and those in need of workers. As a result, in 1992, a National Foundation for Integration was established by a consortium of industrialists, supported by the government which offered financial incentives to firms investing in neighbourhoods with high levels of social and economic need.

Yet, as Jean-Francois Gazeau and Vincent Pryre (1998) have observed, the results of the SPI were uneven and dependent upon local conditions. It was for this reason that we chose, in our research, to make a comparison with the Flaubert estate, because of a widespread recognition that it was one of the neighbourhoods in which many of the objectives of the SPI had been realised. This is not, therefore, an account of what happened in 'France' per se. It is an account of what happened in one French neighbourhood when the time was right, the political will was present and motivated people got organised (Le Gales, 1994). Nonetheless, its significance for the development of social exclusion and community safety strategies in the UK in the twenty-first century will, I hope, be evident.

A Tale of Two Housing Estates

A key difference between the Flaubert and Dickens estates was that the neighbourhood, the geographical space occupied by the Flaubert estate, was not the object of contention between different racial groups. There was racial conflict but this tended to occur in the town of Monet or on the estate's boundaries. On our arrival at the estate in a large coach with UK number plates, local young people surrounded us shouting, in a very pleasant way, 'you are in Africa now', suggesting what was, for us, a very unfamiliar separateness. In France, African and Maghrebian people are likely to live on relatively remote, geographically demarcated, largely non-White estates on the periphery of towns and cities; a spatial pattern more akin to the 1960s housing projects of the United States than social housing in the UK. The residents of the old town of Monet had no desire to reclaim the estate, while the families of the White residents on the estate arrived at around the same time as people of other races and appeared to feel no special racial or cultural affinity with it. In contrast with the young people on the Dickens estate, the young people we interviewed on the Flaubert estate, 'Black' and White, felt 'excluded' rather than 'embattled', their geographical remoteness from the town centre serving as an apt metaphor for the social distance which they saw as separating them from both the town, and access to the opportunity and power, which they associated with the town. The struggle for these young people concerned what they perceived to be an oppressive educational system which denied them opportunity, and an oppressive police force which has sometimes responded to their protests with brutality.

On the Dickens estate the struggle for 'racialised' space and the defence of territory against a group of 'incomers' with whom there was no shared 'working-class' history, was central to the violent conflict. The key issue in the BNP campaign of 1993 concerned whether or not 'local housing' was to be occupied by 'local people'. Inter-racial conflict was evident throughout the research and local young people, and local professionals, Black and White, attributed this to a desire on the part of some White residents and their children to defend 'their' school and 'their' neighbourhood against a perceived 'invasion' of Bangladeshi school students and homeless Bangladeshi families.

A Politicised Practice

The mayor of Monet, like the majority of town mayors in France, served on the National Council for the Prevention of Delinquency, chaired by the Prime Minister. 'Prevention' in this context refers to the prevention of social marginality and spans concerns about crime, educational attainment and family poverty. The mayor's office (the *Mairie*) co-ordinated the expenditure of national and EU poverty funds and served as a meeting point for the statutory and voluntary agencies involved in local initiatives. Another meeting point between the politicians and the people was *La Pagode*, a centre constructed by the *Mairie* where young people met *animateurs sociaux* to undertake the recreational, educational and political activities in which they were interested. Over the three years it had been in existence, the 500 or so users had produced a regular newsletter *Alors Quoi Neuf* which discussed issues affecting the estate and the young people on it. About 60 young people attended monthly meetings at *La Pagode* with the mayor or his deputy at which these issues were discussed and policy options were considered. These developments flowed from the new political possibilities created by the policies of de-centralisation and deconcentration, social prevention and the *politique de la ville* introduced by the Mitterrand administration in the 1980s. By allowing space for political innovation at a local level, they created the ground for the type of localised *Nouvelle Démocratie* described by Jazouli, who is quoting Farid Bouali, a young community leader who was a leading member of the main Maghrebian youth organisation in France, and a prime mover in the development of the *Conseil de Quartier* on the Flaubert estate:

> *Les élus ont souvent la fâcheuse tendance de vouloir mettre la légitimité des gens en jeu, et là on est irréprochable…dit-il. L'Idée, c'était de cogérer les affaires du quartier. Il fallait un contre-pouvoir, pas un anti-pouvoir. S'associent, par cooptation, des parents d'élèves, commerçants, militants du quartier, policiers, pompiers. Deux élus de la commune sont aussi présents. La municipalité est souveraine, mais le Conseil de quartier propose des projets. Des projets élaborés, discutés longuement avec la population, pas seulement les idées.*

The *Conseil de Quartier* emerged as an additional tier of local government in the *quartier* in the late 1980s. All residents of 16 and over, irrespective of immigration status, were allowed to vote for the *Conseil* and around 40 per cent did. The *Conseil* was concerned with policy on the estate but also served as a political conduit, via the *Mairie*, to the National Council for the Prevention of Delinquency where the mayor of Monet served and was pledged to represent their views. The National Council oversaw the development of the SPI and co-ordinated the work on the ground with relevant policy developments in government. This made it possible to influence the priorities of local officials of central government departments, the manner in which these departments cooperated and the way in which their resources were deployed in the attempt to realise shared goals which were, in part at least, formulated in consultation with local citizens in the *Conseil de Quartier*. This structure made it possible to institutionalise this activity, politically, administratively and professionally at national, regional and local levels and, apparently, to do so without too much bureaucratic stultification at local level. This was a politically driven system with a range of political, administrative and professional feedback loops which appeared to ensure that there was some connection between policy, provision, professional practice and the needs, interests and wishes of the intended beneficiaries. Crucially, it was also a system which created the possibility of dialogue within and between different system levels.

These structures have been central to the realisation of the developments on the Flaubert estate, but so too has the congruence between the political values of the citizens and professionals engaged in them and those articulated within French public policy. Grévôt (1994) notes that the vocabulary of Mitterrand's *politique de la ville* was derived in large part from French social work, whose personnel was increased, and whose professional status and political influence were enhanced significantly, by the crucial role it played in the realisation of the *politique de la ville*. This stands in marked contrast with the, sometimes open, hostility with which the social work profession in Britain has been regarded by central government in the 1980s and 1990s (Parton, 1985, 1991; Cooper et al., 1995). Beyond this, British social workers in the 1980s faced the problem that many of them worked in socially-deprived Labour-controlled local authorities which were locked in a struggle with central government to maintain services in the face of 'rate-capping'. Social workers were therefore subject to additional pressures from 'friendly' councils which found themselves powerless to provide the services they believed to be necessary.

The De-politicisation of the Dickens Estate

The borough in which the Dickens estate was located had been a 'cradle' of London socialism. Always a radical borough, the Labour council gained its strength from its close associations with the docks, the dock workers' unions, the elaborate familial networks which developed around the docks and the distinctive culture which they spawned. This was a personalised, face-to-face politics, where families in trouble would often turn to their councillor. By the 1980s this relationship had changed beyond all recognition, with many White residents regarding Labour councillors as 'do-gooders', a euphemism for middle-class professionals and politicians perceived to be too 'pro-Bangladeshi' (Cohen, 1995).

The professionals serving the Dickens estate were all concerned about the falling standard of the services they were able to provide, but sceptical about the efficacy of grassroots or local political pressure to effect change upon those factors which generated the problems encountered by the children and young people to whom they were attempting to provide a service. They appeared to have reconciled themselves to a narrowing of the professional focus, defining their primary task as the efficient exercise of the statutory functions of their agency.

Public professionals from statutory agencies concerned with children and young people and crime and victimisation on the Dickens estate felt themselves to be under growing political pressure to reconcile their commitment to inter-agency and inter-professional co-operation with their statutory responsibilities. In the field of child care and youth justice, professionals had experienced an annexation of the professional task (Pitts, 1988) as, increasingly, they pursued priorities and discharged functions specified by central government departments, in accordance with detailed national standards and codes of practice and locally derived 'performance indicators', and having to do so within ever diminishing local authority budgets. This inevitably meant that their scope for innovation and responsiveness to the 'public' was restricted. Asked to describe what role the local authority Social Services Department might play *vis-à-vis* the high level of assaults on Bengali schoolchildren, two senior officers of the authority ironically observed that, at best, the victim might be made the subject of a child protection investigation and the perpetrators, if they were ever apprehended, could be required to pursue a correctional programme at the Youth Justice Centre.

Respondents did not perceive any positive local or central government political leadership behind the changes they experienced, and their actions were shaped defensively by the attempt to avoid attracting sanctions from local politicians or central government departments if the agency 'fell down on the job' by failing to discharge its statutory responsibilities adequately. This anxiety was heightened during the research because a new Labour administration was re-organising services, thus raising the spectre of demotions and redundancies.

The sense of the absence of political leadership was experienced particularly acutely by professionals when they confronted the thorny issue of the council's responsiveness to racial victimisation. There was a widespread suspicion in the Bangladeshi community that the Housing Department, the schools and the police were failing to take serious action against racist abuse and attack, for fear of provoking a 'White backlash' on the estate. Many Bangladeshi citizens also believed that the schools and the police were pinpointing Bengali youth as troublemakers when, in fact, they were merely responding to 'White' provocation.

Lacking political leadership on the issue, professionals on the estate tended to be unwilling to discuss the victimisation of, or offending by, Bengali school students, or professional responses to it. This apprehension was compounded by an uncertainty, and in some cases acute anxiety, about whether, and to what extent, they would be supported, or sanctioned, by local politicians or senior managers in their agencies if they were perceived to be taking a 'position' or committing their agency to action on these issues.

It is difficult to establish the veracity of the suspicions among the Bangladeshi community. However, it was the view of the deputy chief clerk of the local magistrates' court that, despite anecdotal evidence that very few incidents of violent group conflict on the estate were precipitated by Bangladeshi young people, equal numbers of Bangladeshi and White defendants came before the courts on charges of affray and assault. Youth justice professionals also thought that Bangladeshi children and young people were more likely to be formally processed through the local youth justice system than their White counterparts.

As a result of these political uncertainties and anxieties, professional constraints and a recognition that to engage with the public would, necessarily, bring them into a confrontation with deep-rooted inter-communal conflict, some public professionals on the Dickens estate demonstrated a marked reluctance to engage the 'public' in a process of defining problems, and then devising solutions to them. These tasks were therefore undertaken, inasmuch as they were undertaken at all, beyond the public gaze in a 'depoliticised', corporatist, professional realm (Crawford and Jones, 1995). In the case of the Dickens estate, this was a corporatism which the research strategy inadvertently threatened to disrupt by attempting to introduce the voice of a 'public', albeit a very youthful public, with strongly held views about the nature of the problem, into the deliberations of the professionals. Thus, the Charles Dickens school's invitation to local public professionals to attend an open forum to discuss the victimisation of school students, evoked responses ranging from surprised enthusiasm to unconcealed panic.

The quiescence of local politicians, the absence of any formal connection between them and their constituents, alongside the intense political violence which sometimes characterised life on the Dickens estate, stood in marked contrast with the level of political engagement between politicians, professionals and residents on the Flaubert estate. The political quiescence on the Dickens estate flowed, in part, from the growing incapacity of a politically beleaguered, local authority to move beyond tightly demarcated service provision to a sustained engagement with social conflicts in the neighbourhood over which, notionally at least, it presided.

The Practice of Prevention

In discussing 'prevention', Anglo-American criminologists have tended to distinguish between primary, secondary and tertiary prevention. 'Primary prevention' attempts to modify or eradicate criminogenic aspects of the social, economic and physical environment; 'secondary prevention' attempts to reduce the risk of future involvement in crime by individuals or groups thought to be 'at risk' because of social, economic, personal or familial characteristics or their physical or social environment; 'tertiary prevention' focuses upon the behaviour, beliefs, attitudes, values, modes of thinking and opportunities available to individuals or groups, who are already involved in crime.

As we have seen, the form of prevention identified in the youth justice provisions of the Crime and Disorder Act 1998 is tertiary, while the community safety provisions of the Act make implicit reference to individualised forms of tertiary and secondary prevention. The distinctiveness of the French SPI is that its preventive strategy spanned all three levels of intervention. At the primary level, the government intervened in the economy to redirect business and industry towards pockets of social and economic disadvantage. It improved and expanded social housing to inject greater stability into de-stabilised neighbourhoods.

In education, schools in under-achieving neighbourhoods were given additional resources while long-term education and training programmes which aimed to equip trainees for primary sector employment, were introduced for unemployed young people and adults.

The Family

And then there was family policy. Although the French SPI had little to say about the role and responsibilities of the family in stemming youth crime and disorder, far from neglecting the family, it aimed to create the social, political and cultural conditions under which the family could discharge its central function as 'the material and primary institution, the actor in social and political activity, and the keeper of national values' (Commaile, 1994).

If the family in Britain, at an ideological level at least, is a 'private trouble', in France it is, emphatically, a 'public issue' (Mills, 1959). Whereas in France the 'family' and its future are regarded as a legitimate concern of governments and an appropriate target for state policy, in the UK political responses to the 'family' are characterised by a deep ambivalence. This became evident in the run-up to the 1997 general election in which New Labour's much-vaunted 'family policy' eventually emerged as an adjunct to its youth justice strategy. In French law and policy, families are the building blocks which constitute the state and this is reflected in levels of benefits, in cash and in kind, which mean that far fewer families in France, however constituted, fall below the median wage level than in the UK (Cooper et al., 1995). Commaile (1994) has argued that: 'If familialism has had and continues to have so much value at the core of French society, this is because the family has been given an essential role within the social and political structure of society.'

Specialised Prevention

In France, the bulk of secondary preventive interventions target geographical areas, groups and social processes rather than the deficiencies of individuals. This form of intervention has its origins in the Specialised Prevention which emerged in France in the 1950s in response to concerns about accelerated North and Central African migration into urban neighbourhoods, a consequent rise in inter-racial and racist violence, marked increases in unemployment and drug-taking among young people and the emergence of a flamboyant, oppositional youth subculture, the *blousons noirs*. Specialised Prevention was modelled on North American models of 'street gang work' and British detached youth work (Gazeau and Pryre, 1998). Whereas, in the UK, this approach to prevention went into decline in the 1980s, in France it is a model which has grown, and in growing has been continuously refined. With the advent of Francois Mitterrand's SPI in 1983, an expanded Specialised Prevention service became one of its central props.

Pioneered originally by the voluntary sector, by the mid-1990s Specialised Prevention services were provided by 320 voluntary organisations deploying specialist teams in most medium and large French towns with a population of more than 10,000 people. These services were funded by *départements* on the basis of service level agreements with the voluntary sector from departmental children's services budgets and the central government family benefits fund (CAF). At national level, a liaison committee promotes and supports Specialised Prevention services. Specialised Prevention is defined in law as a range of actions aimed at preventing social marginalisation and promoting the social integration of young people facing social problems (*Article 45: Code de la Famille et de l'Aide Sociale*). Yet Specialised Prevention workers have no formal links with, or accountability to, the justice system. In practice Specialised Prevention provides:

1. Street social work – with young people and some adults in targeted neighbourhoods.
2. Prevention clubs – which offer support to families in crisis, access to legal advice and representation, health promotion, school homework support, advocacy and support for children facing exclusion from school.
3. Holiday play schemes and activity programmes, the *été jeunes*, for children in areas of poverty and high crime.
4. Training and employment – helping youngsters access the best schemes, working with local employers to develop opportunities, working with young people to start their own businesses and cooperatives.
5. Collaboration with mainstream agencies – to help local people gain access to them and helping the agencies to evaluate and enhance their impact locally.
6. Development of community problem-solving capacities – through the support of local people to develop residents' and tenants' associations and promote self-help networks, skills exchanges and purchasing collectives.

This 'collective' approach to 'social work' or 'prevention' is less extraordinary in France than in the UK:

> *If social work in Britain is primarily concerned with the needs, rights and responsibilities of individuals, French social work focuses more on work at a collective level to promote support networks and to ensure that those in difficulty are integrated into the social and economic life of the community.*   (Mitchell and Gelloz, 1997)

Specialised Prevention is rooted in the idea that some children and young people are denied the cultural and emotional experiences, and the social space, in which to grow to maturity. In consequence, they find it difficult, and sometimes impossible, to handle the adult world and its institutions. This has strong echoes of the findings of Detleif Baum in predominantly Turkish neighbourhoods on the outskirts of Koblenz, discussed in Chapter 7.

The task of the Specialised Prevention worker, on the street, is to make and sus
with these young people, on their terms, in order to help them build a more positi
perception, devise more satisfying, yet attainable, personal goals; to facilitate their contact w
the agencies and individuals with the resources they need to achieve these goals and to suppor
them through adversity. But the key to the apparent success of this strategy is time. Workers
sometimes maintain relationships with the most troubled young people for five or six years.

Each member of Specialised Prevention teams will normally be assigned a particular
quartier which can be covered easily on foot. The team in Bourg-les-Valence, for example,
had four workers who served a population of 27,000, each team member having their own
'patch' (Walden-Jones 1993). Teams undertook an analysis of local patterns of youth crime
and disorder and the location of young people believed to be at risk in a variety of ways. In
doing so they drew upon data supplied by the Education Department, the *Mairie*, the police
and their own local knowledge. On the basis of these assessments, certain neighbourhoods
or groups were targeted for intervention. One team identified a group of young drug users,
hanging around the bus station, as their target. The Service gave the team 18 months to
establish relationships with the targeted group and up to five years to locate and work with
a broader network of around 300 opiate-using young people in that part of the city. Walden-
Jones offers a breakdown of a Specialised Prevention team member's week (cf. Table 9.1).

Table 9.1: Breakdown of a Specialised Prevention Team Member's Week

Activity	Percentage of time devoted to it
On the street	28
In the office	15
Meeting other social workers	2
Managing a homework project	9
Management meetings	9
In transit	9
Running activities	8
Meeting individuals	6
Meeting families	4

th Crime: Discipline or Solidarity?

Iden Jones utilised a range of approaches to achieve their 'away from offending and disaffection and towards 'normal' ion'. All the team's work was carried out with the agreement ver as a condition of a sentence or a magistrate's directive. ıl and accepted practice that no information was passed to ıily, without the young person's permission:

.ıt behind a desk and call you in to give you a hard time', said one 16-year-old, 'it's (the worker) who moves' ('C'est lui qui bouge'). 'They're realistic about what you can and can't do. They know we're not intellectuals and can only do so much'... 'I only trust (the worker) apart from my own family.' But this loyalty was based on mutual respect: the prevention workers treated the young people much as they would adults and I saw no examples of patronising attitudes by workers.

(Walden Jones, 1993)

Padieu and Sanchez (1994) note that 84 *départements* spent FF700m. on 650 Specialised Prevention services in 1991, enabling some 2,500 staff, mainly street social workers in the voluntary sector, to be deployed. A *Ministère de la Santé* assessment of Specialised Prevention in 1975 calculated that if each project only prevented two young people from entering secure care or custody each year, the service could be considered cost-effective.

'Youth Justice'

In France, 'youth justice' and 'child care and protection' are both the responsibility of DPJJ (*Direction de la Protection Judiciaire et de la Jeunesse*). DPJJ employs all the children's judges and court social workers in France. It works through its *Action Educative bureaux* (akin to UK pupil referral units) with children who are unwilling or unable to stay in mainstream schooling. In the late 1970s the Ministry of Justice *Instituts Fermés*, akin to reformatory schools, were shut down as a result of protracted industrial action by their staff, and political pressure from high-profile activists like François Truffaut, the film director, and the philosopher, Michel Foucault, who protested against the imprisonment of children. Many of the staff were redeployed as DPJJ detached or street workers with young people, similar to the ones employed by Specialised Prevention. Today DPJJ employs over 1,000 detached or street youth workers.

The French 'youth justice' system was created at the end of the Second World War and was based upon the paternalistic, nineteenth-century, Latin, 'social defence' model which gives a privileged place to prevention, rehabilitation and the needs of the child, and a relatively minor one to the claims of 'justice'. 'Youth justice' in France is deeply imbued with 'welfarist' assumptions about the origins of, and solutions to, the problem of youth crime. However, whereas in the UK 'welfarism' tends to be associated with a preoccupation with family functioning, DPJJ social workers are required to work collaboratively with other professionals, groups, organisations and agencies to enhance the educational and vocational opportunities available to socially disadvantaged children and their families, and the quality of life within their neighbourhoods (Ely and Stanley, 1990; Cooper et al., 1995).

As such, the *welfare versus justice dichotomy*, the resolution of which was central to the development of the justice-oriented, minimalist youth justice strategies of the 1980s in England and Wales, presents itself in France as an inevitable tension to be worked with by way of discussion between judges, social workers, families and young people in trouble (Morris et al., 1980; Pitts, 1988, 1996; King and Piper, 1990; Krisberg and Austin, 1993). DPJJ social workers work under the direction of the children's judge, which circumscribes their professional autonomy. In England and Wales, the advent of corporatism in youth justice, and closer co-operation between youth justice workers, the police and the courts in the 1980s accompanied the effective abandonment of attempts, by youth justice professionals, to address the social factors deemed to be associated with youth crime, in favour of more narrowly focused systems management strategies aimed at the attainment of diversionary targets. In France by contrast, DPJJ social workers have been at the forefront of innovations in the 'social sphere'. From 1983, DPJJ workers were to play a central role in Francois Mitterrand's SPI, which led to a broadening of the 'social work' role to include a concern with 'social prevention' and the 'social insertion' of 'socially marginal' young people in education, training and employment. This initiative was inspired in large part by concerns about the 'integration' of young people of North and Central African origin into the mainstream of French cultural and economic life (Bonnemaison, 1983; King, 1986).

Over the period, Mitterrand's SPI led to a redefinition of the social work role and a refocusing of the social work task. In some cases, this has meant the recruitment of new personnel with new skills and perspectives and the construction of new political alliances (Picard, 1995). Crescy Cannan (1996) has observed that some social workers found involvement in collective action with neighbourhood groups difficult, preferring to play a more traditional role with individual service users. As a result, some departments and communes have grown impatient with professional social work's reluctance to grasp the new roles and new opportunities on offer, and have employed people like sociologists and geographers, who have been more attuned to the goals of the SPI, which often concerned economic development and employment.

Employment

David Downes (1990) has observed that employment schemes on the Dickens estate had, for their duration, been effective in diverting young people from crime, or minimising their involvement in it but, when the funding ran out, and the schemes terminated, their impact was quickly dissipated. This points up two key differences between the Dickens and the Flaubert estates. 'Crime prevention' on the Dickens estate had traditionally taken the form of time-limited 'projects' emanating from beyond the estate and unintegrated with the activities of the established local and central government agencies operating there. Not only were they unintegrated at agency level, they rarely articulated with the plans and strategies of the local council. Moreover, as the 1990s progressed the quest for funds became increasingly competitive and unpredictable and this promoted an arbitrary opportunism among local agencies and local politicians. This meant that those projects which were funded tended to come with fully formed and non-negotiable 'targets', and unrealistic 'exit strategies' which required the under-funded local authority to make improbable commitments to future spending in order to sustain them. This process had led to considerable cynicism among our research participants, both professionals and local residents, about the viability of developing a 'safer neighbourhood' on a project-by-project basis, a feeling articulated most clearly by English participants who visited the Flaubert estate with us.

On the Flaubert estate local employment policy aimed to offer local jobs on the estate to local people in order to reduce local unemployment and reinforce contacts between local residents. A national youth and adult training agency, *Association Jeunesse, Culture, Loisirs, Technique* (JCLT) was contracted by the *Mairie* and the *Mission Locale*, to offer long-term youth and adult training leading to nationally recognised qualifications which would enable residents to enter skilled, higher paid, jobs in primary sector employment in the *département* and in Paris. This policy was devised by the *Mairie*, the *Mission Locale* and the *Conseil de Quartier*.

Housing Policy

Housing policy was developed in the same way. It aimed to pursue demographic stability by locating the children and relatives of local residents in local accommodation in order to strengthen the ties of friendship and kinship which underpin networks of informal social support and social control. The pursuit of this policy led to the construction of new, larger, low-rise apartments on the Flaubert estate and an expanded range of community facilities. As a result of this policy, however, many apartments were overcrowded, being unsuitable for the larger families on the estate. However new, larger, council homes and a new hospital were being constructed alongside the estate. The Neighbourhood Council had previously initiated a project with the mayor's office in which consecrated rooms were established at the town abattoir where Islamic religious rites could be practised. Also, an African market and food co-operative had started where residents could buy the food they needed at reasonable prices. One of the consequences of these developments had been that requests for transfers off the estate had dwindled, while the waiting list for transfers onto the estate had grown significantly.

This is of particular interest when we remember that the key issue in local elections, and the 'space-specific ideology of race and nation' espoused by some White residents of the Dickens estate and the neighbouring Isle of Dogs, concerned the paucity of decent public housing (Jackson and Penrose 1993; Cohen 1995). The Housing Department operated a system of housing priority points, determined on the basis of social need. This was a policy which was increasingly difficult to implement in the face of the erosion of good-quality local housing stock occasioned by central government's 'Right to Buy' strategy and 'Tenant Incentive' schemes. This meant that 'disruptive' tenants, those who did not pay their rent regularly, the homeless, often young single-parent and Bangladeshi families, and successive waves of refugees were allocated to the unpopular and underused tower blocks on the estate which were notorious for their high levels of predatory crime and drug dealing. This had produced a less stable, less cohesive, often fearful, neighbourhood with fewer ties of kinship and friendship.

The Violent Victimisation of Children and Young People

Bangladeshi children and young people at the Charles Dickens School on the Dickens estate were victimised more frequently and more seriously than the other students. Whereas Richard Kinsey et al. (1990) found that the victimisation of children and young people differed very little between youngsters from poor or prosperous neighbourhoods or different social classes, but differed markedly from the victimisation experienced by their parents, we found that the heightened vulnerability of Bengali and Somali school students was consistent with the heightened vulnerability of their parents. In their study of the estate undertaken in 1991, Sampson and Phillips (1995) found that 67 per cent of the Somali and Bengali families who were subject to racially motivated crime were multiply victimised and this tallied with the findings of contemporaneous studies in adjacent boroughs (see, for example, Hesse et al., 1990). In our study 69 per cent of Bengali students, against 44 per cent of Whites, reported being violently victimised 'a few times' or 'often' in the preceding year.

The high levels of violent victimisation, racial and otherwise, on the Dickens estate, in comparison with adjacent areas, most of which had much larger Bengali and Somali populations, suggested that this victimisation was not simply precipitated by the characteristics of the victims or 'White racism' per se. Something else was at stake. It seems more likely that the exceptionally high levels of violence inflicted upon Bangladeshi youngsters who attended the Charles Dickens School and lived on the estate were related to the symbolic significance of the school and the estate. For many White residents, the Dickens estate was a 'racially defined space' (Goldburg, 1993), a beleaguered White enclave, struggling to resist against Bangladeshi 'encroachment' (Cohen, 1995).

The Struggle for the School

As public services withdrew from the Dickens estate, the Charles Dickens School, as the remaining accessible public resource, was forced to assume new responsibilities. Parents, and other adults, turned increasingly to the school for advice about problems with housing, health, racial harassment and the law, advice which was previously dispensed by state agencies and voluntary organisations. As a result secretarial, ancillary and teaching staff spent more and more time 'counselling' distressed parents, and other local adults. In the late 1990s, the influx of political refugees and economic migrants from Eastern Europe meant that schools like Charles Dickens, in areas of settlement were also acting as a point of referral to local authority refugee services, embassies and refugee support groups.

However, their very responsiveness to the growing social and cultural diversity of the children and young people they served, and their families, rendered such schools vulnerable to the charge from other parents that they were advancing the interests of some social, racial or cultural groups over others. For some established, 'local', White residents, the school, like the despised local council, came to represent an official world of 'do-gooders' who, by their 'politically correct' responses to newcomers, were rejecting 'local people' who had sent generations of their families to the school (Cohen, 1995).

The children and young people in these households were not impervious to their parents' desire to retrieve a, partly-remembered, partly-fantasised, cohesive, mono-racial community (Cohen, 1995). And some of these youngsters, like some of their parents, came to see the neighbourhood as a place which had to be defended against the incursions of outsiders. This said, many of the White children and young people we interviewed did not take this line, and some youngsters whose parents held racist attitudes felt that the school should equip them with stronger arguments with which to challenge their bigotry.

In earlier periods of economic expansion, the young people on the Dickens estate would have cut their ties with the school and school-age friends and got on with adult life. Now, young people of 18 and older, particularly those with few qualifications, were condemned to seek such status as they could within the neighbourhood, from a peer group, many of whose members were still at school. Thus, they were only semi-detached from the school, its social networks and its tensions. In fact, the de-stabilising changes which had occurred on the estate in the late 1980s and early 1990s, had primarily involved the replacement of older, more prosperous White residents with younger, poorer White residents, and an increase in the number of non-White students attending the school.

Thus the Bangladeshi students at Charles Dickens school, and the handful of Bangladeshi and Somali families living on the estate, had become a potent metaphor for change for certain socially and occupationally immobile White residents and their friends and associates, posing a threat to what Webster (1995) has described as their 'embattled identity'.

The White young people were aware that the increasingly sophisticated forms of social organisation, improving levels of educational attainment, and growing, albeit fairly modest, levels of relative prosperity achieved by members of the local Bengali community, stood in marked contrast with what they could hope to achieve. As Cohen (1995) has observed: 'Their aggressive assertion of localised working class nativism was incoherent, and dogged with self-doubt, rather than an expression of a belief in White supremacism'. This aggression and self-doubt sometimes found expression through bullying and violence. On the Dickens estate, school students tended not to reveal the extent of their victimisation to their parents. This reluctance, also noted by Sampson and Phillips (1995), was promoted by a desire not to worry their parents on the one hand and to limit the restrictions their parents might otherwise impose upon their social lives if they knew the 'whole story'. Whereas Kinsey et al. (1990) found adults unwilling to listen to, or believe, children, we found a more collusive relationship between parents and children which served to contain the anxieties of parents while keeping open a broad, albeit risky, range of recreational and social opportunities for their children.

In the secondary school on the Flaubert estate, a semi-formal organisation, *Femmes Relais*, a network of Senegalese, North African, Kurdish, Iranian and Portuguese mothers, supported by *animateurs sociales* from the mayor's office, which had developed over a decade, met regularly with representatives of the schools, the police, the local administration and relevant welfare agencies, to discuss problems of victimisation, underachievement, truancy, bullying, drugs etc., in the school and in the neighbourhood, and to devise strategies for tackling them. One of the fruits of these meetings had been the recruitment by the *Mairie* of ex-school students, undertaking national service, to work as teachers' assistants in the school and to monitor and control student-student violence in the school and the neighbourhood. This often involved 'mentoring' both perpetrators and victims. This appeared to have had the effect of rendering both the playground, and the journey to and from school, far safer than on the Dickens estate.

Action in the School

On the basis of national educational 'league tables', the Flaubert estate had been designated a *Zone Educationale Prioritaire* by the French Ministry of Education. This meant that additional resources had been directed towards all the schools on the estate. These resources included additional specialist staff, additional staff hours for coaching individual students and helping with homework, and the construction of a radio station which provided public service broadcasting to the surrounding region in an attempt to form closer and more positive social and economic links between the Flaubert estate and the region. *Femmes Relais*, in conjunction with JCLT, also offered language tuition and vocational training to parents.

Levels of attainment in the Charles Dickens School were roughly similar to those in the secondary school on the Flaubert estate, *vis-à-vis* the national league tables. However, the implementation of the National Curriculum and Local Management of Schools had generated an enormously increased administrative load which made it increasingly difficult for the school to sustain pastoral, sporting and social activities. These pressures were placing at risk the very close staff-student relationships and high standards of pastoral care for which the school was renowned.

A few low-achieving White boys, those most likely to be the perpetrators of racial violence, continued to pose a serious problem to the school and, largely as a result of the pressures identified above, staff were resorting to exclusion more frequently. Already feeling marginalised and scapegoated, these boys became even more frustrated and angry by their exclusion from school. The Charles Dickens School, like others in adjacent areas, had attempted to respond to these difficulties by developing a parent-teacher association, but mistrust among some Bangladeshi parents and an apparent lack of interest among many others, had confounded their efforts. However, despite the formidable problems with which the school was attempting to wrestle, rather than the promise of additional support and resources, staff were 'motivated' by the threat of the intervention of OFSTED if standards measured by the schools' league table ranking fell further.

Multi-agency Partnership

On the Flaubert estate, official initiatives to reduce victimisation through inter-agency and inter-professional collaboration had been established since the early 1980s. The mayor had been central to this process and the arrangements for co-operation grew out of protracted, and continuing, negotiations, between him and his fellow politicians and representatives of the adults and young people on the estate (Le Gales, 1994; Jazouli, 1995; Picard, 1995). As we have noted, these negotiations had spawned the *Conseil de Quartier*. Partly because of this painstaking groundwork, the efforts and ambitions of the *Conseil de Quartier* articulated fairly closely with the efforts of local authority departments, locally based offices of central government, central government departments, voluntary sector agencies and the DPJJ 'youth justice' professionals. However, this 'will to collaboration' was due in no small part to pressure exerted by central government ministries and the National Council for the Prevention of Delinquency which required statutory and voluntary agencies, as a matter of policy and a condition of their funding, to collaborate on all relevant projects which aimed to resolve problems of community life and neighbourhood conflict. They were required, in particular, to focus upon problems of social marginality and social exclusion, and to promote the social insertion of young people into significant educational and vocational opportunities. At the time of our research these partnerships had been in existence for 15 years and had, to a large extent, become institutionalised within political and professional practice and within the network of local services.

French children's judges were expected to be active in their neighbourhoods, using knowledge gained through dealing with child care and youth offending cases to help focus the efforts, and develop the activities of local welfare, educational, training and employment agencies. They too were enjoined to promote social insertion as a way of reducing crime and public disorder (Ely and Stanley, 1990). On the Flaubert estate they were pursuing these objectives through membership of the management committees of local voluntary and neighbourhood organisations and regular meetings with the staff of DPJJ.

On the Dickens estate there was a clear separation between local crime prevention initiatives, which incorporated some 'social', but mainly 'situational', elements, and the local authority youth justice service which was wedded to an offence-focused 'delinquency management' strategy. Regardless of their sympathies with the political orientation of the local council, the public professionals we interviewed were deeply sceptical about the ability of any local authority to defend existing levels of service, let alone innovate in the current political climate. Crime prevention programmes, Safer Neighbourhoods, Safer Cities etc., had come and gone and had, for their duration, had some effect, but because they were never planned to mesh with the practices of local agencies they had little lasting impact. As a result, both professionals and local people had grown cynical about such short-term initiatives. Increasingly, agencies found themselves in competition for dwindling central government crime prevention resources which limited still further their motivation and capacity to collaborate. It does not appear that the implementation of community safety provisions of the Crime and Disorder Act 1998 at local level has changed this situation significantly.

The UK magistrates approached during the research chose not to participate. Although they had sentenced young people and adults from the neighbourhood, not infrequently for racially motivated crimes and inter-racial fighting, they claimed to be insufficiently familiar with the neighbourhood and its problems to be of any help to the research team. Moreover, they feared that too close a knowledge of these problems might cloud their objectivity.

Conclusion

In 1981 in both Britain and France, approximately 3.5 million offences were recorded by the police. Both countries had witnessed steady increases in recorded crime in general, and recorded youth crime in particular, and both confronted youth riots on the streets of their major cities. However, by the end of the 1980s the number of offences recorded in

Britain was approaching 6 million, while in France, from 1986 recorded youth crime declined to around 3 million from where it rose gradually to the end of the decade (Parti Socialiste Français, 1986; De Liege, 1991; Home Office, 1994). Gazeau and Pryre (1998) note that:

> *After a period of relative stability between 1972 and 1976, the general trend shows a rapid increase up until the early 1980s...after reaching a peak then levelling out, a rapid decrease was observed in 1986, followed by a slight increase...all the statistical variations can be explained by changes in the political situation and in public policy concerning criminal behaviour.*

As we noted in Chapter 7, in Britain crime appears to have risen fastest in the poorest neighbourhoods (Hope, 1994). However, in France it was in the poorest neighbourhoods that the fall in the crime rate was most marked (King, 1989; De Liege, 1991).

Not since the American Poverty Programme of the 1960s has there been a governmental assault upon the problem of social cohesion on the scale of the French SPI of the 1980s. The American Poverty Programme, orchestrated by the Kennedy-Johnson administrations, aimed to circumvent existing political and administrative structures and provide alternative vehicles for political participation among the poor (Marris and Rein, 1967; Moynihan, 1969; Cloward and Fox-Piven, 1972). Like the neo-conservatives of the 1980s and 1990s, the architects of the American Poverty Programme located the problem in hidebound, oppressive and self-serving state services and bureaucracies which, while claiming to ameliorate the condition of the poor, merely compounded it. In pursuing the consequences of this analysis, however, the state found itself in a situation which was both unprecedented and extremely uncomfortable since it effectively sanctioned the expenditure of central government funds on the subversion of local government structures.

The ensuing popular protests and riots notwithstanding, the alternative structures developed in the struggle against the 'establishment' in the USA were never integral to the processes of political decision-making and social change. Although these alternative structures offered some members of the indigenous Black leadership a means of entering an emergent Black middle class, they failed to institutionalise mechanisms whereby the bulk of the poor, who were for the most part Black or Hispanic, could be reconnected with the organised working class, which was predominantly White (Wilson, 1987). In the end therefore, as Cloward and Fox-Piven (1972) have argued, 'relief-giving turned out to be the most expeditious way to deal with the political pressure created by a dislocated poor, just as it had been many times in the past'.

The French initiative of the 1980s emerged from a different political tradition, adopted a different political strategy and, in consequence, had a different effect upon the relationship between those on the social margins and the state. At the core of the political culture of both the USA and the UK is a notion of the state as a potentially antagonistic force which, unless it is rigorously controlled, may at any moment encroach upon the lives and arrogate the liberties of citizens. Thus 'freedom' consists in minimising the role of the state. In France, and many other Western European states, by contrast, the state is conceived as a potentially creative force, constituted by, and representative of, the collective interest of its citizens:

> *...within Europe, what it means to 'belong' varies from one nation state to another...French researchers often distinguish between the French 'way of doing things' and the 'Anglo-Saxon tradition'. Behind this dichotomy lies a conception of the distinctiveness of the French nation state which is seen to originate with the French revolution... This distinction is structured by universalism, by the notion of the French nation as the expression of the collectivity of equal and active citizens, a structuring that is thought to be absent in Britain and the Netherlands, which are characterised alternatively (and in polar opposition) as social formations shaped by institutional pluralism and decentralisation.* (Miles, 1993)

Although both of these perspectives are, necessarily, idealisations, they open doors to quite different political possibilities for governments trying to fashion responses to the problems of crime and social cohesion.

Rather than circumventing the state apparatus, the task defined by Mitterrand and Bonnemaison concerned the construction, and then the institutionalisation, of a new relationship between the political centre and the social margins. This was to be achieved through the reform and co-ordination of the relevant ministries and devolution of state power which aimed to depoliticise, democratise and localise key areas of state activity and transform the practices of their agents. In consequence, for a time, the French initiative achieved the prize which had eluded the Kennedy Johnson administrations, the construction of a political 'hotline' between the head of state and the ghetto.

Although the French initiative adopted many of the techniques pioneered in the American Poverty Programme, it was designed to solve the very different social and economic problems of the 1980s. The American Poverty Programme of the 1960s and 1970s aimed to break down the political, educational, bureaucratic and racial barriers which excluded the poor from full participation in a traditional, three-tier class structure in an expanding economy. The French initiative of the 1980s was born of a recognition that economic globalisation and a burgeoning new technology had transformed class relations and fragmented the working class, and that now, the key social division was between a contracting, relatively prosperous and skilled workforce and the growing body of, usually young and often non-White, people who appeared to be effectively excluded from economic activity altogether (Donzelot and Roman, 1991; Wilson, 1987).

The social and political analysis upon which the French initiative was based marked an early recognition of the forces which were transforming advanced industrial societies throughout Europe and beyond. Its unique contribution was to devise new forms of social solidarity, and new routes to citizenship, to replace traditional but defunct social and political structures rooted in the workplace. Its other unique features were the precision of its aims and the exhaustiveness and inclusiveness of the process by which those aims were arrived at. Its objectives were clearly specified and the interventions to which they gave rise were targeted precisely on the basis of detailed local assessments (Gallo, 1995).

The painstaking construction of the French SPI bore fruit at neighbourhood level. On the Dickens estate, the social and economic forces making for de-stabilisation had proceeded more or less unchecked by central or local government. On the Flaubert estate, the economic interventions aimed at opening up primary sector employment opportunities beyond the estate by the *Mission Locale*, the local housing strategies devised by the Neighbourhood Council, the training initiatives of JCLT, the social action and anti-racist programmes of the DPJJ were co-ordinated by the mayor's office. This meant that a housing strategy, which located several generations of the same family in close proximity, articulated with an employment strategy which, by placing local young people and adults together in work groups on the estate, reinforced relationships between the generations and created a higher degree of social interaction and mutual dependency between residents. These initiatives grew out of, and articulated with, negotiations between the mayor, the Neighbourhood Council, *Femme Relais*, and the 'socially excluded' young people of the estate whom the mayor met at his monthly meetings at the Pagoda.

In the 1980s and 1990s, under successive governments, youth crime policy in Britain, came to focus primarily upon the functioning of the youth justice system. In France during the same period, policies inspired by governmental concerns about the erosion of social cohesion, culminated in the development of a complex national 'social prevention' programme which brought together politicians, professionals and citizen groups at national, regional and local levels in a programme which linked concerns about poverty, drugs, mental health, educational attainment, racial conflict and unemployment with questions of crime and social disorder.

In contrasting these two neighbourhoods we encounter one in which a politically engaged public is devising new forms of social solidarity and another in which social atomisation is accelerating. These differences have little to do with the proclivities or potential of local residents, or the skills and abilities of the public professionals who serve them. Rather they speak to the social and political possibilities which can be opened up by a belief among politicians that an extension of citizenship as the key to social cohesion matters, and that such cohesion can best be achieved by involving the children, young people and adults most closely involved in these problems, in the political process.

References

Abel-Smith, B. and Townsend, P. (1964) *The Poor and the Poorest.* London: G. Bell and Sons.

Althusser, L. (1965) *For Marx* (trs. Ben Brewster). Harmondsworth: Penguin Books.

Altschuler, D. and Armstrong, T. (1984) Intervening with Serious Juvenile Offenders. In Mathias, R. and DeMuro, P. (Eds.) *Violent Juvenile Offenders.* San Francisco: National Council on Crime and Delinquency.

Audit Commission (1996) *Misspent Youth.* London: The Audit Commission.

Audit Commission (1999) *Safety in Numbers.* London: The Audit Commission.

Aymer, C. and Bryan, A. (1996) Black Students' Experience on Social Work Courses: Accentuating the Positives. *British Journal of Social Work,* 26: 1–16.

Bailey, R. and Williams, B. (2000) *Inter-agency Partnerships in Youth Justice: Implementing the Crime and Disorder Act 1998.* Social Service Monographs Research in Practice/Community Care.

Baldwin, J. (1964) *Nobody Knows My Name.* London: Michael Joseph.

Ballieau, F. (1998) A Crisis of Youth or of Judicial Response. In Ruggerio, V., South, N. and Taylor, I. (Eds.) *The New European Criminology.* London: Routledge.

Bandura, A. (1969) *Principles of Behaviour Modification.* London: Holt, Rinehart and Winston.

Barberan, J.M. (1997) 'Mediation in Spanish Youth Justice'. *Social Work in Europe,* 3(3).

Barry, M. (1998) Social Exclusion and Social Work: an Introduction. In Barry, M. and Hallett, C. (Eds.) *Social Exclusion and Social Work.* Lyme Regis: Russell House Publishing.

Baum, D. (1996) Can Integration Succeed? Research into Urban Childhood and Youth in a Deprived Area in Koblenz. *Social Work in Europe,* 3: 3.

Bazemore, H. et al. (1997) *The Declaration of Leuven.* Brussels: The Catholic University of Leuven.

Becker, H. (1963) *Outsiders: Studies in the Sociology of Deviance.* New York: Free Press.

Bellow, S. (1997) *The Actual.* London: Viking.

Bennington, J., Bond, N. and Skelton, P. (1975) *Community Development Project. Part 1: Coventry and Hill fields: Prosperity and the Persistence of Inequality.* London: Home Office and City of Coventry.

Blagg, H. and Smith, D. (1989) *Crime and Social Policy.* London: Longman.

Blatier, C. and Poussin, G. (1997) New Concepts of Intervention in the Judicial Field. *Social Work in Europe,* 4: 1.

Bohn, I. (1996) Action against Aggression and Violence. *Social Work in Europe,* 3(1): 32–6.

Bonnemaison, H. (1983) *Face à la Delinquence: Prévention, Répression, Solidarité: Rapport au Premier Ministre de la Commission des Maires sur la Securité.* Paris: La Documentation Francaise.

Borutsky, S. (1991) The Chicago Boys: Social Security and Welfare in Chile. In Glennester, H. and Midgley, J. (Eds.) *The Radical Right and the Welfare State: An International Assessment.* London: Harvester, Wheatsheaf.

Bottoms, A. and McWilliams, W. (1979) A Non-treatment Paradigm for Probation Practice. *British Journal of Social Work*, 9: 159–202.

Bottoms, A.E., Brown, P., McWilliams, B., Mc.Williams, W. and Nellis, M. (1990) *Intermediate Treatment and Juvenile Justice*. London: Home Office.

Bourdieu, P. (1998) *Acts of Resistance: Against the New Myths of Our Time*. Cambridge: Polity Press.

Braithwaite, J. (1989) *Reintegrative Shaming*. Cambridge: Cambridge University Press.

Braithwaite, J. and Daly, K. (1994) Masculinities, Violence, and Communitarian Control. In Stanko, T. and Newburn, T. (Eds.) *Just Boys Doing Business*. London: Routledge.

Bratton, W. (1997) Crime is Down in New York City: Blame the Police. In Dennis, N. (Ed.) *Zero Tolerance: Policing a Free Society*. London: Institute of Economic Affairs.

Bright, J. and Petterson, G. (1984) *The Safe Neighbourhoods Unit*. London: NACRO.

Bromwich, D. (1999) Review Article: The Origins of Postmodernity by Perry Anderson, The Cultural Turn by Fredric Jameson. *London Review of Books*, 21(3): 4 Feb.

Burroughs, D. (1998) *Contemporary Patterns of Residential Mobility in Relation to Social Housing in England*. York: The Centre for Housing Policy, University of York.

Campbell, B. (1993) *Goliath, Britain's Dangerous Places*. London: Methuen.

Cannan, C. (1996) The Impact of Social Development and Anti-Exclusion Policies on the French Social Work Professions. *Social Work in Europe*, 3(2): 1–4.

Cantle Report (The) (2002) *Violent Community Disorders in Bradford, Burnley and Oldham*.

Catholic Education Service (1997) *A Struggle for Excellence, Catholic Secondary Schools in Urban Poverty Areas*. London: Catholic Education Service.

Centre National de Formation et d'Etudes de la Protection Judiciaire de la Jeunesse (1995) *Annual Statistics*. Veaucresson: CNFEPJ.

Centrepoint (1995) *Statistics: April 1994–March 1995*. London: Centrepoint.

Chapman, S. and Savage, P. (1999) The New Politics of Law and Order: Labour, Crime and Justice. Powell, M. (Ed.) *New Labour, New Welfare State: the Third Way in British Social Policy*. Bristol: Policy Press.

Christie, N. (1977) Conflicts as Property. *British Journal of Criminology*, 17: 1–15.

Church, R. (1963) The Varied Effects of Punishment on Behaviour. *Psychological Review*, 70: 5.

Cicourel, A. (1968) *The Social Organisation of Juvenile Justice*. New York: Wiley.

Ciefu, D. (1997) Reforming Romanian Youth Justice. *Social Work in Europe*, 4(2): 32–6.

Clarke, J., Cochrane, A. and McLaughlin, E. (1994) *Managing Social Policy*. London: Sage Publications.

Cliffe, D. (1990) Warwickshire's Minefield. *Community Care*, 837(8): 25 Oct.

Cloward, R. and Fox-Piven, F. (1972) *Regulating the Poor: the Functions of Public Welfare*. London: Tavistock Publications.

Cloward, R. and Ohlin, L. (1960) *Delinquency and Opportunity*. London: Routledge and Kegan Paul.

Cohen, P. (1995) *Island Stories: Real and Imagined Communities in the East End*. London: Runnymede Trust.

Cohen, S. (1979) *How do we Balance Guilt, Justice and Tolerance*. London: Radical Alternatives to Prison.

Commaile, J. (1994) France: from Family Policy to Policies for the Family. In Dumon, W. (Ed.) *Changing Family Policies in the Member States of the European Union*. Bonn: Commission of the European Communities DGV.

Conrad, J. (1896) *Under Western Eyes*.

Cooper, A. and Lousada, J. (2000) *The Meaning of Welfare*. London: Venture Press.

Cooper, A., Hetherington, R., Baistow, K., Pitts, J. and Spriggs, A. (1995) *Positive Child Protection: a View from Abroad.* Lyme Regis: Russell House Publishing.

Crawford, A. (1998) Delivering Multi-Agency Partnerships in Community Safety. In Marlow, A. and Pitts, J. (Eds.) *Planning Safer Communities.* Lyme Regis: Russell House Publishing.

Crawford, A. and Jones, M. (1995) Inter-agency Co-operation and Community Based Crime Prevention. *British Journal of Criminology*, 35: 1.

Cressey, D.R. (1973) Adult Felons in Jail. In Ohlin, L. (Ed.) *Prisoners in America.* Englewood Cliffs, NJ: Prentice Hall.

Crimmens, D. (1991) Running out of Care: Developing a Service for Young Runaways. In Dennington, J. and Pitts, J. (Eds.) *Developing Services for Young People in Crisis.* London: Longman.

Crimmens, D. (forthcoming) *Having Their Say: Young People, Rights and Participation.* Lyme Regis: Russell House Publishing.

Crimmens, D. and Pitts, J. (2000) *Positive Residential Practice: Learning the Lessons of the 1990s.* Lyme Regis: Russell House Publishing.

Currie, E. (1985) *Confronting Crime: an American Challenge.* New York: Pantheon.

Currie, E. (1991) International Developments in Crime and Social Policy. In NACRO, *Crime and Public Policy.* London: NACRO.

Dahrendorf, R. (1994) The Changing Quality of Citizenship. In van Steenbergen, B. (Ed.) *The Condition of Citizenship.* London: Sage Publications.

De Liege, M-P. (1991) Social Development and the Prevention of Crime in France: a Challenge for Local Parties and Central Government. In Farrell, M. and Heidensohn, F. *Crime in Europe.* London: Routledge.

Dean, H. (1999) Citizenship. In Powell, M. (Ed.) *New Labour, New Welfare State: the Third Way in British Social Policy.* Bristol: The Policy Press.

Dean, M. (1997) Tipping the Balance. *Search*, 27: Spring.

Delors, J. (1993) *Growth, Competitiveness, Employment, the Challenges and Ways Forward into the 21st Century.* Brussels: Commission of the European Community, COM (9.3) 700.

Dennis, N. (Ed.) *Zero Tolerance – Policing a Free Society.* London: Institute of Economic Affairs.

Department of Health (1989) *The Children Act 1989.* London: HMSO.

Department of Health (1998) *Final Report on Glenthorne Youth Treatment Centre.* London: DoH.

DHSS (1969) *Children and Young Persons Act 1969.* London: HMSO.

Donzelot, J. and Roman, J. (1991) Le Déplacement de la Question Sociale. In Donzelot J. (Ed.) *Face à l'Exclusion.* Paris: Editions Esprit.

Downes, D. (1990) *Public Violence on Two Estates.* London: Home Office.

Downes, D. (1995) Serious Diversions: Juvenile Crime and Justice in Europe: the Lessons for Britain. *Social Work in Europe*, 1: 2.

Dubet, F., Jazouli, A. and Lapeyronnie, F. (1985) *L'Etat et les Jeunes.* Paris: Editions Ouvrieres.

Durkheim, E. (1964) *The Division of Labour in Society.* New York: Free Press.

Eagleton, T. (1991) *Ideology: an Introduction.* London: Verso.

Elejabarrieta, F. et al. (1993) *Els Programes de Mediacio: Que Pensen i Com Els Viuen Les Parts Implicades.* Universitata Autonoma de Barcelona.

Elliott, D., Hunzinga, D. and Morse, B. (1986) Self-report Violent Offending: a Descriptive Analysis of Juvenile Violent Offenders and their Offending Careers. *Journal of Interpersonal Violence*, 1: 472–514.

Ely, P. and Stanley, C. (1990) *The French Alternative: Delinquency Prevention and Child Protection in France.* London: NACRO.

Esping Anderson, G. (1990) *Three Worlds of Welfare Capitalism.* Cambridge: Polity Press.

Essler, G. (1998) *The United States of Anger.* Harmondsworth: Penguin.

Etzioni, A. (1995) *The Spirit of Community.* London: Fontana.

Fagan, J. (1991) *The Comparative Impacts of Juvenile and Criminal Court Sanctions on Adolescent Felony Offenders, Final Report, Grant 87-IJ-CX-4044, to the National Institute of Justice.* Washington DC: US Department of Justice.

Farrington, D. (1996) *Understanding and Preventing Youth Crime.* York: Joseph Rowntree Foundation.

Farrington, D. (2000) Explaining and Preventing Crime: The Globalisation of Knowledge. *Criminology,* 38(1): 1–24.

Farrington, D. and Burrows, J. (1993) Did Shoplifting Really Decrease? *British Journal of Criminology,* 33: 57–69.

Farrington, D. and West, D. (1993) Criminal, Penal and Life Histories of Chronic Offenders: Risk and Protective Factors and Early Identification. *Criminal Behaviour and Mental Health,* 3: 492–523.

Feeley, M. and Simon, J. (1992) The New Penology: Notes on the Emerging Strategy of Corrections and its Implementation. *Criminology,* 30(4): 452–74.

Feld, B. (1988) The Juvenile Court Meets the Principle of the Offense: Legislative Changes in Juvenile Waiver Statutes. *Journal of Criminal Law and Criminology,* 78: 471–533.

Fischer, T. (1994) *The Thought Gang.*

Forrester, D., Frenz, S., O'Connell, M. and Pease, K. (1990) *The Kirkholt Burglary Prevention Project: Phase II.* London: Home Office.

Foucault, M. (1977) *Discipline and Punish: the Birth of the Prison.* London: Penguin Books.

Foucault, M. (1980) *Power, Knowledge.*

Foucault, M. (1986) What is Enlightenment? In Robinson, P. (Ed.) *The Foucault Reader.* Harmondsworth: Penguin.

Friedman, M. (1962) *Capitalism and Freedom.* Chicago: University of Chicago Press.

Fukyama, E (1992) *The End of History and the Last Man.* New York: The Free Press.

Gallo, E. (1995) The Penal System in France: from Correctionalism to Managerealism. In Ruggerio, V., Ryan, M. and Sim, J. (Eds.) *Western European Penal Systems: a Critical Anatomy.* London: Sage Publications.

Gardiner, D. and Nesbitt, D. (1996) Cognitive Behavioural Group Work with Male Offenders, the Newcastle upon Tyne Intensive Probation Unit. In Newburn, T. and Mair, G. (Eds.) *Working with Men.* Lyme Regis: Russell House Publishing.

Gardner, J., von Hirsch, A., Smith, A., Morgan, R., Ashworth, A. and Wasik, M. (1998) Clause 1: The Hybrid Law from Hell. *Criminal Justice Matters,* 31: 25–6.

Gazeau, J-F. and Pryre, V. (1998) France. In Mehlbye, J. and Walgrave, L. (Eds.) *Confronting Youth in Europe: Juvenile Crime and Juvenile Justice.* Denmark: AKF Forlaget.

Gendreau, P. (1996) The Principles of Effective Intervention With Offenders. In Harland A. (Ed.) *Choosing Correctional Options That Work.* Thousand Oaks: Sage Publications.

Gewisty, S., Ball, S. and Bowe, S. (1995) *Markets, Choice and Equity in Education.* Milton Keynes: Open University Press.

Giddens, A. (1998) *The Third Way: the Renewal of Social Democracy.* Cambridge: Polity Press.

Gilroy, P. and Sim, J. (1985) Law, Order and the State of the Left. *Capital and Class,* 25: 15–55.

Ginsberg, N. (1992) *Divisions of Welfare.* London: Sage Publications.

Glennester, H. and Midgley, J. (Eds.) *The Radical Right and the Welfare State.* London: Harvester/ Wheatsheaf.

Goldburg, T. (1993) *Racist Culture.* Oxford: Blackwell.

Goldson, B. (1997) Children, Crime, Policy and Practice: Neither Welfare nor Justice. *Children and Society*, 11: 77–88.

Goldson, B. (1998) Re-visiting the 'Bulger Case': the Governance of Juvenile Crime and the Politics of Punishment – Enduring Consequences for Children in England and Wales. *Juvenile Justice Worldwide*, 1(1): 21–2.

Goldson, B. (1999) Youth (In)justice: Contemporary Developments in Policy and Practice. In Goldson, B. (Ed.) *Youth Justice: Contemporary Policy and Practice*. London: Ashgate.

Goldson, B. (Ed.) (2000) *The New Youth Justice*. Lyme Regis: Russell House Publishing.

Goldson, B. and Peters, E. (2000) *Tough Justice: Responding to Children in Trouble*. London: The Children's Society.

Gottfreidson, M. and Hirschi, T. (1990) *A General Theory of Crime*. Palo Alto: Stanford University Press.

Gouldner, A. (1971) *The Coming Crisis in Western Sociology*. London: Heinemann Educational.

Graham, J. (1988) *Schools, Disruptive Behaviour and Delinquency. Home Office Research Study No. 96*. London: Home Office.

Graham, J. (1993) Crime Prevention Policies in Europe. *European Journal of Crime, Criminal Law and Criminal Justice*, 1: 2.

Graham, J. and Bowling, B. (1995) *Young People and Crime*. London: Home Office.

Grevot, A. (1994) French Chronicle. *Social Work in Europe*, 1(3): 31.

Habermas, J. (1983) *Moralbewusstein und Kommunikatives Handeln*. Frankfurt: Suhrkamp.

Habermas, J. (1994) *The Past as Future*. Cambridge: Polity Press.

Hagan, J. (1993) The Social Embeddedness of Crime and Unemployment. *Criminology*, 31: 455–91.

Hagan, J. and McCarthy, B. (1997) *Mean Streets: Youth Crime and Homelessness*. Cambridge: Cambridge University Press.

Hagedorn, J. (1998) *People and Folks: Gangs, Crime and the Underclass in a Rustbelt City*. Chicago: Lakeview Press.

Hagell, A. and Newburn, T. (1994) *Persistent Young Offenders*. London: Policy Studies Institute.

Haines, K. (1997) *Restorative Justice for Juveniles: Limitations on a Good Idea*. (Unpublished paper presented to the British Criminology Conference, 15–18 July 1997.)

Hall, S., Critcher, C., Clarke, J., Jefferson, T. and Roberts, B. (1978) *Policing the Crisis*. London: Macmillan Press (now Palgrave).

Harrison, B. (1972) *Education, Training and the Urban Ghetto*. Baltimore: Johns Hopkin University Press.

Hawkins, D. and Catelano, R.E. (1998) *Effective Prevention for Today's Youth Problems*. Seattle: Developmental Research and Programmes.

Heidensohn, F. (1990) Introduction, Convergence, Diversity and Change. In Farrell, M. and Heidensohn, F. (Eds.) *Crime in Europe*. London: Routledge.

Herrnstein, R. and Murray, C. (1994) *The Bell Curve*. New York: The Free Press.

Hesse, B. et al. (1990) *Beneath the Surface: an Enquiry into Racial Harassment in the London Borough of Waltham Forest*. London: London Borough of Waltham Forest.

Hiro, D. (1992) *Black British, White British*. London: Paladin Press.

Hirschi, T. and Hindelang, M. (1977) Intelligence and Delinquency: a Revisionist Review. *American Sociological Review*, 42: 571–7.

Hobbs, D. (1988) *Doing the Business*. Oxford: Oxford University Press.

Hobbs, D. (1993) *Bad Business*. Oxford: Oxford University Press.

Hoghughi, M. (1983) *The Delinquent*. London: Burnett Books.

Home Office (1982) *Criminal Justice Act 1982*. London: HMSO.

Home Office (1990) *Crime, Justice and Protecting the Public* (White Paper). London: HMSO.

Home Office (1991) *The Criminal Justice Act 1991*. London: HMSO.

Home Office (1994) *The Criminal Justice and Public Order Act 1994*. London: HMSO.

Home Office (1996) *Crime (Sentences) Bill 1996*. London: HMSO.

Home Office (1997) *Crime (Sentences) Act 1997*. London: HMSO.

Home Office (1998a) *The Crime and Disorder Act 1998*. London: HMSO.

Home Office (1998b) *Chief Inspector of Prisons Report on Werrington YOI*. London: Home Office.

Home Office (1998c) *Aspects of Crime: Youth Offenders*. London: Crime and Criminal Justice Unit Research and Statistics Directorate. London: Home Office.

Hope, T. (1994) *Communities, Crime and Inequality in England and Wales*. Paper presented to the 1994 Cropwood Round Table Conference *Preventing Crime and Disorder*, 14–15 Sept., Cambridge.

Hope, T. (1995) Inequality and the Future of Community Crime Prevention. In Lab, S.P. *Crime Prevention at a Crossroads*. Cincinnati: Anderson Publishing.

Hope, T. and Foster, J. (1992) Conflicting Forces: Changing the Dynamics of Crime and Community on a Problem Estate. *British Journal of Criminology*, 32: 92.

Howell, J., Krisberg B., Hawkins, D. and Wilson, J. (Eds.) (1995) *Serious, Violent and Chronic Juvenile Offenders: a Sourcebook*. London: Sage Publications.

Hughes, G. (1996) Communitarianism and Law and Order. *Critical Social Policy*, 16(4): 17–41.

Humphreys, J. (2000) *Devil's Advocate*. London: Arrow.

Hutton, W. (1995) *The State We're In*. London: Jonathan Cape.

Hutton, W. (1999) Another War is Being Fought and the Enemy is Poverty. *The Observer*, 4 April, 30.

Jackson, P. and Penrose, B. (1993) *Constructions of Race, Place and Nation*. London: University College.

Jazouli, A. (1995) *Une Saison en Banlieue*. Paris: Plon.

Jenkins, S. (1995) *Accountable to None: the Tory Nationalisation of Britain*. London: Hamish Hamilton.

Johnstone, G. (2000) Penal Policy Making: Elitist, Populist or Participatory? *Punishment and Society*, 2(2): 161–80.

Karger, H.J. (1991) The Radical Right and Welfare Reform in the United States. In Glennester, H. and Midgley, J. (Eds.) *The Radical Right and the Welfare State: an International Assessment*. London: Harvester, Wheatsheaf.

Karger, H.J. and Stoesz, D. (1990) *American Social Welfare Policy: a Structural Approach*. New York: Longman.

Kelling, G. and Bratton, W. (1998) *Declining Crime Rates: Insiders' Views of the New York City Story*. New York: Rutgers University, unpublished.

King, D. and Wickham-Jones, M. (1999) Bridging the Atlantic: the Democratic (Party) Origins of Welfare to Work. In Powell, M. (Ed.) *New Labour, New Welfare State: the Third Way in British Social Policy*. Bristol: The Policy Press.

King, M. (1988) *How to Make Social Crime Prevention Work – the French Experience*. London: NACRO.

King, M. (1989) Social Crime Prevention a la Thatcher. *The Howard Journal*, 28: 291–312.

King, M. (1991) Child Welfare in the Law: the Emergence of a Hybrid Discourse. *Journal of Law and Society*, 18: 218–36.

King, M. and Piper, C. (1990) *How the Law Thinks about Children*. Aldershot: Gower.

Kinsey, R. et al. (1990) *Cautionary Tales*. University of Edinburgh Centre for Criminology.

Krisberg, B. and Austin, J.F. (1993) *Reinventing Juvenile Justice*. London: Sage Publishing.

Le Gales, P. (1994) The Political Dynamics of European Policy Implementation: Poverty III in Mantes-la Jolie. *Local Government Policy Making*, 20(5): 39–44.

Le Grand, J. (1995) Quasi-Markets in Welfare. In Trevillion, S. and Beresford, P. (Eds.) *Social Work, Education and the Community Care Revolution.* London: NISW.

Lea, J. (1998) *The Return of the Dangerous Classes: Crime Control in the 21st Century.* Inaugural professorial lecture, 10 Dec.

Lea, J. and Young, J. (1984) *What is to be Done about Law and Order.* Harmondsworth: Penguin.

Lemert, E. (1986) Juvenile Justice Italian Style. *Law and Society Review,* 20: 4.

Lemierre, R. (1994) Juvenile Services of the French Ministry of Justice. *Social Work in Europe,* 1: 2.

Lilley, R., Cullen, F. and Ball, R. (1995) *Criminological Theory.* London: Sage Publications.

Lipsey, M. (1995) What Do We Learn from 400 Research Studies on the Effectiveness of Treatment with Delinquents? In McGuire, M. (Ed.) *What Works in Reducing Offending. Guidelines from Research and Practice.* Chichester: John Wiley.

Local Government Management Board (1996) *Deprivation, Poverty and Education.* Luton: Local Government Management Board, unpublished.

London Youth Justice Managers Group (1998) *Remand Rescue at Feltham YOI.* Unpublished.

Loveday, B. and Marlow, A. (Eds.) (2000) *Policing after MacPherson.* Lyme Regis: Russell House Publishing.

Lyotard, J-E. (1979) *The Post-Modern Condition.* Manchester: Manchester University Press.

Mailer, N. (1998) Clinton for Pres. No, not you Bill, Hilary, Your Country Needs you. *The Observer,* 8 Feb.

Mair, G. and Mortimer, G. (1996) *Electronic Tagging.* London: Home Office.

Mair, P. (2000) Partyless Democracy. *New Left Review,* 2: Mar/Jun.

Mandelson, P. and Liddle, R. (1996) *The Blair Revolution.* London: Faber.

Marlow, A. (1999) Youth, Minorities, Drugs and Policing. In Marlow, A. and Pearson, G. (Eds.) *Young People, Drugs and Community Safety.* Lyme Regis: Russell House Publishing.

Marquand, D. (2000) From Baldwin to Blair. *New Left Review,* 3: May/Apr.

Marris, P. and Rein, M. (1967) *Dilemmas of Social Reform: Poverty and Community Action in the United States.* New York: Atherton Press.

Marshall, T.H. (1950) *Citizenship and Social Class.* Cambridge: Cambridge University Press.

Martinson, R. (1974) What Works? Questions and Answers about Prison Reform. *The Public Interest,* Spring: 22–54.

Marx, K. and Engels, F. (1888) *The Communist Manifesto.* Moscow: Progress Publishing.

Mathieson, T. (1974) *The Politics of Abolition.* London: Martin Robertson.

Matza, D. (1969) *Becoming Deviant.* Englewood Cliffs, NJ: Prentice-Hall.

McGahey, R.M. (1986) Economic Conditions, Neighbourhood Organisation and Urban Crime. In Reiss, A.J. and Tonry, M. (Eds.) *Communities and Crime.* Chicago: Chicago University Press.

Mehlbye, J. and Sommer, B. (1998) Denmark. In Mehlbye, J. and Walgrave, L. (Eds.) *Confronting Youth in Europe: Juvenile Crime and Juvenile Justice.* Denmark: AKF Forlaget.

Messerschmidt, J.W. (1993) *Masculinity and Crime: Critique and Reconceptualisation of Theory.* Maryland: Rowman and Littlefield.

Messner, S. and Rosenfeld, R. (1994) *Crime and the American Dream.* Belmont, CA: ITP.

Mika, H. and Zehr, H. (1997) *Fundamental Concepts of Restorative Justice.* Harrisonburg: Mennonite Central Committee.

Miles, R. (1993) Explaining Racism in Contemporary Europe. In Rattansi, A. and Westwood, S. (Eds.) *Racism, Modernity, Identity on the Western Front.* Cambridge: Polity Press.

Millham, S. (1973) *Locking Up Children.* Basingstoke: Saxon House.

Millham, S. (1978) Intermediate Treatment: Symbol or Solution? *Youth in Society,* 26: 22–4.

Mills, C.W. (1959) *The Sociological Imagination.* Harmondsworth: Penguin.

Ministry of Health (1933) *Children and Young Persons Act 1933*. London: HMSO.

Mitchell, J. and Gelloz, N. (1997) Supporting Families and Strengthening Communities: the Role of the 'Specialised Prevention' Movement in France. *Social Work in Europe*, 4: 3.

Mooney, J. (1993) *The Hidden Figure: Domestic Violence in North London*. Middlesex University Centre for Criminology.

Moore, M. (1997) *Downsize This: Random Threats from an Unarmed American*. New York: Boxtree.

Morgan Report (The) (1991) *Standing Conference on Crime Prevention, Safer Communities: the Local Delivery of Crime Prevention through the Partnership Approach*. London: Home Office.

Morran, D. (1996) Working in the CHANGE Programme: Probation-based Groupwork with Male Domestic Violence Offenders. In Newburn, T. and Mair, G. (Eds.) *Working with Men*. Lyme Regis: Russell House Publishing.

Morris, A. et al. (1980) *Justice for Children*. London: Macmillan Press (now Palgrave).

Moynihan, D.P. (1969) *Maximum Feasible Misunderstanding. Community Action in the War on Poverty*. New York: Free Press.

Muncie, J. (1999) *Youth and Crime*. London: Sage Publishing.

Murray, C. (1984) *Losing Ground: American Social Policy 1950–1980*. New York: Basic Books.

Murray, C. (1994) *Underclass: the Crisis Deepens*. London: Institute of Economic Affairs.

NACRO (1988) *Diverting Juveniles from Custody*. London: NACRO.

NACRO (1997) *Young Offenders Committee Report*. London: NACRO.

National Association for Youth Justice (1998) *ADJUST Now*, 41: Jan.

Novak, T. (1997) Young People, Class and Poverty. In Jones, H. (Ed.) *Towards a Classless Society*. London: Routledge.

OFSTED (1997) *From Failure to Success*. London: OFSTED.

Olds, D., Henderson, C., Tatelbaum, R. and Chamberlain, R. (1986) Improving the Delivery of Pre-natal Care and Outcomes of Pregnancy: a Randomised Trial of Nurse-Home Visitation. *Paediatrics*, 77: 16–28.

Padieu, C. and Sanchez, J-L. (1994) *L'Action Sociale Décentralisation 1984–1994*. Paris: ODAS Editeur.

Page, D. (1993) *Building for Communities: a Study of New Housing Association Estates*. York: Joseph Rowntree Foundation.

Parsons, C. (1996) *Permanent Exclusions from Schools in England: Trends, Causes and Responses*. London: The Children's Society.

Parti Socialiste Français (1986) *Les murs d'argent. Manifeste contre la privatisation des prisons*. Paris: Parti Socialiste.

Parton, N. (1985) *The Politics of Child Abuse*. London: Macmillan Press (now Palgrave).

Parton, N. (1991) *Governing the Family*. London: Macmillan Press (now Palgrave).

Patten, J. (1991) Making the Punishment Fit the Frame. *The Guardian*, 12 Apr.

Pawson, R. and Tilley, N. (1997) *Realistic Evaluation*. London: Sage Publications.

Pearce, J.J. (1995) French Lessons: Young People Comparative Research and Community Safety. *Social Work in Europe*, 1(3): 32–6.

Pearson, G. (1975) *The Deviant Imagination*. London: Macmillan Press (now Palgrave).

Pearson, G. (1987) *The New Heroin Users*. London: Batsford.

Pearson, G. (1993) The Role of Culture in the Drug Question. In Lader, M., Edwards, G. and Drummond, D. (Eds.) *The Nature of Alcohol and Drug Related Problems*. Oxford: Oxford University Press.

Penal Affairs Consortium (1994) *The Case against the Secure Training Order*. London: The Penal Affairs Consortium.

Penal Affairs Consortium (1997) *The Crime (Sentences) Bill.* London: The Penal Affairs Consortium.

Perfect, M. (1998) Presentation to Youth Justice and Community Safety Conference, New Hall, Cambridge (unpublished).

Phillips, M. (1994) Is the Male Redundant Now? *The Observer,* 26 Jun: 27.

Picard, P. (1995) *Mantes-la-jolie: Carnet de Route d'une Mairie de Banlieue.* Paris: Syros.

Pitts, J. (1988) *The Politics of Juvenile Crime.* London: Sage Publications.

Pitts, J. (1991) Less Harm or More Good? Politics, Research and Practice with Young People in Crisis. In Dennington, J. and Pitts, J. (Eds.) *Developing Services for Young People in Crisis.* London: Longman.

Pitts, J. (1993) Developing School and Community Links to Reduce Bullying. In Tattum, D. (Ed.) *Understanding and Managing Bullying.* London: Heinemann.

Pitts, J. (1995) Public Issues and Private Troubles: a Tale of Two Cities. *Social Work in Europe,* 2(1): 3–11.

Pitts, J. (1996) The Politics and Practice of Youth Justice. In Mclaughlin, E. and Muncie, J. (Eds.) *Controlling Crime.* London: Sage Publications/Open University Press.

Pitts, J. and Hope, T. (1997) The Local Politics of Inclusion: the State and Community Safety. *Social Policy and Administration,* 31: 5.

Pitts, J. and Smith, P. (1995) *Reducing School Bullying.* London: Home Office.

Pitts, M. (1992) *Somewhere to Run: a Statistical Analysis of the Work of the Central London Teenage Project for Young Runaways.* Unpublished BA dissertation, Exeter University.

Pollard, C. (1997) Zero Tolerance: Short-term Fix, Long-term Liability? In Dennis, N. (Ed.) *Zero Tolerance – Policing a Free Society.* London: Institute of Economic Affairs.

Porteous, D. (2001) Mentoring. In Factor, F., Chauhan, V. and Pitts, J. (Eds.) *The Russell House Companion to Work with Young People.* Lyme Regis: Russell House Publishing.

Power, A. and Tunstall, T. (1995) *Swimming Against the Tide: Polarisation or Progress.* York: The Joseph Rowntree Foundation.

Power, A. and Tunstall, T. (1997) *Dangerous Disorder: Riots and Violent Disturbances in Thirteen Areas of Britain 1991–92.* York: The Joseph Rowntree Foundation.

Power, M., Benn, R. and Norris, J. (1972) Neighbourhood, School and Juveniles before the Court. *British Journal of Criminology,* 12: 111–32.

Praedrie Report (1991) *Enterprises and Neighbourhoods.* Paris: Ministry of Internal Affairs.

Pratt, J. (1989) Corporatism, the Third Model of Juvenile Justice. *British Journal of Criminology,* 29: 236–54.

Preston, R.H. (1980) Social Theology and Penal Theory and Practice: the Collapse of the Rehabilitative Ideal and the Search for an Alternative. In Bottoms, A.E. and Preston, R.H. (Eds.) *The Coming Penal Crisis.* Edinburgh: Scottish Academic Press.

Raynor, P. and Vanstone, M. (1994) *Effective Probation Practice.* London: BASW/Macmillan.

Reiss, J.A. and Tonry, M. (1986) *Communities and Crime.* Chicago: Chicago University Press.

Riley, K. and Rowles, D. (1997) *Learning from Failure.* Roehampton: Centre for Educational Management.

Roberts, K. (1998) Youth Training. In Jones, H. (Ed.) *Towards a Classless Society.* London: Routledge.

Robinson, D. (1995) *The Impact of Cognitive Skills Training on Post-release Recidivism Among Canadian Federal Prisoners.* Canada: Ottowa Correctional Services.

Room, G. (Ed.) (1995) *Beyond the Threshold: the Measurement and Analysis of Social Exclusion.* Bristol: Polity Press.

Rorty, R. (1989) *Contingency, Irony and Solidarity.* Cambridge: Cambridge University Press.

Ross, R. and Fabiano, E. (1985) *Time to Think: A Cognitive Model of Delinquency Prevention and Offender Rehabilitation.* Johnson City, Tenn: Institute of Social Science and the Arts.

Ross, R. et. al. (1988) Reasoning and Rehabilitation. *International Journal of Offender Therapy and Comparative Criminology*, 32: 29–35.

Rowntree Foundation (1995) *Joseph Rowntree Inquiry into Income and Wealth.* York: JRF.

Rutherford, A. (1986) *Growing out of Crime.* Harmondsworth: Penguin.

Rutter, M., Maughan, B., Mortimore, P., Ouston, J. and Smith, A. (1978) *Fifteen Thousand Hours.* London: Open Books.

Said, E. (1994) *Representations of the Intellectual.* London: Vintage.

Sampson, A. and Phillips, C. (1995) *Reducing Repeat Racial Victimisation on an East London Estate.* London: Home Office.

Sampson, R. and Laub, J. (1993) *Crime in the Making: Pathways and Turning Points.* Harvard University Press.

Sampson, R.J., Raudenbush, S.W. and Earls, F. (1997) Neighbourhoods and Violent Crime: a Multi-Level Study of Collective Efficacy. *Science*, 277: 15 Aug.

Scarman, L. (1982) *The Scarman Report: the Brixton Disorders 10–12 April 1981.* Harmondsworth: Penguin.

Schlossman, S., Zeuman, G. and Showelter, R. (1984) *Delinquency Prevention in South Chicago: a Fifty-year Assessment of the Chicago Area Project.* Santa Monica, CA: RAND.

Schur, E.M. (1973) *Radical Non-Intervention.* Englewood Cliffs, NJ: Prentice Hall.

Scull, A. (1977) *Decarceration.* New Jersey: Spectrum Books.

Segal, L. (1990) *Slow Motion: Changing Masculinities, Changing Men.* London: Virago Press.

Shaw, C. and McKay, H. (1942) *Juvenile Delinquency and Urban Areas.* Chicago: Chicago University Press.

Shaw, S. and Sparks, C. (2000) Young People in Penal Establishments. In Crimmens, D. and Pitts, J. *Positive Residential Practice: Learning the Lessons of the 1990s.* Lyme Regis: Russell House Publishing.

Sherman, L., Gottfredson, D., MacKenzie, J., Reuter, P. and Bushway, S. (1998) *Preventing Crime: What Works, What Doesn't, What's Promising.* Washington DC: US Department of Justice.

Shriane, H. (1995) *Luton Runaways Profile.* Luton: Luton Community Links Project.

Smith, J. (1984) *No Lessons Learnt: a Survey of School Exclusions.* London: Children's Society.

Social Exclusion Unit (1998) *Bringing Britain Together.* London: HMSO.

Stoesz, D. and Midgley, J. (1991) The Radical Right and the Welfare State. In Glennester, H. and Midgley, J. (Eds.) *The Radical Right and the Welfare State.* London: Harvester/Wheatsheaf.

Straw, J. (1997) *Supporting the Role of the Police: Building a Responsible Society.* Speech by Home Secretary to the Police Federation. London: Home Office.

Sullivan, M. (1989) *Getting Paid: Youth Crime and Work in the Inner City.* London: Cornell University Press.

Szymanski, L. (1987) *Statutory Exclusions of Crimes from Juvenile Court Jurisdiction.* Unpublished manuscript. Washington: National Center for Juvenile Justice.

Thornberry, T. (1994) *Violent Families and Youth Violence. Fact Sheet No. 21.* Washington DC: Office of Juvenile Justice and Delinquency Prevention.

Thorpe, D., Smith, D., Green, C. and Paley, J. (1980) *Out of Care.* London: Allen and Unwin.

Utting, W. (1997) *People Like Us.* London: DoH.

Utting, W., Bright, J. and Hendrickson, W. (1993) *Crime and the Family.* London: Fabian Society.

Van Gunterstein, H. (1994) Four Conceptions of Citizenship. In van Steenbergen, B. (Ed.) *The Condition of Citizenship.* London: Sage Publications.

Van Steenbergen, B. (1994) *The Condition of Citizenship.* London: Sage Publications.

Vidal, G. (1998) *The Virgin Islands.* Harmondsworth: Penguin.

Wacquant, L. (1996) The Comparative Structure and Experience of Urban Exclusion: 'Race', Class and Space in Chicago and Paris. In McFate, K., Lawson, R. and Wilson, W.J. (Eds.) *Poverty, Inequality and the Future of Social Policy.* New York: RAND.

Walden Jones, B. (1993) *Crime and Citizenship: Preventing Youth Crime in France through Social Integration.* London: NACRO.

Walgrave, L. (1994) Beyond Rehabilitation: in Search of a Constructive Alternative in the Judicial Response to Juvenile Crime. *European Journal of Criminal Justice Policy and Research,* 2: 57–75.

Wallis, E. (2000) *A New Choreograhy: Integrated Strategy for the National Probation Service for England and Wales: Strategic Framework 2001–2004.* London: National Probation Service.

Wallis, L. (1995) French Lessons. *The Guardian.* Education Section, 3 Apr. 4–5.

Warner Report (The) (1996) *Choosing with Care.* London: DoH.

Webster, C. (1995) *Racial Attacks in Northern England: Qualitative Aspects of the Keighley Crime Survey.* British Sociological Association Conference, Apr. 1995, University of Leicester.

West, P. and Sweeting, H. (1996) Nae job, nae Future: Young People and Health in a Context of Unemployment. *Health and Social Care in the Community,* 4(1): 50–62.

Whyte, W.F. (1943) *Street Corner Society.* Chicago: Chicago University Press.

Wieviorka, M. (1994) Racism in Europe: Unity and Diversity. In Ratsani, A. and Westwood, S. *Racism, Modernity, Identity on the Western Front.* Cambridge: Polity Press.

Wikstrom, T. and Loeber, R. (1997) Individual Risk Factors, Neighbourhood SES and Juvenile Offending. In Tonry, M. (Ed.) *The Handbook of Crime and Punishment.* New York: Oxford University Press.

Wilkinson, C. (1996) 'The Drop Out Society'. *Young Minds.* London: MIND.

Wilkinson, G. (1994) *Unfair Shares: the Effects of Widening Income Differentials on the Young.* Ilford: Barnardos.

Wilson, J.J. (1994) *The Future of the Juvenile Justice System: Can We Preserve It?* Paper presented at the 21st National Conference of Juvenile Justice, Boston.

Wilson, J.Q. (1975) *Thinking about Crime.* New York: Basic Books.

Wilson, J.Q. and Herrnstein, R.J. (1985) *Crime and Human Nature.* New York: Simon and Schuster.

Wilson, J.Q. and Kelling, G. (1982) Broken Windows. *The Atlantic Monthly,* Mar.

Wilson, W.J. (1987) *The Truly Disadvantaged: the Inner City, the Underclass and Public Policy.* Chicago: University of Chicago Press.

Wilson, W.J. (1994) *Citizenship and the Inner-city Ghetto Poor.*

Wolfgang, M. (1982) Abolish the Juvenile Court System. *California Laywer,* 17: 12–3.

Wright, M. (1991) *Justice for Victims and Offenders: a Restorative Approach to Crime.* Milton Keynes: Open University Press.

Young, J. (1998) Zero Tolerance: Back to the Future. In Marlow, A. and Pitts, J. (Eds.) *Planning Safer Communities.* Lyme Regis: Russell House Publishing.

Young, J. (1999) *The Exclusive Society.* London: Sage Publications.

Youth Justice Board (2001) *Pilot Youth Offending Team Evaluation Undertaken by the Universities of Sheffield, Hull and Swansea.* London: Home Office.

Zeldin, T. (1994) *An Intimate History of Humanity.* London: Minerva.

Zizeck, S. (1998) *The Obscure Object of Ideology.* Cambridge: Polity Press.

Zizeck, S. (2000) Casting our Maiden. *New Left Review,* Mar–Apr.

Index